HEGEL AND THE SPIRIT

PHILOSOPHY AS PNEUMATOLOGY

Alan M. Olson

PRINCETON UNIVERSITY PRESS

PRINCETON, NEW JERSEY

LIBRARY OF CONGRESS CATALOGING-IN-PUBLICATION DATA
OLSON, ALAN M.
HEGEL AND THE SPIRIT : PHILOSOPHY AS PNEUMATOLOGY / ALAN M. OLSON.
P.   CM.
INCLUDES BIBLIOGRAPHICAL REFERENCES AND INDEX.
ISBN 0-691-07411-9 (HARD)
1. HEGEL, GEORG WILHELM FRIEDRICH, 1770–1831.   2. SPIRIT—
HISTORY—19TH CENTURY.   I. TITLE.
B2949.S75047   1992   193—DC20   91-41996   CIP

THIS BOOK HAS BEEN COMPOSED IN LINOTRON BASKERVILLE

PRINCETON UNIVERSITY PRESS BOOKS ARE PRINTED ON ACID-FREE PAPER,
AND MEET THE GUIDELINES FOR PERMANENCE AND DURABILITY OF THE
COMMITTEE ON PRODUCTION GUIDELINES FOR BOOK LONGEVITY OF THE
COUNCIL ON LIBRARY RESOURCES

PRINTED IN THE UNITED STATES OF AMERICA

1   3   5   7   9   10   8   6   4   2

For Janet, Maren, and Sonja

The Holy Spirit is, in fact, the one wholly credible and indubitable member of the Divine Trinity. Even if we doubt the existence of the sources from which it is alleged to proceed, a doubt which, in our twilight state, cannot but afflict us at every moment of our life, we cannot yet doubt its living presence *within* us, above all when we fall short of our higher aspirations, but also when it confers upon us the guidance, strength, peace, and joy that it at times does.

(John N. Findlay, "Thoughts Regarding the Holy Spirit")

CONTENTS

ACKNOWLEDGMENTS

RESEARCH for this book commenced by way of a *Forschungssti-pendium* from the *Deutsche Akademische Austauschdienst* in 1982, and also by a Fulbright Senior Research Fellowship in the Federal Republic of Germany during 1986. I have many to thank for these rewarding opportunities—especially Professors Rüdiger Bubner, Jürgen Moltmann, Heiko Oberman, Hans Küng, Eberhard Jüngel, and the late Professors Klaus Hartmann and Ludger Oeing-Hanhoff, who were my hosts at the University of Tübingen during these periods.

Much of the material herein was tested, as it were, on the faculty and students of Ripon College, Cuddesdon, Oxford, when I was the Karl Jaspers Lecturer there during the spring semester of 1989. For the honor of being selected, and for their wonderful hospitality and stimulating conversation, I wish to thank the Reverend John Garton, Principal of Ripon, the Reverend Jonathan Draper, Professor of Systematic Theology, and the rest of the faculty and students of Ripon College, Cuddesdon, Oxford.

I also wish to express my gratitude to all who have supported this project through critical evaluations, recommendations, and numerous other encouragements, especially President John R. Silber, Provost and Executive Vice President Jon Westling, and my colleagues in the Departments of Religion and Philosophy at Boston University. A special word of thanks is due to Dr. Ana-Maria Rizzuto who graciously shared her professional expertise as a psychiatrist in reading the chapter on Madness, and to my friend and colleague Professor Klaus Brinkmann, who shared his critical eye in checking the German passages.

The late Professor John N. Findlay of Boston University, and Professor Hans-Georg Gadamer of Heidelberg, were my principal sources of inspiration for this work. These two great scholars are among those chiefly responsible for the renaissance in Hegel studies during the past forty years, and I count it as one of the great blessings of my life to have known them both as teachers and as friends.

Finally, it has been a great pleasure to work with the editorial staff at Princeton University Press throughout the production of this book. I am particularly grateful to Ann Himmelberger-Wald, Editor of Philosophy and Religion, and to Lauren Oppenheim, Manuscript Editor, whose keen perceptions have greatly helped to refine this book, in both form and substance.

Boston, 1992

PRIMARY TEXT ABBREVIATIONS

All references in German are to G.W.F. *Hegel, Werke in zwanzig Bänden* (Frankfurt: Suhrkamp Verlag, 1979).

A   *Aesthetics: Lectures on Fine Art*, 2 vols. Trans. T. M. Knox. Oxford: Clarendon Press, 1975.

B   *Briefe von und an Hegel*, 4 vols. Ed. J. Hoffmeister and R. Flechsig. Hamburg: Felix Meiner, 1961.

D   *The Difference between Fichte's and Schelling's Systems of Philosophy*. Trans. H. S. Harris and W. Cerf. Albany: SUNY Press, 1977.

DS   *Differenzschrift*, Werke 2. Jenaer Schriften. Frankfurt: Suhrkamp Verlag, 1970.

E   *Enzyklopädie der philosophischen Wissenschaften*, Werke 8, 9, and 10. Frankfurt: Suhrkamp Verlag, 1970; *Encyclopaedia of the Philosophical Sciences*, 3 vols. Trans. W. Wallace and A. V. Miller. Oxford: Clarendon Press, 1971.

ETW   *Early Theological Writings*. Trans. T. M. Knox. Philadelphia: Pennsylvania University Press, 1971.

FK   *Faith and Knowledge*. Trans. W. Cerf and H. S. Harris. Albany: SUNY Press, 1977.

FPS   *First Philosophy of Spirit* (1803). Ed. and trans. H. S. Harris and T. M. Knox. Albany: SUNY Press, 1979.

FS   *Frühe Schriften*, Werke 1. Frankfurt: Suhrkamp Verlag, 1970.

GP   *Einleitung in die Geschichte der Philosophie*, Werke 18, 19, and 20. Frankfurt: Suhrkamp Verlag, 1970.

GW   *Glauben und Wissen*, Werke 2. Jenaer Schriften. Frankfurt: Suhrkamp Verlag, 1970.

HD   H. S. Harris, *Hegel's Development*, 2 vols. Oxford: Clarendon Press, 1972 and 1983.

HL   *Hegel: The Letters*. Trans. Clark Butler and Christine Seiler. Bloomington: Indiana University Press, 1984.

HP   *Lectures on the History of Philosophy*, 3 vols. Trans. E. S. Haldane and F. H. Simpson. New York: Humanities Press, 1974.

JS   *Jenaer Schriften* (1801–07), Werke 2. Frankfurt: Suhrkamp Verlag, 1970.

LPR   *Lectures on the Philosophy of Religion*, 3 vols. Ed. and trans. Peter C. Hodgson. Berkeley and Los Angeles: University of California Press, 1984, 1985, and 1987.

PG   *Phänomenologie des Geistes*, Werke 3. Frankfurt: Suhrkamp Verlag, 1970.

PR   *Philosophy of Right*. Trans. T. M. Knox. Oxford: Clarendon Press, 1967.

PS   *Phenomenology of Spirit*. Trans. A. V. Miller. Oxford: Clarendon Press, 1977.

RP   *Grundlinien der Philosophie des Rechts*, Werke 7. Frankfurt: Suhrkamp Verlag, 1970.

SEL   *System of Ethical Life* (1802–03). Trans. and ed. H. S. Harris and T. M. Know. Albany: SUNY Press, 1979.

SL   *Science of Logic*. Trans. A. V. Miller. New York: Humanities Press, 1976.

TE   *Three Essays, 1793–1795: The Tübingen Essay, Berne Fragments, and The Life of Jesus*. Trans. Peter Fuss and John Dobbins. Notre Dame: Notre Dame University Press, 1984.

VA   *Vorlesungen über die Ästhetik*, Werke 13, 14, and 15. Frankfurt: Suhrkamp Verlag, 1970.

VPR   *Vorlesungen über die Philosophie der Religion*, Werke 16, and 17. Frankfurt: Suhrkamp Verlag, 1970.

WL   *Wissenschaft der Logik*, Werke 5, and 6. Frankfurt: Suhrkamp Verlag, 1970.

HEGEL AND THE SPIRIT

I

INTRODUCTION

Der Geist erkennt nur den Geist.
(*Frühe Schriften*)

SPIRIT *(Geist)* is Hegel's grand philosophical category. Of this
there can be little doubt. He stakes his claim on Spirit in what
arguably is his first major philosophical essay, "The Spirit of
Christianity and Its Fate" (1797–98), and devotes the rest of his life to
showing how it works.[1] What Spirit ultimately is and means, after this
massive effort, is exceedingly difficult to specify with any real precision. Of this difficulty too, and as nearly two centuries of commentary on Hegel bear witness, there can be little doubt. The reason for
this categorical imprecision lies in the fact that Hegel's conception of
Spirit, as in the case of Aristotle's conception of Being, quite literally
has to do with everything and with nothing. As such it is the most basic
and also the emptiest of categories. Unlike Aristotle's conception of
Being, a category a priori in the order of logic, and a posteriori in the
order of time, Hegel's conception of *Geist* encompasses both dimensions of the question in such a way that they cannot really be separated
one from the other. Therefore, while Spirit is the most immediate and
least differentiated of categories, it also provides Hegel with the basis
of infinite mediation and differentiation through a form of logic that
can only be called hermeneutical. This is the uniqueness of Hegel's
category of Spirit—namely, that Spirit and the dynamic life of the concept are one and the same.

Failing to understand or appreciate this, many doubt whether Spirit
is a meaningful category at all. Such individuals might argue, in the
manner of Bertrand Russell, that those who evoke the language of
Spirit, being contemptuous of conventional logic, do so in order to
confound categorical coherence for the sake of advancing metaphysical claims that would be otherwise untenable. But there also are metaphysical objections. Nicolas Berdyaev, for example, believes that
Hegel's Spirit and Aristotle's Being are necessarily vague because both
are monists. He argues that Hegel, in fact, played Aristotle to Kant's
Plato thus signaling a major theoretical shift in both instances from
the cosmo-ontological dualism implicit in classical Greek philosophy
prior to Aristotle's unified worldview, to some form of monism or pan-

theism. The traditional dualism in Western thought that is reinforced by the Judaeo-Christian-Islamic traditions of supernatural revelation, and preserved and reinstated by way of the Kantian *noumenon*, is dissolved, Berdyaev argues, in the transcendental monism of Fichte and his successors, including Hegel. Thus Hegel's Absolute Spirit turns out, after all, to be another instance of human spirit, and this alone. What is important for Berdyaev, and more recently for Derrida, is the preservation of the ontological status of Spirit as wholly *Other*. Berdyaev believes that he accomplishes this by way of an ethical personalism grounded in the philosophy of freedom; and it is from the standpoint of a personalist ethics especially, Berdyaev contends, in a Kierkegaardian way, that Hegel's system and the conception of Spirit upon which it is based falls short of the mark.[2]

Among other twentieth-century philosophers sympathetic to Hegel, Jaspers's notion of *das Umgreifende* (the All-Encompassing or All-Comprehensive) probably comes closest to the overall intent and purpose of Hegel's conception of Absolute Spirit. But Hegel would have been uncomfortable with the spatialized ontotheological nuances in Jaspers's formulation that, like those of Berdyaev and Findlay, have a certain theosophical quality and probably owe more to Schelling and other mystical sources, especially Jacob Böhme, than to Hegel. Jaspers, in turn, was uncomfortable (as many remain today) with the many crudely temporalized, teleo-eschatological versions of Hegel's *Geist* that have accumulated in the scholarly literature inspired by and indebted to Hegel—especially neo-Marxist interpretations in which freedom tends to be absorbed by necessity.[3] On the other hand, Jaspers's contemporary and erstwhile rival, Martin Heidegger, was a thinker simultaneously obsessed with and repulsed by the Hegelian legacy of *Geist*—so much so, as Derrida has observed, that the early Heidegger strenuously "avoided" all references to "Spirit" and the "spiritual" because of the allegedly ontotheological, semantic overload contained in post-Hegelian conceptions of Spirit. After his infamous *Rektoratsrede* in 1933, however, Heidegger (for reasons highly questionable) removed the brackets with respect to "Spirit" and the "spiritual" in the attempt to go beyond or, as the case may be, behind Hegel.[4]

But Heidegger's "origin-heterogeneous" return, as Derrida calls it, to *Geist* can scarcely be viewed as definitive unless one is inclined to subscribe to the quasi-Romantic view whereby Spirit, as Ricoeur puts it, is always identified with an Other "anterior" to human experience.[5] Needless to say, Heidegger, while he certainly has the virtue of having studied Hegel very carefully (in contrast to many of his contemporaries), does not elucidate the meaning of the mature Hegel's understanding of *Geist* in ways that get to the bottom of its religious dimension, nor is he interested in doing so. Nor was it really possible for the early twentieth-century sympathetic critics of Hegel, such as Jaspers and Berdyaev, or unsympathetic ones like Popper and Voegelin, to abstract Hegel from the Left interpretations that so dominated Hegel studies during the war years. Indeed, until the revival of Hegel studies in the mid-twentieth century, prudentially motivated scholars were inclined to conclude that the Spirit of Hegel, whether in its Right or Left instantiations, was best left alone.

Rather than survey the vast literature concerned with the *Spirit of Hegel*, my concern in this study is to probe the religious dimension of *Hegel and the Spirit* by way of a highly specific religious and theological hypothesis. The definite article in the title of this work, therefore, is to be taken seriously since the focal point of my argument is to show that Hegel's philosophy of Spirit is a *speculative pneumatology* drawing its primary spiritual energies in this regard from the Christian doctrine of the Holy Spirit. By the qualifier "Christian," however, I certainly do not suggest that Hegel was preoccupied with the theology of Spirit in a conventional sense, nor do I claim to measure Hegel's conception against the wildly diverse conceptions of Spirit within Christianity as a whole. My concern rather is to indicate the manner in which Hegel's conception of Spirit, and especially Absolute and Free Spirit are directly inspired by and contiguous with Luther's understanding of Spirit—*not* the Luther so long debated by historians and theologians, but the household or catechetical Luther familiar to every thoughtful student of his *Small Catechism*. As such, I am distinguishing the catechetical Luther's conception of Spirit from an officially Lutheran dogmatic conception and from whatever doctrine of Spirit might be extrapolated from painstaking analyses of Luther's massive and notoriously unsystematic *Werke*. My argument turns rather upon what I view as being the performative character of the catechetical Luther's notion of Spirit as the "symbol giving rise to thought," in the phrase of Ricoeur, for those who, like Hegel, were very close to it. As such, it is my contention that the dialectic implicit in Luther's formulation provides a great deal of the trajectory, both formally and materially, to Hegel's philosophy of Spirit. By implication, I will also be arguing that the major impetus of German Idealism, for all of its variegated complexity, cannot be properly understood apart from this simple background, and that Hegel's philosophy of Spirit may be viewed therefore as a theoretical completion of the pneumatology deeply embedded in the religious and philosophical *Lebenswelt* of Germany.

The identification of Holy and Absolute Spirit, needless to say, is problematical—especially for the many theologians who regard He-

gel, and Hegelian philosophy generally, as the enemy of all things sacred, including the Holy Spirit. While many scholars certainly concede
that Hegel's philosophy is inspired by Christianity, at least initially,
they also tend to agree that he offers very little in its support, especially as regards the Christian doctrine of the Holy Spirit, or pneumatology, in the strict theological sense. Thus Hegel's philosophy, they
surmise (but usually not in ways as profound as Berdyaev's), may be
about *human* but not *Holy* Spirit. Like all things human, Hegel's finite
Spirit must *end*, Hegel's system being fittingly identified, therefore,
with the *end* of philosophy.

Oddly enough, something akin to this view is shared by many entirely secular, antireligious thinkers who, especially in the modern period, tend to view all talk about Spirit as being obscure, mythical, and
a subject to be strenuously avoided. This probably accounts for the
predilection of many analytical philosophers, at least until recently, to
discuss Hegel's philosophy of Spirit in terms of a philosophy of Mind
and to avoid, thereby, any association with theology or contamination
by religion.[6] But the alleged dichotomy between human and divine
Spirit, between psychology and metaphysics, has greatly contributed
to misinterpretations of Hegel, and it certainly has greatly inhibited
the development of a truly comparative philosophy of religion. Until
the advent of Pietism in the late seventeenth century, in fact, not even
Western theologians wrote much about Spirit; and philosophers have
yet to appreciate, much less appropriate, what phenomenologists have
to say about Spirit in the history of religions. What is written about
Spirit, especially in the Latin tradition of Christianity, has frequently
been suppressed or deemed heretical, as in the case of Joachim of
Fiore, the Spiritual Franciscans generally, and also the Anabaptist
traditions of the Reformation. This legacy of alleged heterodoxy associated with Spirit has no doubt also contributed to the semantic association of Free Spirit with "free thinking"—especially in the late nineteenth and early twentieth centuries. But serious philosophical and
theological reflections on Spirit are conspicuous for their scarcity. Indeed, because the Holy Spirit, in the modern period, is primarily associated with conversion-oriented spiritualist religious movements both
within and without Christianity (e.g., Pentecostal, Holiness, neo-Pente-
costal, neo-Evangelical, Transpersonalist New Age movements, etc.),
this benign neglect regarding the nature and meaning of Spirit has
continued by way of what might be regarded as an elitist default by
mainline, late-modern theologians, Spirit being hopelessly abandoned
to the utterly banal and superficial rhetorical formulations that
abound in popular religion.

Pneumatology thus remains the "orphan doctrine" in Christian intellectual history, as Adolf von Harnack once put it. By the term "or-

phan" Harnack means that Spirit seems always to have been treated as a subspecies of its own genus, so to speak, pneumatology being subordinated to a host of other theological considerations, especially christology and above all ecclesiology. A simple explanation for this neglect, of course, is that christology, with few exceptions, has always been the *Anknüpfungspunkt* of Christianity and, as such, its constant point of reference and controversy. Nor is this surprising since the doctrine of the atonement or redemption through the sacrifice of the God-man Jesus as satisfaction for the sins of the world is the metanarratological foundation of Christianity's *ordo salutis*. By this supreme metanarrative "the power of death and the devil," according to Saint Paul, has been "overcome" existentially and ontologically. The institutional task, *zwischen den Zeiten*, is to explain how this action is efficacious and salutary at practical, procedural, institutional levels. Having once established the hypostatic unity of the Father and the Son at Nicaea and Chalcedon, theologians necessarily turned their efforts to the business of defining soteriologically and instrumentally the proper mediation and appropriation of the divine-human identity.

At more subjective levels, of course, Christianity has always understood the personal appropriation of this mediation to be the gift of faith through the work of the Holy Spirit—whether by way of the simple confession, in the early Church, that "Jesus is Lord," of baptism and participation in the cultic Eucharistic fellowship meal, or the rather more complex doctrine of John Calvin regarding the *testimonium spiritus sancti internum*. Nevertheless, with the transition from what Max Weber has called the *charismatic* to the *institutional* phase of Christianity, there also commences what might be regarded as the gradual subversion of the simple truths of the trinitarian mediation by the monarchical-triumphalist tendency of the church to identify itself with Spirit—whether through the vast mediational-sacramental structure of Catholicism or through the foundationalistic biblicism of Protestantism.

Obviously, what tends to get lost in this transition is a living sense of the *power* immanent to experiences of Spirit. Such experiences of transhuman powerfulness have been left to historians of religion and phenomenologists such as E. B. Tylor, R. H. Codrington, Rudolf Otto, Gerardus van der Leeuw, and Mircea Eliade, to identify and to explicate as *das Numinose* in ways that frequently imply Christianity itself has lost this power. Unfortunately such assessments and implications are, in many instances, painfully true. Indeed, the entire history of the development of religions, and certainly the development of the philosophy of religion, has in many ways been the history of the negation of Spirit. For it is precisely the power of the *whole* that the Holy qua Spirit most deeply signifies—and not only signifies but *presences*, in being one with what it signifies. Clearly, such awarenesses inform the scrupulousness of the ancient world with respect to the names of the Divine, and it is very likely the case that Jesus himself refers precisely to this aspect of Spirit when he says to his disciples that "you will receive power when the Holy Spirit comes over you"—in other words, that Spirit is the power underlying any possible existential bliss and moral serenification.[7]

That the simplicity of such soteriological allusions should change with the growth of institutional Christianity, that there should be a movement from immediacy to mediacy, of course, is the point of Weber's Hegel-inspired hypothesis. Many feminist scholars today tend to understand this shift almost entirely in terms of the victory of patriarchy over matriarchy, the supreme dramatic example being the Petrine theory of Apostolic succession with the bishop of Rome or the Holy Father as supreme authority over all things, sacred and secular. By this thesis, the advent of male-dominated ecclesial absolutism signals the shift from the immediate and intuitive to highly mediated spiritual consciousness by way of fidelity to paternally administered sacraments deemed efficacious by their mere performance, *ex opere operato*.

Hegel's analysis of Spirit, of course, does not begin or even end with what might be termed the bare outlines of the Christian *idea* of Spirit in its classical and medieval forms. Historical considerations alone will not suffice to isolate the essence of Christianity—nor will what has now fashionably come to be called the sociology of knowledge, unless philosophers of religion wish to be reduced to the status of "counting clerks" (which Hegel believed to be the inevitable consequence of historicism). What counts is philosophy's ability to explicate the meaning of the "consciousness of God" or, more properly, "God consciousness," which, for Hegel, is identical with the consciousness of Spirit (*LPR* 1, §§74, 278–85). Absolute Spirit must be comprehended therefore in ways that are *true to its concept*, which means that Objective Spirit, understood ecclesiologically, must give way to—indeed, must constructively prepare the way for—an adequate philosophy of the state or whatever shape the "spiritual community" might assume in the future. This is precisely what Hegel was attempting to clarify, I argue, during the Berlin period when he was presenting, side by side, his lectures on religion, history, aesthetics, and the philosophy of law.

By this pneumatological thesis I do not mean, of course, that Hegel should be viewed as a philosopher of spiritual immediacy. On the contrary, Hegel is preeminently a philosopher of mediation by way of his insistence on the primacy of the logic of the concept. Nevertheless Hegel's philosophy of Spirit, inclusive of its religious roots, provides the dialectic of conceptual mediation with its existential and metaphysical energy. Hegel's philosophy of the concept, therefore, ultimately derives its force from his position with respect to the immediacy of Being since the mystery of Being and the mystery of the concept, for him, are ultimately one and the same—the foci being encompassed by *Geist*. It is the central thesis of this work, then, that Hegel's religious apprehension of the power of Spirit provides the nonfoundational ground of Absolute Self-Consciousness, that he elucidates this spiritual ground through a lifelong correlation of the categories of faith and knowledge, and that he completes it through his comparative philosophy of religion. As such, Hegel's philosophy of Spirit may be viewed as a uniquely original and highly constructive speculative pneumatology.

My pneumatological approach to Hegel is therefore hermeneutical in the sense of being an attempt to view Hegel *in context*, to use Dieter Henrich's phrase, while nevertheless attempting to be true, as Klaus Hartmann insists, to Hegel as a category theorist.[8] In this instance context has to do with the historical, social, cultural, and especially the religious and existential situation of late eighteenth-century Württemberg Pietism; and the logical category has to do with the doctrine of Spirit as developed in Christianity and especially by Luther. It is precisely in Luther, and what I term the submerged legacy of Luther in German Idealism, that context and category overlap. Indeed, I argue that much in the complex tradition of German Idealism is doomed to remain something of a closed book unless one attends to the influence of Luther at this basic level of cultural and religious mediation. This is especially true in the case of Hegel since, as J. N. Findlay reminds us, Hegel was first and foremost a theologian, and a unique kind of Lutheran philosophical theologian he remains—even though in the present confused theological situation this may be difficult both to recognize and to accept.

With respect to situating Hegel in historical context, I offer a study broader in scope than the more specialized recent work of Lawrence Dickey[9] without attempting to replicate in any manner the massive biographical-textual project of H. S. Harris.[10] My historical and biographical inquiries are designed rather for the purpose of showing that the category of Spirit has an unusually fertile context for development in late eighteenth-century Württemberg Pietism. As such, I argue that Hegel's philosophy of Absolute Spirit may be viewed as an answer to the obvious inadequacies in traditional Christian pneumatology, and suggest that when Hegel's doctrine of Spirit is elucidated within the discourse of *Selbstbewußtsein*, one obtains a better understanding of its critical place not only in Christian intellectual history but also in the broader arena of the comparative philosophy of religion.

Of course, it may be objected that a pneumatological exposition of Hegel's philosophy is presumptive since Hegel himself speaks of pneumatology only in connection with the old medieval rational psychology (as distinct from the new empirical psychology—i.e., sensationalism).[11] My rejoinder is twofold: first, I argue that Hegel avoids the pneumatological designator precisely because of its status as a *terminus technicus* in conventional theology; and second, I argue that the philosophy of religion, as Hegel conceives it, is concerned with the establishment of something altogether different from the manner in which pneumatology is ordinarily construed. Nevertheless, and as we will see, Hegel's rather extensive comments on pneumatology in the *Enzyklopädie* are suggestive on their own terms since he makes it quite clear that the old rational psychology is to be viewed, in spite of its obvious faults, as infinitely superior to the new empirical psychology (*E*, §34); for the new psychology, Hegel observes, treats only *sensible* data, whereas pneumatology treats the *rational* nature of the soul—its energizing element being the bond between the mind and the body, a bond that is nothing less than Spirit-itself. One can scarcely underestimate the importance of recognizing that this mediational function is identical, both formally and materially, with the work of the Holy Spirit as Luther understood it. One can also see, from the overall structure of the *Enzyklopädie*, that Hegel could easily have called Part C of his *Philosophy of Subjective Spirit* a "pneumatology" rather than a "psychology"; but he did not choose to do so, the reason being that the whole of Book 3 of the *Enzyklopädie* is really a *Pneumatologie*. In other words, if Hegel had used this term as the substitute for *Psychologie*, a substitute that might have been more accurate in the narrow semantic sense, such a designation would also have prevented his readers from recognizing what is, I argue, the deeper meaning Spirit for Hegel. The distinction between psychology and pneumatology therefore follows from differentiating the *intentio recta* of the category of *Geist* from the *intentio obliqua* absolutely central to the larger horizon of Hegel's philosophy of Spirit.

It is interesting to note in passing that the pneumatological thesis first originated, to my knowledge, in the satirical *Hegel-Spiel* of O. H. Gruppe. This play, which appeared during 1832, the year following Hegel's death, was entitled *The Wind, or an Entirely Absolute Construction of World History through Oberon's Horn* (*Der Wind, oder eine ganz absolute Konstruction der Weltgeschichte durch Oberons Horn*). By Gruppe's choice of this ethereal designator, it was his intent to demonstrate that Hegel's philosophy was metaphysically spurious, politically objectionable, and entirely without substance. Written under the pseudonym *Absolutulus von Hegelingen*, Gruppe ridiculed Hegel's rustic Swabian origins—origins that served to explain how one otherwise so brilliant could so easily be politically duped.[12] In any case, Gruppe, a young Berlin theology and philology student, makes reference in this farce to Hegel's so-called *Geister-Lehre* as a *Pneumatologie*, the dramatic analogues of Hegel's windy philosophy being Oberon, *König von der Elfen*, and Titania from Shakespeare's *Midsummer Night's Dream*. Hegel himself is portrayed as the *Nuß Knackerchen* intent upon disclosing the innermost secrets of the Aristotelian *nous*. However, the recent editor of this play, Heiner Höfener, observes that Gruppe remained blissfully unaware of the larger implications of such references and associations, for by aligning *Geist* with *Luft* and *Atem*, Gruppe does not thereby invalidate Hegel's concept of *Geist*. On the contrary, by such allegedly primitive phenomenological identifications, and their wider associations with the other aspiratives of Spirit in the history of religions, the politically bigoted Gruppe[13] inadvertently places Hegel's philosophy of religion squarely where it belongs, namely, within the larger context of a comparative philosophy of religion or a cross-cultural, speculative metaphysics. Hegel's Berlin *Lectures on The Philosophy of Religion*, in fact, clearly indicate that he was moving in the direction of a distinctively comparative philosophy of religion. Thus, far from being impervious to the manner in which religious people actually experience Spirit, Hegel increasingly viewed the history of religions as a way in which he might better assess his own experience of Spirit in the lifelong task of developing a philosophy of Spirit. Such associations, far from being spurious, can and should alert the sensitive reader to the phenomenological complexity and deep significance of Spirit in religion and in philosophy. Indeed, it is just the richness and density of *Geist* and its cognates in the history of religion and philosophy that makes Hegel's philosophy of Spirit such fertile ground for continued phenomenological and hermeneutical exploration.

· · · · ·

We begin this study by briefly exploring the place and, more specifically, the neglect of pneumatology in Western religious and philosophical thinking. This discussion establishes the groundwork for my thesis that Hegel's philosophy of Spirit may be viewed as an attempt to rescue and rehabilitate pneumatology and, a fortiori, the Christian *Trinitätslehre* that had fallen into disrepute under the onslaught of rationalism—whether rationalism in its objectivist deistic form, on the one hand, or rationalism in its subjectivist neo-Pietist form, on the other. Far from being inadequate or obsolete, Hegel believed, I argue, that the doctrine of the Trinity itself provides, through its category of Spirit, the key to religious and philosophical self-understanding. Much of the trouble with Enlightenment Christianity, therefore, lies in the neglect of its own conceptual resources, the chief resource being nothing less than Spirit-itself.

The religious and philosophical consciousness of many late eighteenth- and early nineteenth-century German (and in the case of Kierkegaard, Scandinavian) thinkers was heavily influenced by Pietism. Thus Pietism must be appreciated as the distinctive *Lebenswelt* out of, through, or over against which eighteenth- and nineteenth-century German philosophy develops. I try to show in Chapter 2 how Hegel interacted with the particularly orthodox form of Pietism that developed in the conditions peculiar to Württemberg. Although the neo-Pietism of Hegel's day had degenerated from its earlier forms, I nevertheless argue that key elements in Pietistic self-understanding remain embedded in Hegel's philosophy by way of Luther, Johannes Brenz, and C. F. Sartorius. My catechetical hypothesis with respect to Hegel's doctrine of Spirit, first introduced in connection with a discussion of *Trinitätslehre* in Chapter 1, takes on material significance as a primary leitmotif in his philosophy only when considered against this Pietist background.

I consider the categories of Transcendence and Dialectic historically and biographically in Chapters 3 and 4. Here I focus on the Frankfurt period of Hegel and his poet friend, Hölderlin, since it is in Frankfurt, I argue, where a pneumatological transformation of dialectic opens up a double path of Transcendence and, with it, the eventual split between Hegel and Hölderlin with respect to the meaning of dialectic. Hölderlin's position, as evidenced by the thematic of renunciation in his *Hymns*, introduces a path of thinking that extends to Heidegger and the deconstruction of ontotheology; Hegel's position, on the other hand, opens a path of thinking that will take him beyond Fichte, Jacobi, and Schelling to Absolute Idealism. But Hegel's intellectual conversion in Frankfurt, together with his subsequent abandonment of Hölderlin, has another important dimension. This I identify as Hegel's persistent fear of Madness, and it is this fear, I argue, which defines the relentlessly constructivist nature of the Hegelian dialectic and also his critique of the subjectivist Enlightenment. These topics are explored in Chapters 5 and 6, where, by considering the extremities of Madness and Enlightenment, the pneumatological leitmotif in Hegel becomes particularly pronounced in its religious, theological, and psychological aspects. The supreme work of the Holy Spirit, it will be recalled, is to serenify the religious self-consciousness through sanctification. In Hegel's case the work of sanctification and serenification—that is, the task of reconciling and making whole what is otherwise in a self-estranged state—is identical with the work of the concept, namely, *the binding together feeling's emotion and memories reflection in thought.*

This Hegel accomplishes by means of what I term the "pneumatological transformation of dialectic," and, to the extent that Hegel's philosophy of Spirit culminates in the teleo-eschatological goal of Absolute Self-Consciousness, I argue that this transformation also functions as an *ordo salutus.* This is the existential, Platonic dimension in Hegel's otherwise Aristotelian approach to Spirit—namely, philosophy as the means of eternalization. However, such an assertion makes sense only if it can be shown that Hegel's conception of Holy Spirit and of Absolute Spirit are one and the same. The final chapters on Absolute Spirit and Free Spirit are dedicated to showing how and why this is the case by reading Hegel's *Logic* against his treatment of the history of philosophy and religion—the subjects that so preoccupied Hegel during his final years. Indeed, it is precisely here where Hegel introduces a criterion of measure drawn directly from his *Logic* with respect to determining the essence of philosophy and religion: "How true," he asks, "are philosophy and religion to their concept?" But since the logic of the concept at its highest level and the Spirit both Absolute and Free are identical for Hegel, what he poses is in fact a pneumatological criterion that can be answered only by reconceiving philosophy as speculative pneumatology.

II

PNEUMATOLOGY

Glauben ist eine Erkenntnis des Geistes durch Geist.
(Frühe Schriften)

THE DOCTRINE of the Holy Spirit or pneumatology was a point of general theological controversy between Orthodox and Pietist Lutherans in Hegel's time, the point at issue being that Orthodox Lutherans held to what might be termed, in Hegel's terms, an objective notion of Spirit, whereas the Pietists leaned toward a subjective notion. Obviously this Hegelian characterization is inaccurate if taken to imply that such debates were pneumatological in the strong sense, that is, debates regarding the nature and essence of Spirit-as-such—which they were not. The arguments between Orthodoxists and Pietists were focused rather on the perennial soteriological issue of "justification (*Rechtfertigung*) by grace through faith" as this doctrine had been advanced by Luther and Melanchthon during the Reformation and formulated in the Lutheran Confessions of the sixteenth and seventeenth centuries.

Briefly stated, the principal issue between Orthodoxists and Pietists continued to be Pelagianism or, more precisely, Synergism, with respect to whether individual believers "cooperate" with the means of effective grace and, if so, on what terms. For the Orthodox no such subjectivism was admitted, emphasis being placed upon the objectivity of grace and its instantiated infusion through the "Word rightly preached and the Sacraments rightly administered" within the institutional framework of the Church. The Holy Spirit certainly "operates upon the heart" (*intus operans*), they contended, but only by way of the externally objective and authoritative agencies of Word and Sacrament, the Orthodox emphasis being *fides quae creditur* or the faith *that* is believed. The *inner word* must therefore be viewed as subordinate to the *outer word* for, as the reformed Augustinian Friar, Martin Luther, once argued, "the outward part shall and must precede, and the inward come afterward and through the outward because he [God] has determined to give the inward part to no man except through the outward part."[1]

Pietists, while agreeing with what they deemed to be the spirit of Luther, had difficulty with the letter of the Confessions and, as a result, placed increased emphasis upon the subjectivity of the subject with respect to the meaning of Spirit—that is, paid closer attention to *how* one believes, *fides qua creditur*. Against high-handed Orthodoxism, the Pietists believed that Word and Sacrament had to be not only "properly administered" but also felt or "experienced" by the believing subject. Only through experience could the "confirmation" by the Holy Spirit be demonstrated, not only personally but also in terms of improving the overall spiritual character of the *communio sanctorum*.[2]

Although Hegel was never directly involved in these theological squabbles, it must be recalled that his self-stated philosophical project at the turn of the century is an attempt to overcome the "difference," as he puts it, between the systems of Fichte and Schelling (the subjective and objective poles of idealism, respectively). Hegel's discussion of Fichte, Schelling, Reinhold, Jacobi, and later the theologians Schleiermacher and Tholuck is framed throughout by the Kantian formulation of the subject-object relation with respect to the determination of knowledge. In each and every instance, Hegel attempts to dissolve the problem of priority, whether subject or object, self or nature, infinity or finitude, through Reason-itself understood as Spirit—Spirit being understood as the Absolute encompassing ground of reason and, as such, the power by which the determinations of objectivity and subjectivity are both posited and reconciled. This difference, with respect to the problem of differentiating the internal structures of idealism and, by implication, the meaning of Enlightenment, has its direct, albeit less sophisticated, theological analogue in the above-mentioned "difference" between Pietism and Orthodoxy. Because Hegel takes religion far more seriously than many of his contemporaries, and because he is of the firm conviction that the religious or theological meaning of experience precedes the philosophical—indeed, prepares the way for "the life of the concept," which is nothing less than "life in the Spirit," Hegel's philosophy not only begs to be considered against this theological background but can also, I argue, be amplified by it.

In order to do so, we begin this chapter by briefly discussing the place of pneumatology in the history of Christian theology. I say discuss "briefly" because it is, in fact, a relatively short history, pneumatology being, in Harnack's words, the "orphan doctrine" in Christian theology since it has never enjoyed the attention attributed to the doctrines of God, christology, or ecclesiology. Following this, we focus more directly upon the role of pneumatology in the conflict between Pietists and Orthodoxists by way of a consideration of Ritschl's critique of Pietism. Finally, we take up what I consider to be the pneumatological pulsar driving Hegel's philosophy of Absolute Spirit—namely, Luther's catechetical explanation of the Holy Spirit—where I contend that the incipient dialectic in Luther's *Trinitätslehre*, especially as evidenced in his doctrine of the Holy Spirit, is decisive with respect to the manner in which Hegel's philosophy might be understood as a pneumatology.

· 1 ·

As Paul Tillich and others have indicated, the doctrine of the Holy Spirit has long been the nemesis of Christian theology—this nemesis being the historical result of the monarchical element in Western christology, which has tended to subvert any sustained or truly creative development of pneumatology.[3] Obviously there are many complex social, cultural, and political reasons for this dogmatic shortfall, a full account of which transcends the scope of this study. Suffice it to say that a significant side effect of the christomonism that has dominated Western theology is manifest in the inability of theologians to provide an adequate account of *how* the merits of Christ are to be appropriated by the believer apart from falling into the trap of mechanistic objectivism, as in the case of Western Orthodoxists, or into an emotivistic subjectivism, as in the case of the Pietists.[4]

To some extent, the theological truncation of pneumatology is a logical consequence of the normative credal adoption of the *filioque* clause by the Latin Church in the early ninth century. This insertion was perceived by the Eastern Church as the subordination of the Spirit to the Son, and it was this action, together with the iconic controversy and a host of other political, cultural, and economic problems, which produced the Great Schism between Byzantium and the Latin West. Therefore even though Eastern Orthodox theology continues to be Spirit-oriented, much of its discourse on Spirit remains spiritualized in the abstract, Platonic sense and remains socially and politically otherworldly.[5]

Thus there is little that can be identified as critically substantive pneumatology reflection in Christian theology, even during the period of definitive credal formulation. Indeed, the articles on the Holy Spirit in the Apostles', Nicene, and Athanasian Creeds are conspicuously sparse with respect to any exposition on the nature and meaning of Spirit-as-such and, when considered against later additions and redactions, the doctrine of Spirit can only be viewed as a kind of potpourri of postulates and assertions designed to include everything that cannot be said of the Father and the Son. One finds simple assertions *that* Spirit exists, but little or no attention to what it *is*, or *how* it exists. Indeed, the what and the how remain a kind of unintentional mystery when contrasted with the finely tuned delineations concerning the reality and proper relationship of the Father and the Son.

The exigent questions during the century and a half between Nicaea and Chalcedon, of course, had to do with christology—especially the monophysitism of Platonistic followers of Arius. One might surmise that sustained attention to pneumatology during the conciliar period would have compromised the primary concern of the Fathers, which was to establish, in a definitive way, the nature and scope of the mediational authority of the Church. This it achieved by way of what turned out to be a dynamically monarchical christology (even though modalistic monarchianism was officially condemned). The obvious doctrinal extension of this monarchianism was not pneumatology but ecclesiology, since sustained attention to pneumatology would compromise what Hegel came to regard as the *Positivität* or extrinsicism of its foundationalistic christology. Given the astonishing success of Christianity as the victorious trans-imperial mystery cult in the late classical world, and given the inevitable political and institutional struggles that followed as the Church made its way, in Max Weber's terms, from a charismatic to an institutional stage, it was probably inevitable that functional necessities would quickly displace mystically speculative concerns of theology. The charismatic feature of pneumatology, moreover, makes it a necessarily vague, mystical doctrine inviting subjectivism; and vagueness and ambiguity were not what the business of running a Church was about, especially during a time when it viewed itself as the successor to a collapsing Imperium. Hence, theological inquiries regarding the nature of Spirit necessarily shifted to questions regarding its work, and with that shift pneumatology largely becomes ecclesiology. Following the ecclesiological *Aufhebung* of pneumatology (which, in this instance is not really a sublation but a near-cancellation, or *aufgehoben*), the doctrine of the Holy Spirit becomes identical with highly complex articulations of the proper institutional or material agencies for the effective mediation of grace and the exoteric actualization of salvation[6] with little or no attention to esoteric questions regarding the ontological or the existential meanings of Spirit-as-such. Indeed, theological affirmations regarding the co-equality of the Spirit with the Father and the Son, as Harnack points out by way of Athanasius,[7] seem from the outset to have been important only as a means of insuring the symbolical economy of the Trinity.

But there are also significant epistemological problems underlying the inability of the Church to reconcile the formal and substantive properties of Spirit—or what Hegel would eventually come to identify as Absolute Spirit. Bernard J. F. Lonergan points out in his brilliant study, *De Deo Trino*,[8] that it was the fate of the Christian or Nazarene sect, once having been accepted wholesale by the Greco-Roman world, to have its theological roots formulated in a philosophical culture already dialectical, but in a mode of dialectic insufficient to comprehend the richness of the Trinity. This deficiency was not formal, however, but material, since the mythological roots of primitive Christianity were of a rhetorical and narrative order wholly alien to middle and late Platonism. The Christian story was not grounded in the mode of *Phantasie* that typified the other mystery cults; it was grounded rather within the order of incipient history—but for the Gentile world, obscure Semitic history. Until the rise of Christianity it had been the express function of Platonic dialectic to overcome the mode of mythical fantasy or, at the very least, to domesticate it by allegory (as in the case of Philo with respect to Judaism)—something that in fact continued in Christianity among the Alexandrine theologians. Wholesale adoption of this hermeneutical strategy, however, would have been tantamount to subordinating the mythical to the eidetic in ways that would lead, as the victorious Athanasians determined, to the destruction of its popular soteriological appeal. The element of fantasy, so essential to religion, was therefore retained by the early Church in a different way: narrative fantasy was raised to the level of historical fact while remaining, at the same time, something culturally alien to the experience of an ever-increasing number of those who avowed it. But it is precisely this alien element that, somewhat ironically, also provided the emergent Christian mythos with its unique peculiarity. The cosmological postulation of absolute truth grounded in a historical narrative that otherwise remained culturally and psychologically alien to the now-dominant Gentile Church strangely enabled it also to survive. At the same time, *logos*, unable to overtake the mythos of the Christian story completely, places mythos into the perpetual jeopardy of *paradoxus*—the terms of this paradox being the foci of endless debate in the history of theology until Paradox-itself becomes the principal focus of theological and philosophical reflection as in Luther, Hegel, and especially Kierkegaard.[9]

Owing to the contradictory nature of the Platonic metaphysical dialectic and quasi-mythical Hebraic historical narrative, it is difficult, therefore, to locate with exactitude the precise nature of the trinitarian conception. This is why, I argue, pneumatology remains the "orphan doctrine" in Christian theology.[10] This being the case, it is not surprising that theologians tended to shift their attention from questions of Being to questions of meaning regarding the Trinity—that is, to questions regarding the *persons* as distinct from the *nature* of the

Trinity. In Hegelian terms, this meant a turn away from the concept (*Begriff*) of the Trinity, and a turn toward the meaning of its instantiated mythological representations (*Vorstellungen*). These mythic-historic representations, manifestations, or revelations, depending on one's perspective, are all present in the biblical record as well as in the early Apostolic and Patristic traditions, where God is variously portrayed as a creator, father, lawgiver, redeemer, preserver, judge, and so forth.[11] It is the language of persons rather than natures, therefore, which provides these symbols with their popular institutional authority since God is understood as that being who inspires certain individuals, especially the prophets, by the breath of his Spirit, and, for Christians, becomes incarnate in the Son by the power of the Spirit, as the Lukan account of the visitation of the Blessed Virgin testifies. Given the phenomenology implicit in such assertions, it was also natural to assert that Enlightenment, Inspiration, and Illumination, in the classical and medieval world, were all perceived as coming "from above"—*supra nos*—whether from the gods or the upper world of Platonic *Eide*. In the Christian case, however, this fusion of discourse ultimately represents the contradictory blending of two entirely different orders of rhetoric—the question of Being (the central concern of Greek metaphysics) and that of Meaning (the central concern of the Hebrew religious experience), and a mode of paradox that, as Kierkegaard later put it, is absolute.

The meaning question in Christianity, however, was no longer confined to *halakic* questions regarding ethics and the moral law as had been the case in Judaism. The meaning question now required or at least implied meta-ethical clarification of properties, relations, and attributes within the being of God. The ante-Nicene apologists attempted to accomplish this by way of the economic Trinity by differentiating the relations between Father, Son, and Holy Spirit in ways that would obviate suspicions of tritheism. And while the gradual emergence of trinitarian dogma during the conciliar period represents at least the beginning of Christianity's attempt, in the phrase of Hegel, "to be true to its concept" (that concept being for Christianity, by the time of Athanasius at Nicaea, *Dreieinigkeit*), the truth of this concept was itself neglected and even subverted, I argue, until the advent of Hegel's speculative pneumatology.[12]

Far from glorifying the primitive as being the true element in religion or in the authentic religious consciousness, Lonergan asserts in a manner close to Hegel that "the further back we go . . . the less differentiated the consciousness of all [religious peoples]. . . . That is why among the primitives the sphere of the sacred and the profane interpenetrate without benefit of distinction or separation."[13] Like Hegel,

Lonergan therefore rejects the Romantic notion that the lack of differentiation somehow represents a higher degree of originality and authenticity in matters religious. This judgment does not reflect disdain for the value of immediate religious experiences, or that religion (or what we come to identify as religion) originates in the human attempt to make sense out of numinous experiences—experiences of power.[14] It rather reflects the judgment that the decisive element in religious experience is not experience-itself but "the will to differentiate" the meaning of this experience. As the will to differentiate intensifies, consciousness changes with respect to what one is likely to identify as being the essence of religion. The instability of what we call religion therefore originates in the fact that "religion [is] no ready-made eternal and immutable Platonic form," as Lonergan puts it. Recognizing this, religious consciousness must be understood as being hermeneutical consciousness, since "whatever is received is received after the manner of the receiver" and the consciousnesses of all receivers (whether as mediated or mediating) have structures that texture the meaning of what is received.[15]

The complexity of this mediating structure is evident in the semantic density and overlap of key terms having to do with the nature of the deity in early Christian theology: *onoma, logos, nomos, rama,* and so on. The Gnostics, of course, harmonized the name and the Being of God in highly mythical ways through numerous imaginative constructions—whether the *Aeons* of the *logos spermatikos,* or the *probolan* or "emissions" of his *pleroma* or "fullness" in and through the creative process. In Judaism, by contrast, the Being of God was accessible only through Torah—the moral law, whether written or unwritten, Torah being synonymous with the hidden essence and unspeakable name of God.[16] But the "split reference" of the early Christian apologists, if we may call it that, necessarily led to the overlapping of the ontological and moral attributes of the manifest One, whether in law, word, thought, or name. And although the incompatibilities of these categories and concepts are reconciled, at least for most believers, in the Christian story, there is a radical element within this process that continually resists theology's attempt to harmonize the rhetorical modes of questions of meaning and questions of being. It is precisely this radical element, this principle of nonidentity or difference, which raises questions of subordinationism, in one form or another, regarding the persons within the economic Trinity, and the problem of radical *Alterity,* as Levinas and others call it, in philosophical theology.

This tendency toward subordinationism, as Lonergan rightfully indicates, is particularly evident in Tertullian's predilection for "images of generation" as a way to mount an argument against Praxeas regarding the distinct and separate personae of the Father and the Son.[17] Tertullian argues that parents and offspring are separate and not the same, for "if one thing comes out of another, it is necessarily a second thing, different from that out of which it came, but it is not on that account separate from it. But where there is a second, there are two, and where there is a third, there are three. For the Spirit is third, with God and the Son, as the fruit is third, coming from the root and the shoot, and the stream is third, coming from spring and the river, and the point of light is third, coming from the sun and the Beam." Hence the unity and power of God is "one substance" just as the power of a monarchy is "one" and undivided—even within the monarchical family—"until overthrown by another monarch" of equal or greater rank and power.[18]

By this reasoning, however, and as Lonergan shows, substance or *ousia* does not really remain identical with itself because it is still understood in terms of representations, even though Tertullian's formulations are more sophisticated conceptually than the mythical images of the Gnostics. The cognitive structures of *Vorstellungsdenken* or "representational thinking," to use Hegel's term, are therefore critical with respect to understanding the complexity of the christological debates since no one at that time, according to Lonergan, really understood dialectic as cognitional process; that is, classical theology was not equipped to comprehend the dialectical process of Mind or Spirit-itself.

However Lonergan is not willing to acknowledge finally, as Hegel does, the negative implications of "picture thinking"—especially in the monarchical instance of Tertullian. Such an acknowledgment would clearly compromise the authority of Catholic teaching. Lonergan points rather to the differences between naive dogmatism and critical realism, suggesting that transcendental Thomism alone ultimately resolves this problematic in ways that make the *Dreiheit* cognizable and also affirm the integrity of the Catholic symbols of belief and faith. For example, Lonergan argues that the failure to differentiate between the strictly material and eidetic principles of dialectic generates the contradictions that are precisely the assigned task of dialectic to reconcile. Lonergan's argument therefore runs parallel to Hegel's (as we will see in Hegel's treatment of the pre-Socratics in the chapter on Absolute Spirit) since the problem with the arguments of the early fathers, according to Lonergan, are analyses that remain largely in the material sphere. Like the Miletian pre-Socratics, the Fathers either attempt to harmonize the contradictions between Father and Son by way of monarchic-social-organic reasoning (e.g., Tertullian), or attempt to dissolve these contradictions through a negative, apophatic theology (e.g., Origen and Irenaeus). Neither side recognizes that the one-sidedness of this logic of incompatibles originates in the intentional consciousness of the believer qua subject. In short, the ancients did not fully comprehend, according to Lonergan, the eidetic-transcendental nature of dialectic even though the *Trinitätslehre* of Christianity owes its very existence to it.[19]

A related problem in the early trinitarian debates is the propensity of the Fathers to treat "spirits" (*pneumatakoi*) as "things" or substances on the notion that even the world "invisible" to humans is "visible" to the omniscient God (as evidenced in the first article of Nicaea, viz., belief in a God who has created all things "visible and invisible"). Hence the realm of spirits (especially the Holy Spirit) is deemed infinitely superior to the realm of angels since semimaterial angels (spiritual beings nevertheless limited in space and time) are only selectively visible to humans, whereas Spirit is fully manifest in the Church (at all times and places) through the means of grace. It was precisely this kind of thinking that probably led to a designation of the Holy Spirit as a "Holy Ghost," an immaterial substance that could be present at all times and places in the material order. Driven by an institutional agenda, this blending of ontological and soteriological categories meant that discourse regarding the nature and meaning of Spirit was bound to remain tertiary to discussions regarding the distribution of power among Father, Son, and Church. This being the case, it is not surprising that so little attention should be paid to Spirit understood as the process implicit in the trinitarian dialectic. It does not follow, then, that the simple formula of Athanasius is as inspired as Lonergan suggests—namely, that "all that can be said about the Father is said about the Son except that the Son is Son and not the Father." As a dogmatic formula, this proposition merely asserts the consubstantial (*homoousian*) unity of the invisible and the visible without specifying how it is possible to make such an assertion.

To be sure, one might identify the root of the problem regarding the meaning of the primary category, *ousia*, in category confusion. For the Fathers, as Lonergan indicates, tended to treat phenomenal and noumenal substances as though they were the same. As one moves from the abstract language of Being (*eidos*) to the language of historical generation (*egenatos*), however, it quickly becomes evident that one cannot easily harmonize such disparate realms—whether by mathematics, which both Plato and Aristotle recognized as the problem in Pythagoras and Parmenides, or by the language of personae, which becomes the soteriologically effective but philosophically problematical strategy of the Church. For the Latin term *substantia*, as Lonergan indicates, does not correspond to the Greek word *ousia*, but to *hyposta-*

sis or "standing under," as in rank and an additional warrant for mon-archicanism. Thus if one is negatively disposed to this rhetoric for political reasons, it is very difficult to go along with Lonergan's con-clusion, to wit, that the ecclesial resolution, while not perfect, is necessary.[20]

The process of the pneumatological dialectic, however, is illuminat-ing in a decisive way for this study since it seems to be the case that it is a process that remains largely uncalculated and therefore uncon-scious in theology until the advent of critical idealism. Obviously this is important for those who, like Hegel and Lonergan, are concerned with a phenomenological and epistemological delineation of the de-velopment of religious and philosophical consciousness. Indeed, the historical consciousness of Spirit's process, as outlined by Lonergan, is nearly identical to Hegel's, namely, a development of religious and philosophical consciousness that moves from a naive realism to a dog-matic realism and finally to a critical transcendental realism. In He-gelian terms, such a movement commences with the harmonization of conflicting biblical images at the level of "sense-certainty," to the rec-ognition that such images must be read symbolically and allegorically because of the limits of "picture thinking" (as in Philo and Clement of Alexandria), and finally, having once made the critical-hermeneutical turn, to the recognition that Reason-itself is "inspired" and even Abso-lute in its ability to comprehend these *Übergänge*. In just this way Christianity is "true to its concept," according to Hegel, and therefore the consummate religion.[21]

Hegel's distinctions between the conception of God as empty, for-mal universality, God as subjectivity, and God as revealed, including the praxis element necessary in moving from the religions of nature and art to religion in the service of specific cultural goals, is another way to elucidate the same point. Indeed, this is precisely the position taken by Lonergan when he suggests that something like the consub-stantial formula of Athanasius was necessary to harmonize, on the one hand, the contradictory positions of the monarchists of the West (es-pecially Tertullian), whose allegorical treatment of the source materi-als was guided by ecclesial, political considerations and, on the other hand, the Alexandrine allegorists of the East, who took refuge in neo-Platonic apophaticism. In both instances, however, the divinity of Christ could only be maintained at the expense of its opposite. The critical choice of institutional praxis over ontology, of course, provided the occasion for curtailing naively realistic "anthropomorphic or metaphorical language" and "by setting aside the Platonic categories introduced by Origen, [Athanasius] posed the question at issue in the Christian categories of Creator and creature. . . . Having thus set up the problem, he resolved it by arguing, in a more or less rationalistic way, to the conclusion that the Son was a creature."[22]

The chief accomplishment of the Athanasian formula, then, is that it preserves the problem for later resolution. However, the general lack of differentiation as regards the nature and meaning of the Spirit also leaves it wide open to the diverse manner of functionalist reductions and emotivist interpretations of Spirit that follow one after the other in the history of Christianity. Only the Eastern Church, with its emphasis upon *theosis, epiclesis,* and its resistance to the *filioque* insertion by the Western Church, managed to maintain phenomenological nuances of the mystical energies inherent to the notion of Spirit-as-such. But this preservation is excessively platonistic and thus trinitarian in the narrow and extrinsic sense, even though phenomenologically contiguous with the oldest attributes of Spirit in the history of religions. In other words, the Eastern Orthodox conception of *hagios pneumatikos* retains, by way of the categories of *dunamis* and *energia,* the immediate force of such aspiratives as the Sanskrit *pranna* in the *Rig Veda* where "the breathless breathes" commencing the cosmic process and the Hebrew *ru'ah* in Genesis. For Spirit encompasses what is both most primordial and least differentiated in the history of religious consciousness, and what has at least the potentiality of being the most differentiated conceptually in metaphysics. It is precisely this conception of Spirit as a *complexio oppositorum* or, as Jaspers would put it, *Geist als das Umgreifende,* that Hegel presupposes in his conception of *Geist.* For it is the power and reality of Absolute Spirit that underlies the very possibility of "a phenomenology *of* the experience *of* consciousness," as Hegel puts it in the first part of his *Phänomenologie,* and, as Heidegger observes accurately, Hegel's philosophy "begins and ends with Absolute Spirit."[23]

· 2 ·

The Eastern Orthodox communions, while remaining true, so to speak, to the Holy Spirit, progressively lost their initial pneumatological vibrancy through platonistic reifications and liturgical conventionalizations of Spirit. As Aristotle became the classical philosopher of choice in the West, Scholasticism drifted into the essentialistic staticism that late medieval mystics such as Eckhart and Tauler, driven by *pneuma,* tried to overcome with little success. And while it might be argued that Protestant reformers, inspired by the mystics, rediscovered the existential and mystical properties of Spirit qua consciousness (i.e., the noetic and the pneumatic poles of faith), such pneumatological insights were subverted by way of prolonged debates as to how, precisely, the "righteousness of Christ" might be "imputed" to the believer "by grace through faith." Indeed, Orthodox Protestant Scholasticism reintroduced Aristotle by way of the eminently unmystical forensic language that soon displaced what was initially, especially for Luther, a passionately existential and clearly dialectical understanding of Spirit-filled faith.[24]

The late seventeenth-century Pietistic *Bußkampf* must be understood, therefore, as the quest for a Spirit-filled experience of faith that might cut through the wooden Orthodox mechanism of Protestant Scholasticism. Conversely, it is against the enormously popular success of the Pietistic *Bußkampf* that Protestant Orthodox and, indeed, Enlightenment reactions to Pietism must also be understood. In the case of the Orthodox, this reaction was fueled by the fear that an excessive preoccupation with the Holy Spirit and the "quest for holiness" through sanctification would lead to subjectivism and christological distortions through the introduction of a new criteriology whereby one might really *know*—that is, *experience immediately* or, as in Calvinism, *demonstrate*—the actuality of one's salvation.[25] The Enlightenment and post-Enlightenment response to Pietism, of course, is characterized by the attempt to discredit the very terms of debate as being "unenlightened" through an increasingly secularized critique of the authority of the symbols through which Spirit had been traditionally understood. Hegel's response to this symbolical devaluation, as we shall see, is one of the most important features of his critique of Enlightenment.

What developed in the theological standoff between the Orthodox and the Pietist factions in seventeenth- and eighteenth-century Lutheran theology is structurally analogous to the eighteenth- and nineteenth-century secularized standoff between the formalistic and Romantic factions in German Idealism. The larger cultural and social implications of this dichotomy are richly illustrated by way of Albrecht Ritschl's late nineteenth-century critique of Pietism. Indeed, Ritschl was particularly concerned about the reduction of the conflict between Pietists and Orthodoxists to the terms of a conventional theological dispute—the proper role of the Holy Spirit in the doctrine of sanctification. The deeper problem, for him, was the ideological conflict implicit in the shape of the new Protestant social order, namely, whether the reformed German social order would be based on Luther's perception of the sanctity of *all* vocations, whether secular or religious, and a strong affirmation of the concept of freedom that informed his theology of vocation; or whether this order would be based on sensibilities and values that facilitated the reinstatement, overtly or covertly, of the medieval ideals of "poverty, chastity, and obedience," which had functioned as the cornerstones of virtue and value in the hierarchically monarchistic vision of Christianity that dominated European religious consciousness for over a millennium.[26] If the latter case prevailed, then Ritschl believed that the traditional gulf between the religious and the secular would be enhanced and widened as it had been in the days prior to the Reformation. Indeed, Pietism, in Ritschl's view, was both consciously and unconsciously oriented in this direction owing to its emphasis upon the highly emotive forms of religious piety, which tended to promote political disengagement as evidenced by the Anabaptist sects that cultivated a separatist social ethic during and after the Reformation.

Aware of the negative social consequences of this dualistic tendency, Luther was firm in the insistance, according to Ritschl, that "the Christian religion [must] lead to spiritual dominion over the world, and [Luther] therefore placed the same value on the service of ethical action toward other men as he placed on those activities which comprise man's reconciliation with God."[27] Faced with the exigencies of social reconstruction, Luther, like Saint Paul, intentionally adumbrated his mystical sensibilities out of the fear that world-negating forms of spirituality tend to foster disunity and sectarianism. In other words, it is very difficult, from the standpoint of *praxis*, to keep the constructive and the deconstructive elements of mysticism distinct and separate. Thus any religious movement that tends to view the attainment of holiness or perfection in terms of the separatistic, ascetical ideals of monasticism, must be rejected, according to Ritschl, by insisting on the unity of both the formal and the material aspects of the Protestant Principle as *primus et principalis articulus*. "The importance of this doctrine," Ritschl insists, "becomes clear only as Christians have to strive after their perfection within the domain of secular society."[28] The Anabaptists, of course, did not agree with this in Luther's time, and the Pietists of Hegel's time also tended to view civil authority as inferior to religious authority. The *sensus communis* of a particular Pietist group or conventical was frequently viewed as inherently superior to that of society in general, since society in general, being unregenerate, has no identifiable *sensus communis*. Because of these dualistic tendencies (viz., divided loyalties informed by evaluative distinctions between divine *Geboten* and civil *Gesetzen*), Pietists tended to be viewed by both the Orthodox and the secular "cultured despisers" of religion, in Schleiermacher's term, as socially and politically divisive and culturally retrograde.

This is not to imply that seventeenth- and eighteenth-century Pietists were antinomian in the manner of the Protestant Left during the sixteenth century. Pietists were dedicated, in fact, to the general moral improvement of the social order and were partisan, as we will see in the next chapter, to causes that even today would be considered progressive. Nevertheless, because Pietists looked to the regeneration of individuals as the exclusive means to the end of improving the social order, and because such efforts were frequently *conventicaled*, or semi-secretive, they tended to create a church within a church, admission to which was based on personal conversion or rebirth. Thus whether in theory or in actual practice, Pietists frequently fostered the suspicion, among their opponents, that they were converting Luther's Gospel of Freedom into a new law of the twice-born.

But the Enlightenment secular adversaries of the Pietists, as we will see, were just as guilty, if not more so, in fostering social disunity and cultural deformation—and with more dramatic and far-reaching consequences. Hence it is against the disenchanted, secularized subjectivists of the nineteenth century who viewed themselves as a "class apart," so to speak (viz., Schleiermacher's "cultured despisers of religion"), that Hegel also directs the brunt of his criticism in the *Phänomenologie* and the *Rechtsphilosophie*. Indeed, this is why Hegel is emphatic, especially in his later works, that subjective or felt virtues become "real" (*wirklich*) only as they are made objective, that is, as actually and constructively present in the life of the community or state. It is in this moral sense that Hegel's famous maxim "what is rational is real [i.e., 'actual'] and what is real is rational" is set forth as the touchstone of any political philosophy that might serve the cause of unity and progress. Political philosophies that cannot make this positive contribution, be they religious or secular, pious or Romantic, fall into the strictly negative category of what Hegel terms "empty reflection" since, as individualistic privatizations of meaning and truth (i.e., privatizations of meaning devoid of spiritual power), they tend to subvert the kind of thinking that might actually contribute to the moral well-being of society.

It is important to note that Hegel's *Rechtsphilosophie* (especially the final sections) seems to be much informed by the latent tradition of speculative mysticism in Württemberg Pietism, for the fundamental question in Pietism has to do with making real or *wirklich* what is asserted as being formally and materially true—that is, *wahr*—in action or in life as lived. More specifically, the critical question has to do with reconciling the formal truth of the doctrine of creation with the efficient truth of redemption accomplishing this within the actual or material truth of sanctification. Herein lies the basic outline of the Hegelian dialectical distinctions between the *an-sich*, the *für-sich*, and the *an-und-für-sich Selbstsein* of Spirit. It is a formula Hegel derives, I argue, from Luther—at least in outline.

28 CHAPTER TWO

· 3 ·

The following lines from Hegel's *Lecture Manuscript on the Philosophy of Religion (1821)*, and thematic throughout his earlier critique of "contemporary philosophy" in the *Differenzschrift* (1801), are among the most compelling in the whole of Hegel's *Werke*. For the purpose of understanding his conception of Spirit in light of Luther, they are perhaps also the most significant: "[When] . . . I raise myself to the Absolute and thus being infinite consciousness I am, at the same time, finite consciousness . . . Both aspects seek and flee each other . . . I am the struggle between them" (*LPR* 1, §120).

This philosophical meditation contains, in abstract, the dynamics of the struggle for possible *Existenz* in the philosophy of freedom Hegel recognizes at the heart of the Protestant Principle. It was Luther who, in the midst of his quest for the meaning of faith, gave eloquent dialectical voice to the same struggle: "When I am raised up to Heaven, Thou castest me down to Hell; and when I am in Hell, Thou liftest me up to Heaven." Far from being an occasional comment, this dialectical conception of faith is found at the heart of Luther's enigmatic catechetical exposition of the third article on the Holy Spirit: "I believe that I cannot, by way of reason or power, believe in Jesus Christ, my Lord, or come to him; but the Holy Spirit has called me through the Gospel" (*Ich glaube, dass Ich nicht, aus eigener Vernunft noch Kraft an Jesum Christum, meinen Herren, glauben oder zu ihm kommen kann, sondern der heilige Geist hat mich durchs Evangelium berufen*).[29]

One might object at the suggestion that something as elementary as a catechetical formula might be determinative in the formulation of something as sophisticated and complex as Hegel's philosophy of Spirit. But this is just the point with respect to the influence of Pietism on Hegel's philosophy of Spirit—that words and phrases committed to memory in one's youth continue to perform one's consciousness throughout life—and this is precisely what Hegel concludes at the end of his *Enzyklopädie*. Not all words and phrases have this power, to be sure, but words and phrases perceived and appropriated as being profound never cease to have an effect on one's life. And when one begins to ponder the negative dialectic embedded within the formulation "I believe that I cannot . . . believe," one can also begin to see how this startling phrase might truly function, in Ricoeur's words, as a "symbol giving rise to thought" in the consciousness of a catecheumen as talented as Hegel.[30]

It is my contention, in fact, that these lines provide the definitive religious horizon not only for Hegel's philosophy of Spirit but also, in a very real sense, for the whole of German Idealism to the extent that its devotees were also familiar with them. Lack of familiarity with respect to early habituation in this unique form of religious dialectic may be the reason, in fact, why German Idealism remains a closed book, so to speak, for many who come into contact with it in only a formal, academic way.

It must be stressed that the conventional response to the meaning of these paradoxical lines "I believe that I cannot . . . believe," is probably one of general passivity as with other matters pertaining to religious instruction. On the other hand, if the catecheumen is pious, he or she probably concludes (given the perceived effects of original sin and the general authority of Luther's words) that human beings simply do not have the rational capacity to comprehend the redemptive unity of the Father and the Son. Indeed, because reason, according to Luther, is helpless in reconciling these cosmo-ontological and historical opposites (what Kierkegaard called the "absolute paradox"), one must, accordingly, wait upon the miracle of faith that is the gift of the Holy Spirit in order to make it real. It makes no difference whether this gift, and the mediation of sanctifying grace, is understood forensically and imputationally, as it was among the Orthodox, or whether it is understood subjectively and emotively, as it was with the Pietists. The conventional Lutheran view is that belief or faith is *pro me, extra nobis*—the result of something that comes "to me" from "beyond me" and remains beyond the powers of rational comprehension.

While Luther himself certainly held this general view (especially with respect to the exigencies of religious *praxis*), subsequent interpretations of his exposition have tended to neglect or miss altogether the transcendental mystery immanent to this dialectical formulation of faith's possibility. For viewed from a transcendental standpoint, Luther's formulation implies that the awareness of an Absolute-Unconditioned is also somehow present in the knowledge of nonknowledge as a datum of consciousness. What we have in Luther, then, is nothing less than an incipient dialectic of consciousness informing the manner in and through which faith and life in the Spirit are to be understood both formally and existentially. I would argue that for Luther this transcendental element probably originates in the tradition of Rhineland mysticism with which he was so familiar and that this consciousness is given powerful voice in this simple catechetical formula.[31]

This transcendental element, raised to epistemological and metaphysical cogency in Kant and Hegel respectively, can be appreciated by looking more carefully at Luther's formulation. Consider, for example, the meanings of the key terms *Kraft*, *Vernunft*, and *Glauben* in Luther and what they come to mean for Hegel. First, it is important to

note that Luther's use of *Kraft* or "power" in this context is not parallel, it seems to me, to his negative assessment of the power of the will
in his diatribe, *de servo arbitrio*, aimed at the voluntaristic Pelagianism
of Erasmus. Will-Power here has rather to do with the much simpler
and more immediate exigencies of catechetical instruction within a
cultural context beset with belief in superstition, witchcraft, necro-
mancy, and the host of spiritualistic permutations and charismata present to the lives of ordinary believers in the late Middle Ages. Thus we
are not dealing here with complex questions regarding the powers
and limitations of the voluntary and the involuntary that have preoccupied philosophers, theologian-philosophers, and theologians over
the centuries. Moreover, Luther's formulation obviously has nothing
to do with the "will to power" in the sense of Nietzsche and Schopenhauer even though, with some creative exegesis, this might come a bit
closer to the mark. Luther's concern, for the most part, is with the
world of the ordinary peasant in the backwaters of Saxony, a world
filled with a living sense of what Saint Paul refers to as the "principali-
ties and powers and present rulers of darkness," including those sha-
manistic devices whereby one might actually be able to make present
the power of the holy through instrumentalistic and utilitarian conceptions of sacramental power.

In a similar vein Luther's radical limitation of reason (*Vernunft*)
does not here have to do with his infamous quarrel with Aristotle and
"the whore, reason" of medieval Scholasticism; and obviously it has
nothing to do with the post-Kantian, neo-Orthodox limitations of reason that have colored retrogressively the more recent interpretations
of Luther. His reference to reason, in this instance, is influenced by
medieval antecedents, especially the Rhineland tradition of speculative mysticism as we find it expressed, for example, in Cusanus's reflections on "the wall (*Mauer*) of reason" as the ultimate barrier to *unio
mystica*. The Rhineland tradition was, in fact, the equivalent of speculative neo-Pietism in Hegel's day. A primary influence on Luther during his formative years, as Bengt Hoffman indicates, was the *Theol-
ogica Germania*, or the "Frankfurter Tractate" (1497) as it is sometimes
called, which Luther brought out in a new edition in 1516 (one year
prior to the posting of his famous theses), making it his first major
publication.[32] Thematic to this work, and in the thought of Eckhart
and Tauler generally, is the notion of faith as a nonobjectifiable datum
of consciousness—a datum that, as a *coincidentia oppositorum*, is best understood in the apophatic terms of *docta ignorantia*, as in Cusanus.
What is ruled out by Luther are reductions of the nature and meaning
of faith by way of the canons of rationalistic formalism and the whims
of subjectivistic emotivism. Hence "faith" (*Glauben*), for Luther, is not

to be viewed as the opposite of "reason" (*Vernunft*) in the speculative Hegelian sense. It is rather the opposite of *Verstand*; that is, faith is different from subject-centered or subject-controlled rational, instrumentalist understanding. Just so in the case of Hegel, since it was from instrumentalistic philosophies of reflection that he struggled (beginning with the turn-of-the-century *Differenzschrift*, and throughout the rest of his work) to free reason in its mystical, religious element. It is precisely this element, I argue, which is identical with Luther's conception of faith as consciousness (*Glauben als Bewußtsein*), with reason or *Vernunft* qua *Geist* being the decisive element within the "process of faith" wherein faith touches and is touched by the True Infinite.

The paradoxical oppositions Luther mentions, creation and redemption (which rational belief alone cannot unify but which Spirit-filled faith alone can reconcile), may be viewed, in Hegelian terms, as the tension between the formal but empty universality (*Allgemeinheit*) of the Father and the material but entirely contingent particularity (*Besonderheit*) of the Son. In Luther, these terms are paralleled, first, by the empty, nonsalutary universality discernible through the efforts of natural theology or what he calls the Law in its "first use" (*usus primus legis*), and second, by the Law in its "second use" (*usus duplex legis*), whereby the individual subject is psychologically overwhelmed by the experience of radical contingency—the existential consequence, as it were, of pondering the *Third Proof* of Thomas Aquinas. Such speculations, according to Luther, are successful only in showing that the God of Nature or the *deus absconditus* is ultimately the "God of Wrath," and that the contingent particularity of the God of Revelation, the *deus revelatus*, remains an utter enigma to reason, apart from an experience of the Law in its second form, *usus duplex legis*. One must choose, therefore, between the illusion of what is metaphysically and ontologically salutary on the one hand, and what is morally and existentially salutary on the other. This is precisely the enigma articulated in Luther's concept of Spirit, and like Luther, Hegel argues that if the relation between these two terms is fashioned on the basis of the logic implicit within each, the two cannot become "determinate" (*bestimmt*) in terms of a "unity" (*Einheit*), but remain in absolute and irreconcilable contradiction.

The logic inherent in the former is precisely what we find, in Hegel's day, in the orthodox idealism of Kant and Fichte, and the logic of the latter is manifest in the rather more Romantic views of Schelling and Schleiermacher. A reduction of religious or metaphysical meaning to one side or the other of this dialectic leads to what Hegel terms the "end of metaphysics" in philosophy and the "end of confessional content" in theology. Indeed, this dilemma is ironically and sarcastically stated by Hegel in the preface to the first edition of *The Science of Logic*, where he says that philosophy, after the downfall of metaphysics,

> can be likened to a temple richly ornamented in other respects but without a holy of holies. Theology, which in former times, was the guardian of the speculative mysteries . . . has given up this science in exchange for feelings, for the popular matter-of-fact, and for historical erudition. In keeping with this change there vanished from the world those solitary souls who were sacrificed by their people and exiled from the world to the end that the eternal should be contemplated and served by lives devoted solely thereto—not for any practical gain but for the sake of blessedness. . . . Thus having gotten rid of the dark utterances of metaphysics, having abandoned the colourless communion of Spirit with itself, outer existence [for philosophy and theology] seems to be transformed into the bright world of flowers, and there are no *black* flowers, as we all know! (*SL*, 25–26; *WL*, 13–14)

Obviously, Luther was not expounding, or better, articulating his answer to the enigma of the Trinity in terms directly analogous to those of Hegel. Nevertheless, a speculative metaphysics is embedded within Luther's formulation and what both have in common is the exigent need to provide an answer through what Hegel comes to term "a phenomenology of the experience of consciousness." For Luther's question has to do with how it is possible, within the midst of the experience of logical contradiction, to come to a meaningful faith. His question is similar, of course, to the processual circularity implicit in the dialectic of consciousness that informs the medieval formulation *credo ut intelligam; intelligo ut credam*.[33] But this quest is given a unique form in the paradoxical formula "I believe that I cannot . . . believe." And Luther's answer is also unique since he asserts that it comes by being "called" (*berufen*) by the "Holy Spirit." Spirit then, for Luther, is intrinsically involved with the mediation of meaning whereby the hiatus between *notitia* and *assensus* is overcome in *fiducia*; in fact, Spirit-itself *is* this mediation—the mediation of the *an-sich* and the *für-sich* becoming *an-und-für-sich-Selbstsein* in and through the life of faith, which is nothing less, as Tillich once put it, than "life in the Spirit." Moreover, this mediation is hermeneutical in the deepest sense of this now somewhat trivialized term since it is the function of Spirit, according to Luther, "to call" through the Gospel—that is, to be mediated through *logos*, which Hegel identifies as being identical with "the work of the concept (*Begriff*)." It is here, then, that both Luther and Hegel reconnect with the speculative pneumatology of Origen and Gregory of Nyssa.

It is also important to note here that Luther, in this brief but cogent catechetical exposition of Spirit, makes no mention of the sacraments as being part of this process of mediation. This omission was not, I think, lost to the sight of Hegel since he emphatically asserts in the so-called *First Philosophy of Spirit* (1802–03) that "language" is the first and primary manifestation (or *potency*, as he puts it, emulating Schelling) of Spirit separating itself from "air" as its primal element and positing itself as "speech" (*FPS*, 206–17). This does not mean that the Sacraments are no longer valued as a "means of grace" for Luther, since they most assuredly are. The point here is that Luther's emphasis is upon linguistic mediation. Faith or authentic self-consciousness and understanding is specifically identified with the primary hermeneutical acts of hearing, reading, and interpretation—in this case, a hearing, reading, and interpretation of the biblical witness. Providing equal attention to the Sacraments in this instance would have reintroduced the passive function he wishes to avoid by way of invoking an external grounding or *thing* that would obviate—even prevent, through external legitimation, the necessity of coming to self-consciousness through the act of faith.

Hegel's reflection on the *Positivität* of the Sacrament of Holy Communion in the "Spirit" essay (1797–98) exemplifies the problem of faith as he muses: "A regret arises" when the devotee "senses the separation, the contradiction" between the "feeling" that is present in this commemorative meal and the "intellect" that "sees" the representational elements of bread and wine for, in the final analysis, the two "remain separate" and cannot become "one." Hence the "serenity" traditionally associated with the *Abendmahl* turns into a "melancholy serenity since feeling's intensity was separate from the intellect and both were one-sided because worship was incomplete since something divine was promised and it melted away in the mouth" (*FS*, 368–69).

This contradiction remains and must remain present to consciousness, as in the case of Luther's *Ich glaube, daß Ich kann nicht . . . glauben,* unless love-filled devotional experience and memory's reflection upon it are "bound together in thought" (*FS*, 370). Such a "binding together" can only take place in Spirit-filled faith: "The essence of Jesus, in terms of the Son's relation to the Father, becomes known and grasped only in faith" (*FS*, 382; *ETW*, 266: *Das Wesen des Jesus, als ein Verhältnis des Sohnes zum Vater, kann in der Wahrheit nur mit dem Glauben aufgefaßt werden*). Such faith cannot be commanded since, as Hegel asserts, "only Spirit grasps and comprehends Spirit." Spirit qua belief, as Hegel makes clear in his early writings, was being "commanded" by both sides in the late eighteenth century—on the side of "objectivity" by Orthodoxists and Rationalists, and on the side of "subjectivity" by

Pietists and Romantics. This is precisely what Hegel finds so objectionable in the "positivity" of both Judaism and Christianity, the former "commanding" actions, and the latter "commanding" feelings (FS, 370). Moreover, it is this extrinsicism that makes the "fate" of Christianity particularly heart wrenching to Hegel, for while it was the destiny of revealed religion to discover the immutable in the mutable, the unconditioned in the conditioned, Spirit in the flesh as incarnate *logos*, it was the fate of Christianity to lose this insight once the Absolute made was into something merely objective or merely subjective.

This is the difference, then, regarding the reality and the identity of Holy Spirit and Absolute Spirit—whether one turns to the *Geist* essay, where Hegel seems first to struggle intensely with the meaning of faith, or in the *Differenzschrift* written two years later, where this theme becomes philosophically explicit, or in *Glauben und Wissen* and the *Phänomenologie*, where the two come together in the quest for "absolute knowledge." Viewed as a whole or a project, it is clear that Hegel thought the impasses between critical Idealism and Romanticism, Orthodoxy and Pietism, could be surmounted only through the *Aufhebung* of Spirit. Indeed, it is just this dialectical understanding of Spirit that brings about, for the mature Hegel, an understanding of faith as mediation. For faith (*Glauben*) does not mean the immediate sense-certainty that neo-Pietism (Jacobi, Schleiermacher, Tholuck, etc.) takes it to mean: "Faith properly has an antithesis within itself, but one that is [initially] more or less indeterminate. Faith is set in opposition to knowledge, *[but] this is a vacuous antithesis because what I believe, I also know—it is a content in my consciousness*" (*LPR* 1, §§283, 284; my emphasis).

It is in just this sense that Hegel's philosophy of Absolute Spirit must be considered as a speculative pneumatology, as faith as the mediation of Spirit; in fact, the meaning of the Hegelian *Aufhebung*, as Heidegger observed, becomes particularly cogent only when viewed in the context of *Erhebung*: "The sublating of *Aufhebung* must . . . be conceived, as always in Hegel, in terms of the resonance of its threefold meaning: *tollere*, removing and eliminating the mere, initial illusion; as *conservare*, preserving and including in the experience; and as an *elevare*, a lifting up to a higher level of knowing itself and its known."[34] It is through this dialectic of Spirit, as Hegel muses, where "the same [religious] doctrine uttered as a child" is now also known as "Idea" and "the sign of an entire life" (*E*, §§288, 289, Z).

With the shift from religious *Vorstellungen* to philosophical *Begriffen* there also takes place, for Hegel, the inversion of *Vernunft* and *Verstand* as regards the priority and ultimacy of these terms. For Luther and the Pietists, but in different ways, "reason" was the villain and "understanding" was the savior—the former being identified with threadbare Scholastic formalism and the latter with the vitality of living faith. For Hegel, three centuries later, "understanding" had become synonymous with the new orthodoxy, the now pseudo-Kantian philosophy of reflection in which everything is understood and nothing is known, whereas "reason" (the *intellectus archetypus* that, qua Spirit, had initially inspired Kant) seemed now completely expired. It is against the new formalism that Hegel again postulates *Vernunft* in its religious, mystical aspect as that region of consciousness where the unconditioned may itself be again perceived as a datum of consciousness and hence as a knowable content. In so doing, Hegel restores to philosophy and to theology its most primordial dimension, the reality of Spirit.

The reinvigoration of philosophy and theology by way of a speculative pneumatology is a lifelong project for Hegel, and it is a process that commences in Frankfurt and his enigmatic relationship with Hölderlin, where their chief tasks had to do with clarifying the relationship between transcendence (metaphysics) and dialectic. This at least Hegel accomplishes, as I will show in Chapters 3 and 4, in dialogue with Hölderlin during the Frankfurt period as evidenced by the essay "The Spirit of Christianity and Its Fate." Hegel's later views on Madness and Enlightenment are also, as I will argue, the direct result of what he accomplishes in Frankfurt and, immediately following, in Jena. To place these developments in historical context, however, it is necessary first to consider Hegel against the horizon of his fertile religious environment in late eighteenth-century Württemberg Pietism.

III

PIETISM

Die Religion ist die Wahrheit für alle Menschen, der Glaube
beruht auf dem Zeugnis des Geistes, der als zeugend
der Geist im Menschen ist.
(*Enzyklopädie*)

H EGEL WAS NOT a Pietist in the ordinary sense. By conventional standards one could reasonably conclude that he was
the contrary of everything usually associated with Pietism.
Some of Hegel's chief antagonists were Pietists, especially during the
Berlin period (1818–31), when he actively identified himself with Lutheran Orthodox conservatism against both Pietism and neo-Pietist
liberalism. The continuing legacy of Pietism, in fact, has produced
most of Hegel's most vociferous religious and philosophical adversaries—whether tender-minded Schleiermacharians or the rather more
tough-minded Kierkegaardians, to use the terms of William James in
an un-Jamesian way. Had not the "heartless Hegel" bitterly, even sarcastically, criticized Christianity, especially in his early Basel and
Frankfurt essays, suggesting that the Church was the chief impediment to the development of an authentic *Volksreligion* and therefore
obsolete? And had not Hegel prepared the way for Nietzsche by way
of his declaration that no other human institution has "greater contempt for man" than the Church?[1] It is not surprising, then, that Pietists should conclude that Hegel's entire philosophical project is motivated by a blasphemous Prometheanism as evidenced by his avowed
intention, in the *Science of Logic*, "to think the thoughts of the Creator
prior to the creation"; nor is it surprising that neo-Pietists, both then
and now, have looked rather dimly upon the "choleric old man" Hegel
and his outspoken condemnation of Schleiermacher as the church
theologian guilty of having reduced Christianity to "feeling" (*Abhängigkeitsgefühl*) and a religion "devoid of content."[2]

It is just because of such emotive diatribes, of course, that Hegel's
work begs to be considered against the cultural horizon of late eighteenth-century Württemberg Pietism. Master dialectician, Hegel himself was deeply aware of the extent to which we are drawn to an opposite Other that provides the basis of self-understanding and possible
Existenz. In Hegel's case, this Other is the Pietist religiousness within

which he was nurtured and trained as a philosopher-theologian, and it is this very religiousness that he transforms into Absolute Consciousness through a philosophy of Spirit that is the equivalent, I argue, of a speculative pneumatology. Considering Hegel "in context," however, does not imply a historicist reduction of the meaning of his work. As the champion of *Wissenschaft*, Hegel's philosophy certainly must be able to stand on its own and be judged accordingly. But standing on one's own is not the same as being altogether disconnected from one's origins. Indeed, it is just the Cartesian duality of form and substance that Hegel's notion of *Wissenschaft* attempts to overcome. One must, therefore, be attentive to the shape of the Hegelian content in order to adjudicate its meaning more accurately, and to do so, one must consider Hegel against his environment.

Hegel's spiritual and cultural environment was that of late eighteenth-century Württemberg—Pietist Württemberg. Accordingly, I argue that the religious and cultural air fueled by the spirit of Württemberg Pietism was so pervasive that neither the thought of Hegel nor his colleagues, Hölderlin and Schelling, can be properly understood apart from an appreciation of its unique *sitz-im-Leben*. And because Pietism and neo-Pietism so permeated the cultural air of *Alt Würtemberg*, the paucity of Hegel's direct references to it are deceptive[3] and have led more than one commentator to conclude that Hegel was a man so preoccupied in his youth with political matters and, in his maturity, so utterly consumed by formal and abstract questions in philosophy, that the exigencies of popular religiosity were of little or no concern to him. Such conclusions, as Emil Fackenheim was one of the first to show, are major oversights with respect to fathoming the deeper meaning of Hegel's work.[4] Thus while formal approaches are to be commended as the way to overcome the distortions sedimented in the so-called Right and Left critical reactions to Hegel, his religious and metaphysical Spirit cannot ultimately be understood properly apart from historical and biographical considerations—as dangerous as it may be to "read between the lines," so to speak. Thus I argue that if there is to be an authentic religious and philosophical reclamation of Hegel, it is necessary to continue the attempt to view more accurately the man and his work over against the spiritual horizon of his time. This horizon is Pietism—and it is this horizon, I argue, that both haunts and nurtures Hegel throughout his life and even beyond it. For we are reminded by Christiane, Hegel's sister, that following the death of her brother, the widow "took refuge among the [Berlin] Pietists . . . having come heavily under their influence," obviously having been previously forbade this association by her husband.[5]

In this chapter we provide a historical overview of Württemberg

Pietism, and we also attempt to situate the religious life of the Hegel family in Stuttgart in order to discern better what this religious and cultural setting means for the development of his philosophy.

· 1 ·

· In taking account of the influence of Pietism on Hegel, it is important first to note that late eighteenth-century Württemberg Pietism was by no means a static thing; rather, it was a movement in the midst of dramatic changes brought about by a host of economic, political, and social circumstances—especially the influence of the historic European Enlightenment whereby Pietism turns into neo-Pietism. Far from being a seamless garment Pietism passes through several major transformations as it unfolds between its *terminus a quo* in Philip Spener in the mid-seventeenth century and its speculative *terminus ad quem* with F. C. Oetinger in the late eighteenth century. As the definitive religious mood of Württemberg for over a century, it is the changing shape of Pietism that both nurtures the speculative philosophy of Hegel and occasions his reactions to "the religion of feeling."

For the American reader, it is also important to emphasize that German Pietism is not to be equated with the freewheeling, anti-intellectual, hysterically emotive manifestations of pietistic evangelicalism so pervasive in the New World. Such characteristics may have typified certain Anabaptist sects during the Reformation (disparagingly identified by Luther as *Schwärmerei*), but eighteenth-century Lutheran Pietism, while always critical of dogmatism and even antidogmatic, remained confessionally grounded (in contrast to other forms of religious enthusiasm, especially in America) and, as a consequence, is considerably more thoughtful and sedate. The religion of *Frömmigkeit* or "devotion" as exemplified, for example, in Philip Spener's classic mid-seventeenth-century text, *Pia Desideria*,[6] is highly differentiated theologically, and far from being confined to the lower classes, Pietism was a movement that, by the end of the eighteenth century, had become the driving intellectual force in several university communities (including Tübingen) and had also become the primary source of missionary energy of the Zinzendorfeans at Halle. As such, Pietism represents the major spiritual force behind the philosophical, theological, social, and political life of Germany for nearly two centuries and, owing to massive mid-nineteenth-century German immigrations, this influence extends to America as well.

Pietism initially emerged as a grassroots religious response to the decimation of the Thirty Years War, which had claimed over half the population of Württemberg. As such, it was directly contiguous, in terms of social activism, with the sixteenth-century reform party within Lutheranism, led by Johann Arndt. After signing the Peace of Westphalia (1648), the Hohenzollerns (the reigning ducal family in Württemberg) and the nobility generally instituted a heavy program of taxation in order to finance the reconstruction and expansion of royal properties. The diverting of scarce resources for projects of self-aggrandizement was an irritant to many frugal Swabian Protestants and provided political as well as religious motives for Pietistic activities. But the Hohenzollerns were also the patrons of Eberhart-Karls-Universität in Tübingen, and it was from this academic site that Pietism eventually established a definitive hold on the cultural life of Württemberg. Indeed, the Pietistic horizon extended for generations up to and including the time when Hegel, together with his friends Hölderlin and Schelling, spent quiet hours strolling along the banks of Neckar receiving the theological education they would eventually challenge and transform through the grand tradition now known as German Idealism.

The date usually cited for the official establishment of Pietism in Württemberg is 1662, when Philip Spener first visited Tübingen. There he met Johann Andreas Hochstetter, a "prominent churchman" with religious views identical to his own, who later "joined the faculty as professor ordinarius of languages and ephor" in 1677.[7] With the addition of Christoph Reuchlin in 1699, who later became dean of the *Stift*, and Johann Albrecht Bengel, Württemberg's most famous Pietist theologian, the foundations for a theological faculty grounded in an activistic form of Orthodox Lutheran Pietism had been firmly established at Tübingen. It was the unique combination of religious elements embodied in these individuals, according to Stoffler, that exemplified "the native Swabian inclination toward personal piety and social sensitivity." Lawrence Dickey rightly calls this *praxis pietatis*[8] since it was the nonretiring *praxis* element that made Württemberg Pietism different from other forms of religious fervor.

These qualities may be viewed as extending all the way back to Johannes Brenz and the founding of the Reformation in *Alt Württemberg* since it had been the appointed task of Brenz, the personal friend and convert of Martin Luther, "to erect a dogmatic bulwark" in order to stave off the Zwinglians and the Anabaptists.[9] Johannes Brenz (1499–1570), from Weil der Stadt (the birthplace of Johannes Kepler in 1571, who also received his education at Tübingen), was the principal architect of Lutheranism in Württemberg under Duke Ulrich and his son and successor, Christoph. Personally converted by Luther to the cause of Protestantism during the latter's Heidelberg Disputation in 1518, it was Brenz who established the institutional structure of the Württemberg Church in ways guaranteed to ensure the triumph of the Lutheran point of view vis-à-vis those reformed parties closer in spirit to Zwingli and Calvin. The efforts of Brenz were especially influential in the immediate vicinity of Stuttgart, the ducal capital, where he was appointed *Probst* (Provost) of the *Stiftskirche*, a position rightly described by James Estes as "the most prestigious ecclesiastical post in the duchy."[10]

While the theological views of Brenz met with some resistance in the more remote areas of the province, they became firmly established in the immediate vicinity of Stuttgart, including nearby Tübingen. Most important, especially for this study, is the fact that the Brenzian edition of Luther's *Catechism* was formulated with the intention of developing systematic theological hegemony and, as the dogmatic rule of instruction, the impact of this edition was felt not only in the parishes but also in university centers, where dogmatics textbooks, such as the one by C. F. Sartorious in the Tübingen of Hegel's day,[11] were in essence elaborate extensions of the Brenzian canonic rule.

What made the Brenzian edition distinctive, and also the Sartorious *Lehrbuch*, was the decision to give first position to Luther's treatment of the *Credo* and its *Drei Hauptartikelen*. Luther himself began with an exposition of the *Geboten* (Ten Commandments or the Law) in both his *Large* and *Small Catechisms*, but Brenz and his associates considered the powers of Zwinglianism and crypto-Calvinism to be so powerful in *Alt Würtemberg* (owing to the geographic proximity of Swabia to Switzerland) that the semipelagian character of its doctrine of salvation by works rather than by grace needed to be directly confronted. It was the view of Brenz that true Christianity would best be served by making certain that impressionable catecheumens and budding theologians first obtained a solid grounding in Luther's *Trinitätslehre*, which they regarded as perfectly mirroring the essence of the Gospel. Only after this fundamental theological grounding in the doctrine of the Trinity, Brenz and his associates believed, could the temptation to "works righteousness" be assuaged, whereupon students could proceed to other matters such as moral theology.[12]

The articles of the *Credo* and their explanations, of course, were the objects of rote memorization by young confirmands, as were the rest of the primary Lutheran confessions. Indeed, the standard pedagogy known as "reading for the minister" in Lutheran communities extended into the middle part of the twentieth century, both in Germany and in the northern European immigrant communities of the New World, since such readings not only served the purpose of religious indoctrination but also constituted an integral part of one's normal education—in many cases, the only education one received beyond the primary grades. By the end of the nineteenth century, however, this reading consisted not only of memorizing Luther's explanation of the catholic symbols of Christendom, but also committing to memory the many Bible-based expositions added in order to combat modernism. The theological exposition of these proof-texts (a strategy that commenced, in fact, during the time Hegel was at Tübingen, as a means of combating Kantianism) is relatively low-grade compared to the brilliant economy and simplicity of Luther's primary exposition. Indeed, Luther himself regarded his *Kleine Catechismus*, together with *De servo arbitrio* (his polemical treatise against Erasmus on *The Bondage of the Will*), as the only works to fall from his pen that were worth "saving from the fire."[13]

Luther's cogent dialectical formulations regarding the nature of "faith" (*Glauben*) and "knowledge" (*Wissen*) in this basic text have always struck perceptive readers as being theologically inspired. And if one may be so bold as to count Hegel an extremely thoughtful catecheumen, then it may very well be the case that the incipient transcendental dialectic informing Luther's exposition of the Trinity made a strong philosophical impression upon him from the moment he first encountered it. Precisely in this sense I argue that Luther's *Small Catechism* (as distinct from his German translation of the Bible, which is usually cited in this regard) may be viewed as being the foundational symbol-text in the future development of German Idealism; for since the mainstream tradition of German Idealism is almost exclusively Protestant, the performative influence of this catechetical foundation-text cannot be underestimated as a common element in the thinking of its devotees.

Hegel "read for the minister" quite literally in the shadow of the Stuttgart *Stiftskirche*, the *Hegelhaus* being just down the street a few hundred meters. This geographic and existential proximity to the ecclesial *axis mundi* of *Alt Würtemberg* is reflected in the very first entry of his *Tagebuch* (which he began on 26 June 1785, when he was just fifteen), where he comments on his pastor's sermon on the Augsburg Confession and other historic facts having to do with his recently confirmed Lutheran identity. Striking, in retrospect, is the symmetry of this entry with one of his final productions, "The Treatise on the Augsburg Confession," written just a year before his death and delivered at Friedrich-Wilhelms-Universität in Berlin on 25 June 1830 on the occasion of the three hundredth anniversary of that famous document.[14]

In order to ascertain more clearly the place of religion in the formation of Hegel's early identity, it is helpful to differentiate Württemberg Pietism into three basic types. First, there is what I would term mainstream *devotional* Pietism, espoused by the mid-eighteenth-century Tübingen theologian, Johann Albrecht Bengel. This mainstream, exoteric, devotional Pietism was directly contiguous with Spener's ideas, and consisted in the practical, heartfelt harmonizations of the Bible, Lutheran dogma, and *Lebenspraxis*. This is the kind of Pietism that most influenced ordinary laypersons and undergirded the development of what has come to be known as *subtiltas applicandi* in the application of the moral law. For this subtile effectiveness in the pursuit of virtue and sanctification consisted not in the application of complex methods and formulas derived from individual insight and cunning. It followed rather from a piety-based *sensus communis*, this common sense regarding value and virtue being the distinctive mark, as Hans-Georg Gadamer observes, of Pietist hermeneutics. In other words, *sensus communis* grounded in *Lebenspraxis*, as contrasted, to the purely formal and highly individualistic approaches to value and virtue that became characteristic of Enlightenment and post-Enlightenment approaches to ethics, provided the moral strength whereby Pietism was able to actualize its ideals.[15]

But experience-oriented mainstream Pietism also tended to stimulate, especially among the more educated, the esoteric form of neo-Pietism exemplified by the late eighteenth-century theosophical Pietism of Friedrich Christoph Oetinger (1702–82). Speculative neo-Pietism, having its historical origins in the seventeenth-century Lutheran heretic, Jacob Böhme, may also be viewed as being an extension of the work of an earlier Reuchlin at Tübingen, Johannes Reuchlin, teacher of Melanchthon and renowned author of *De arte cabbalistica* in 1517—precisely the year in which Luther posted his famous theses on the door of the *Schloßkirche* in Wittenberg. These esoteric sources, combined with the chiliastic aspect of Bengel's otherwise conventional work, flowed into the speculative neo-Pietism of Oetinger. In fact, Oetinger's *Öffentliche Denkmal der Lehrtafel* (or "public educational discourse") was dedicated to Princess Antonia of Württemberg, who, like Schelling and the early Hegel, had considerable interest in the literary forms of esoterism.[16] Deeply imbued with the spirit of Christian Cabbala, Oetinger contends in this treatise that far from being limited to the official sources of revelation, the basic truths of the Trinity and the Incarnation are primordial, that is, revealed in the *sefirot* or the *Leiblichkeit* of the Divine from Eternity. This primordialist hypothesis (previously advanced by the Italian Renaissance philosopher, Pico della Mirandola, in the face of his inquisitors) most assuredly informs, as Ernst Benz argues, the views of Schelling regarding objective [Nature] Idealism and the "expansion of power" out of the Divine *Ungrund*.[17]

Hegel's eventual rejection of speculative neo-Pietism may also be linked to his critique of the third hybrid type of Pietism better known as Romanticism. Indeed, since speculative Pietism was increasingly oriented toward nature and other nontraditional esoteric sources of truth, especially Romantic literary sources, it tended to subordinate the normative, doctrinal content of mainstream Pietism in favor of the cultivation of what might be termed the "feeling of feeling" or the "immediate-immediate" in ways that were altogether profane and hence identical with Romanticism generally.

We will say more about the proximity of speculative neo-Pietism and Romanticism in the chapter on Hegel's critique of Enlightenment. Here it is important to elaborate, in greater detail, some of the significant ways in which neo-Pietism diverged from the mainstream tradition. As already stated, the primary features of conventional Pietism had to do with the ways in which it strove to cultivate *sensus communis* or commonality in moral and spiritual life: intense prayer, Bible reading, and lengthy afternoon and evening worship in informal settings, both on Sundays and midweek. But these ascetical emphases, while initially stimulated by and combined with the chiliastic element (viz., imminent "end of the world" views originating in medieval Spiritual Franciscans such as Joachim of Fiore), eventually gave way (especially in the late-eighteenth-century academic context of Tübingen) to the even more immediate concerns of coming to terms practically with Oetinger and theoretically with Kant.

It was increasingly the position of church authorities, with respect to Oetinger, that the heterodox sources of speculative Pietism placed the faith at risk. No retiring cobbler, like Jacob Böhme—who could be cowed into submission by the inquisitorial Pastor Richter—the charismatic Oetinger commanded a tremendous following both at his pulpit in Murrhardt and in the wider community. While Oetinger took great pains to harmonize his syncretistic Pietism with the orthodox sources of revelation (probably in the hopes of the academic appointment, which never came), he was increasingly perceived, by the faculty at Tübingen, as being theologically divisive.[18] Indeed, the development of Oetinger's career is a case-study illustration regarding the complexity of the late Württemberg Pietism, which influenced Hegel. For Oetinger started out, while a student of Bengel at Tübingen, as a conventional Pietist. But like many of his Enlightenment contemporaries he also "had a craving," as Stoeffler puts it,[19] for the more esoteric, extrabiblical sources of wisdom, including, as mentioned previously, the heterodox illuminations of Valentin Weigel (1533–88), Jewish and Christian Cabbala—including, of course, the speculative theosophical mysticism of Jacob Böhme (1575–1624), with its grounding in the natural philosophy and alchemical "new science" of Paracelsus. Moreover, Oetinger contended (in a manner not unlike Luther, Böhme, Schelling, and the early Hegel) that mere reason (*Vernunft*) had to be combined with understanding (*Verstand*) when it came to matters of faith. But this deeper "understanding" grounded in true piety and the *sensus communis*, was even more dependent on "feeling" (*Gefühl*) or direct experience, and it was this kind of thinking, among neo-Pietists, that led increasingly to the displacement of the Bible by more exotic sources of revelation. Neo-Pietism therefore begins to fuse with Romanticism generally, especially by way of promulgating, with the Romantics, the attitude of *Glückseligkeit* and naive optimism regarding the human prospect as the humanistic *summum bonum*.[20]

Coming to terms with the more challenging development of the Enlightenment, namely, the critical philosophy of Kant, demanded a different kind of move. What emerged was the beginning of a kind of biblicism that would eventually undermine the moral constructivism of Pietism altogether. Hegel's dogmatics professor, Gottlob Christian Storr, and a fellow student, Karl Christian Flatt (who later joined the Tübingen faculty), were instrumental in this effort through their respective attempts to demonstrate the authority of scripture on the notion that, precisely as inspired, the Bible itself embodied the evasive Kantian noumenon. Hence one did not have to look any farther, they contended, than scripture itself in order to answer the thorny questions in epistemology and metaphysics posed by Kant and his followers. As a result, the new dogmatics texts of these *pseudo-Kantians*, as Hegel and Schelling came to call them, soon replaced the classic *Lehrbuch* of C. F. Sartorious, and Christian theology began to drift into the defensive posture characteristic of Pietism in its antimodernist theological phase.[21] The distinctive feature of the turn-of-the-century dogmatics text thus became the inclusion of extensive, prefatory *theologumena* designed to combat growing skepticism by proving, in "pseudo-Kantian ways," the authority of scripture. Indeed, such arguments in many cases became a substitute for reasoned exposition of the traditional symbols of the faith and, as such, marked the beginning of the long and dismal epoch in Protestant dogmatic theology known as biblicism, whereby students were obliged to accept as given and axiomatic the biblically authoritative conditions for a hermeneutic adequate to an actual exposition of the historic confessional symbols of Christianity. On the other hand, this transition also marked the commencement of liberal theology's reactive abandonment of all content, whether biblical or dogmatic, for the alternatives of historicism and subjective immediacy. In both instances, as Hegel observes, "the authority of the canonical faith has been in part degraded, in part removed. The *symbolum* or *regula fidei* is itself no longer regarded as

something totally binding but instead as something that has to be in-
terpreted and explained from the Bible" (*LPR* 1, §78)—or, as Hegel
also holds, from the alleged authority of subjectivity, in which case all
content is superfluous.[22]

This change in pedagogy, occurring as it does on the cusp of Hegel's
education, is of no small significance for understanding his theological
views. On the one hand this change mirrored the growing doubt that
traditional symbols of Christian faith had the power to convey meaning of their own content requiring rather highly specific and exceedingly dubious methodological propaedeutic in order to be understood
and accepted as authoritative. As such, it is a development that clearly
reverses the Brenzian strategy commenced in the sixteenth century
that advanced, so unabashedly, the content of the *Trinitätslehre*. On the
other hand, it opened the way to subjectivism and it may well be that
Hegel's poor performance in dogmatics classes, while he was a student
at the Tübingen *Stift*, can be attributed to his resistance to the newly
defensive pietistic hermeneutical method.[23] When Hegel later comes
to castigate theology for having lost its content, this loss is for him the
consequence of this transition—such content being lost, on the one
hand, to the alleged objectivity of the biblicists and, on the other, to the
subjectivism of the Romantic neo-Pietists.[24]

It is just this passage of the religion of feeling from the traditional
symbols of religious devotion to secular and profane objects that constitutes the transition from Pietism to Romanticism during the late
eighteenth century. What Pietists from both camps had in common
was the subjective emphasis upon immediate experience as a grounding authority. But the goals of an experience of the immediate-immediate were quite different. In the former case the purpose of an experience of the "heart strangely warmed," in Wesley's phrase, was to
strengthen and invigorate the religious life of the community. In the
latter instance, subjectivism became the basis for a pseudoconfirma-
tion of the veracity of the Romantic principle of identity. Both Luther
and Brenz understood the danger implicit in the religion of feeling to
be the sacrifice of content. Hegel also understood these dangers—not
only late in life when he allied himself with conservative Orthodox
Lutheranism vis-à-vis liberal neo-Pietists, but in the very formulation
of the categories of his dialectic of Spirit-in-itself, for-itself, and in-
and-for-itself. Indeed, this dialectic is virtually unintelligible apart
from Pietism since it was the principal contention of Pietists that Spirit
must make a difference—that is, subjective belief must be capable of
translation into the objective or actual well-being of the life of community. For there are, Hegel argues, three principal marks of true piety
as manifest within the life of the cultus: devotion, sacrifice, and ethical

life (*LPR* 3, §§334, 335).[25] But in later Pietism, where the dialectic of Spirit is reduced to mere subjectivity, religion is reduced to a superficial form of the first mark, *Frömmigkeit*; it has no second mark; and the third mark is therefore impossible to realize. Ideologically opposed to "empty rationalism," neo-Pietism turns out to be theoretically identical to it.(E, §573).

Before we say more about these implications, let us look more closely at Hegel's earliest experiences with Württemberg Pietism. Although the record of this experience is fragmentary, what can be garnered is highly suggestive, especially when considered as an essential rather than a merely incidental part of his life experience.

· 2 ·

While the Hegel family was pious enough by late eighteenth-century German standards, it cannot be *proven* that they were self-identified Pietists—as were, for example, the families of Hölderlin and Schelling.[26] Religion was not an all-consuming activity for the Hegel family. They did not see the necessity of sending the young Hegel to a Protestant *Klosterschule* but chose rather the humanistic Gymnasium in Stuttgart. Both Schelling and Hölderlin, by contrast, were from Pietistic homes and attended schools expressly devoted to the ideals of Pietism—Schelling at Bebenhausen, where his father was on the faculty, and Hölderlin at Denkendorf, where the Pietist theologian Bengel taught prior to his appointment to the faculty at the Tübingen *Stift*.

Protestant cloister schools in the eighteenth century (that is, preparatory schools housed in what were, before the Reformation, Catholic monasteries) were distinctive in that they supplied a curriculum especially strong in biblical studies designed to prepare male students for Protestant clerical vocations. Hegel's education at the Stuttgart Gymnasium, by contrast, was devoted to the classics and the humanistic literature of the Enlightenment. It may be surmised that Hegel's poor performance in biblical studies at Tübingen, especially Old Testament (in contrast to Hölderlin and Schelling), was the result of late exposure to biblical languages and literatures. But it may also be surmised that Hegel's less-than-enthusiastic regard for Romanticism (again, in contrast to Hölderlin and Schelling) had much to do with the fact that for him it was never the primary occasion for a full-scale rebellion from a Pietist curriculum.

That Hegel was the product of neither a clerical family, as was Schelling, nor a would-be clerical family, as was Hölderlin, is also significant given the nature of religiously motivated rebellion as, for example, in the famous case of Nietzsche. And although there is distant evidence of Lutheran clergy in the Hegel family tree, as F. S. Harris indicates,[27] there is nothing to indicate that Hegel's parents placed any great importance on this pedigree. Hegel's father was a minor bureaucrat in the ducal offices at Stuttgart and seems to have had no particular interest in religion beyond that of a normal citizen. Yet it is also precisely in this sense that the Hegel family embodied *Frömmigkeit* or "devoutness" anchored in the conventional sense of moral duty and responsible citizenship encompassing religion. The young Schelling, however, as already mentioned, was of the clerical caste, and Hölderlin's widowed mother probably married a *Kapellmeister* to draw both herself and her son closer to institutional religion. In any case, it has long been surmised by Hölderlin scholars that the frail mental condition of the poet was probably exacerbated by the ceaseless reminder, on the part of his neurotic, pietistic mother, that his obligation to God had commenced with his mother's dedication of his life to the Church in his infancy.[28]

Hegel's mother, Maria Magdalena Louisa [Fromm] Hegel, by contrast, seems to have been remarkably free of the characteristics of the doting, enthusiastically religious parent. It is precisely in this regard that she can be taken as the primary formative influence in her son's religious and intellectual development. In fact, Hegel's sister, Christiane, makes much of the "closeness of spirit and temperament" between her mother and brother, noting that Frau Hegel was entirely cognizant of her son's superior mental gifts and that she did everything possible, "within her limited means," to encourage his intellectual development.[29] As a woman "more highly educated than most of her time and station," she was, perhaps, instrumental in the choice of a humanistic Gymnasium over a *Klosterschule* as the appropriate setting for her son's education; she may, in short, have valued the thematic of the humanistic Enlightenment more than the narrow focus upon church-vocational preparation in mainstream Pietism.[30] Hegel's experience was probably similar to Kant's in this respect for, as T. M. Greene recalls, Kant's mother, in contrast to his father, was "more ardently and emotionally religious and seems to have had a far more forceful personality than that of her husband. . . . [And while she was] a woman of little [formal] education, [she had] . . . a large natural intelligence and genuine piety, and although she died when Kant was fourteen he never ceased to speak of the profound influence she had on his life."[31]

Hegel was twelve when his mother died and, in contrast to Kant, remains strangely silent about her influence—even in the *Tagebuch*, which he began to write three years after her death. Is this silence about his mother and, indeed, his enigmatic silence regarding the fate of Hölderlin, the product of insensitivity? Is Hegel's seeming impassivity already the early manifestation of the cold, dispassionate personality with which he has so frequently been charged by his detractors? I do not think so. In fact, I believe that just as the *unsaid* in Hegel's writings is particularly suggestive with respect to his views on conventional religion, so also his silence with respect to his mother and Hölderlin is particularly profound, as we will see when considering Hegel's views on madness.[32]

It is important to note, for example, that Hegel's entries in his diary commence immediately after his confirmation. Obviously his mother was missing from this otherwise normally joyous family occasion.[33] Was Hegel affected so deeply by her absence that he omitted all references to his mother? Are his intellectually ponderous and altogether unemotive diary entries a substitutionary compensation—indeed, a psychological negation, of the confidences he might have otherwise shared? What compacts were made, in 1781, between the dying mother and her husband regarding the future of the son? We can only speculate about such matters, but such deliberations are not at all unusual in such circumstances. There may be more than meets the eye, therefore, in the young Hegel's uncommon predilection toward methodically charting out his own intellectual and spiritual development, in contrast to being "preoccupied," as F. S. Harris notes, "by a host of adolescent trifles."[34]

While such conjectures cannot be answered with any great precision, it is possible, I think, to show that Hegel was haunted, even obsessed, by his mother's death and, as I will later show, by the madness of Hölderlin and the chronic mental depression of his sister, Christiane. In fact, what might today be termed an "unresolved concept of the feminine" is evidenced throughout his writings—not least in Hegel's fascination with Sophocles' *Antigone*—and that it is occasioned by his own sublimated sense of personal loss. These elements, when combined with near-hostility toward the philosophy of feeling and the altogether subordinate role sensation plays in his theory of knowledge, certainly suggest a certain uneasiness with the chthonic. Thus Hegel's relationship to women, like Freud's, remains darkly problematical throughout his life and career.[35]

The most dramatic early evidence for this can be found in Hegel's ponderous but erotically sublime reflections on Maria Magdalena, the harlot friend of Jesus, as developed in the 1798–99 essay "On the Spirit of Christianity and Its Fate." Here we have an essay that has been variously cited by commentators as representing something of a

turning point in Hegel's thought. I believe this is correct—but for reasons different from the political arguments usually developed. It
seems to me that the uncommon existential intensity of Hegel in this
essay takes its direction from a double set of references—his mother,
and Susette Gontard, Hölderlin's lover in Frankfurt. These images
coalesce, it seems to me, in what can be viewed as the passionate quest
of Hegel for his own *Diotima* or poetic muse. We will develop this further in the chapters to follow. Here it is sufficient to point out that
Hegel's peculiar fascination with the name Maria seems to encompass,
for him, both that of *Gottesmutter* and that of *Maria Magdalena*—which
happens to be the given name of Hegel's maternal grandmothers for
generations. Hegel's fascinated idealization of the name Maria is
documented, in fact, in the letters written during his courtship with
Maria von Tucher, his eventual wife—letters in which he seems to evidence greater infatuation with the name of his fiancée than with her
person.[36]

Consider, once again, the familial factors surrounding Hegel's theological education. Hegel, together with his classmate Hölderlin, and
later Schelling, enrolled in the Tübingen *Stift* with the alleged intention of becoming clerics. No doubt his parents viewed this choice as a
step up, so to speak, in the rigid class structure of late eighteenth-
century Germany, since the clerical-academic route to upward social
mobility was one of the best ways this might be accomplished. Neither
Hölderlin nor Schelling, however, ever seemed serious about fulfilling
the clerical part of their intended vocations—Schelling's secular intellectual ambitions were manifest almost immediately (possibly in reaction to his clerical family), and Hölderlin's creative energies provided
clear evidence from the outset that while theology and philosophy
might have been his mistresses, poetry was his true love.[37]

Hegel's resistance to his clerical calling, however, seems to have
been a bit different—and it is a difference that, in retrospect, represents a kind of curious inversion of the *Traumerlebnis* of Luther,
whereby he abandoned jurisprudence for the priesthood.[38] After
Hegel's first year at Tübingen, Christiane reports that her brother informed his father of his intention to pursue a career in law instead of
theology. By Christiane's account, however, Hegel offered little resistance when the resolute father, Georg Ludwig, demanded that
Georg Wilhelm finish his theological course. But why should a father
who, like Luther's father, manifested little or no religious passion insist that his son continue the theological path? As a minor bureaucrat
in the ducal office of finance, Georg Ludwig certainly realized that the
legal profession afforded his son the prospect of much greater social
and material gain than a career in the Church. And why in the end did

the son offer no more than token rebellion? Could it be that the young Hegel was not really serious in his protestation? I think that this may be the case, and it is a conclusion that becomes more credible as one considers the hidden force of the mother at play in a document prepared in 1804 by Hegel in order to secure an academic appointment as *Dozent* under Schelling at Jena.

In this biographical curriculum vitae Hegel begins by indicating how a theological education can be viewed as providing solid background for a career in philosophy. The most interesting comment in this apologia, however, is his assertion that theological training was pursued not only because of "natural inclination owing to the [historic] connection between classical [theological] literature and philosophy," but also "in accord with my parent's wishes" (*JS*, 582–83).[39]

Two things are worthy of comment here. The first has to do with the obvious fact that Hegel saw no necessary conflict between theology and philosophy—both being viewed within the encompassing Enlightenment horizon of science (*Wissenschaft*). Nevertheless, Hegel might as easily have concluded, as did Schelling and Hölderlin during the period immediately following Tübingen, that his theological studies were simply a waste of time.[40] Moreover, Hegel had in 1804 already clearly established his philosophical credentials with the now-famous monographs he published with Schelling in the *Kritisches Journal der Philosophie* in 1801 and 1802. Nevertheless, commentators hostile to Hegel's theological background have frequently taken the view that the Tübingen sojourn is irrelevant to his mature work, or that his mature work is a reaction to it. Such conclusions, however, overlook the subtle nuance in Hegel's comment regarding a theological degree completed "in accord with [his] parents' wishes" (*nach dem Wunsche meiner Eltern*) and the obvious fact that such "wishes" had to be generated prior to his mother's death 1781. This being the case, it is not at all unreasonable to conclude that Hegel's theological education was, to some significant degree, the result of fulfilling a vow or pledge between his mother and father—perhaps by way of a compact made just before his mother's death. Needless to say, religiously motivated vows made in the face of mortal illness have special power. Because Hegel was once reminded of this by his father, one can surmise that he viewed this "wish" or pledge as encompassing the promise to complete at least the theological degree at Tübingen in order to be certified by the Consistory, even though he might forestall ordination. In any event, this is precisely what Hegel did.

It goes without saying that the desire of pious families to dedicate a son, preferably the eldest, to the service of God is nothing new in the history of religion, least of all Christianity, and the religious ethos of the Hegel family seems to have been in keeping with this predilection. It is also self-evident that the piety of one's family, or the absence thereof, can have a profound influence upon the vocational choices of children. This being the case, it seems entirely reasonable to conclude that the piety of the Hegel family, and especially of Hegel's mother, was influential—perhaps even instrumental—in determining the religious and philosophical path of her son. Indeed, Hegel goes on to say in the same vita that following "the death of [his] father" in 1799, six years after receiving his theological degree, he decided to devote his energies entirely to "*der philosophischen Wissenschaft*" (*JS*, 583). With the passing of both parents, therefore, it seems that Hegel considered himself finally released from the promise to pursue a pastoral vocation.

There can be little doubt, then, that piety and Pietism play a significant role in determining the course and the eventual shape and meaning of Hegel's philosophy—especially his philosophy of religion. For while Hegel was later to equate religion with *picture thinking*, a truncated mode of cognition in which representationalism governed by feeling's emotion are the dominant elements, this did not mean for him that what religion claims is wrong, but rather that what it claims is incomplete. This incompleteness notwithstanding, the major elements in Hegel's dialectical formulation are the part and parcel of Pietism, and it was precisely Hegel's personal familiarity with Pietism that, combined with his own experiences, fueled these formulations. This is the origin of his conviction, beginning with his earliest essays, that feeling's emotion, and its object(s) in perception or sensation, need to be mediated by the life of the concept if religion's claims are to rise to critical, scientific intelligibility. However, apart from the presence of profoundly deep feelings and emotions, there is nothing for cognitive sublation (*Aufhebung*) to raise up. As the third part of the "Positivity" essay indicates (having been written after 1800), Hegel quickly came to understand this in spite of his previously critical remarks on Pietism. But Hegel also came to realize that apart from dialectical sublation through the logic of the concept, a life dominated by feeling's emotion can lead to "infinite anguish" and even to madness, as in the case of Hölderlin.[41] Thus neither Pietism nor neo-Pietism, for Hegel, is the final answer—whether for philosophy, theology, or ethics. Nevertheless, Pietism, or something akin to it, is presupposed as the proper point of religious and philosophical departure, and his "infinite anguish" in the later writings has precisely to do with the Enlightenment and post-Enlightenment loss of the "spiritual community."[42]

By the same token, it is not surprising that many commentators, especially those who have themselves never come into contact with anything resembling the fertile religious ground of Pietism, should conclude that it is unimportant and even superfluous with respect to understanding Hegel's system. I argue, to the contrary, that the "young" Hegel's concept of Spirit, and his system in outline, is not really intelligible apart from this consideration. To make this point more clearly, we now turn to a consideration of Hegel's Frankfurt period, the period of his so-called conversion, and the role Hölderlin played in what I term the transformation of Hegel's understanding of dialectic and its relation to Absolute Transcendence. Luther's notion of dialectic, as we will see, plays a significant mediating role in this transformation and, needless to say, Hegel's religious and theological training constituted the lion's share of the intellectual luggage he brought with him to Frankfurt.

IV

TRANSCENDENCE

Du bist der hohe Sinn, der treue Glauben / Der, ein Gottheit,
wenn auch Alles untergeht, nicht wankt.
("Eleusis: An Hölderlin")

C LASSICAL AND MEDIEVAL literature is full of the blazing
presence of the Divine Transcendence.[1] The means of elicit-
ing the presence of Transcendence, more often than not, is
dialectic. But in the modern, post-Enlightenment world, dialectic
seems to have passed over into a strictly negative form—a dialectic
that bears witness to the presence of absence as in Hölderlin, the absence of presence as in Nietzsche, or that testifies to the absence of any
experience whatever, as in Beckett and Pound, which might suggest
either the presence or the absence of Transcendence in human experience.

The blazing presence of the Divine was possible, as Nathan Scott,
Jr., puts it eloquently, because of the "unbroken continuum" of experience "which enabled [classical and] medieval imagination, with extraordinary ease and nonchalance, to find in the quotidian realities of
the everyday a *glass of vision* into the ultimate reality."[2] Bonaventure
exemplifies this ability as he elucidates, with marvelous dexterity by
way of his *Itinerarium ad mentis deum*, the material, emotive, and cognitive "traces" (*vestigia*) leading most assuredly to the Divine. Such a
journey is possible, he believes, because dialectic unfolds itself within
the one Divine reality—the only reality there is. Thus there is analogi-
cal correspondence every step of the way, for Bonaventure and other
contemporaries of the *via antiqua*, between realities without (*extra nos*)
and realities within (*intra nos*)—whether one's sense phantasm be at-
tuned outwardly to the Atrium or "outer court" of Temple phenomena and the ratiocinative ability of mind to know the world as cosmos,
whether it be turned inwardly to the Sanctum or "inner court" of subjectivity transparent to *intellectus* as the *imago dei*, or whether it be di-
rected upward toward the source of all excellences and, in *unio mystica*,
obtain final entry into the "Holy of Holies," where all distinctions between object and subject fade away as speculative consciousness completes itself in *intelligentia* and fusion with the everlasting *eide*. This
breathtaking ascent to the Absolute is possible a priori for the me-

dievals because of the pervasive, enfolding power of Transcendence as the panentheistic "circle of circles"—that Divine Encompassing that, as Bonaventure puts it, is "most perfect and immense" and therefore "within all things, but not enclosed; outside all things, but not excluded; above all things, but not aloof; below all things, but not debased."[3]

Dialectic was the epistemological means of unfolding the meaning of the Transcendent Encompassing because dialectic, as the *Grundoperation* of mind, was itself encompassed ontologically by Spirit or Being. The path of dialectic therefore provided the contemplative thinker with a nearly perfect speculative metaphysical vehicle for attaining the beatific vision. The pagan philosopher Plotinus generously refined the modalities of this path for Christian believers in a Personal One by demonstrating that dialectic has the power of enabling consciousness to rise above the contradictions in human experience and through reason's own oppositions to a knowledge of the Ultimate One "beyond all being" (*epekeina tes ousias*).[4] Indeed, speculative Christian mystics such as Eckhart, Tauler and, indeed, Hegel are generally agreed that dialectical consciousness may rise to a vision of unity so complete and sublime that all temple images are finally left behind. But this is not an ascent that implies, as some have charged, that disincarnate images are superior to those encumbered by matter. It means rather that as consciousness rises to the region of the "flashing forth," in the lucid image of pseudo-Dionysius,[5] representational images of the lower world are no longer helpful and are therefore deemed unnecessary. Thus while dialectic depends upon the accuracy of preliminary images of objectivity and subjectivity, its destiny is to go beyond them. Such a going beyond is not a cancellation, exclusion, or nihilistic negation of God, but quite properly a dialectical overcoming in the sense, as Gadamer reminds us out of Hegel's theory of negation (*Aufhebung*), of "going beyond" (*Übergang*) by "coming to terms with," which sublates, preserves, and "lifts up" (*Erhebung*) what it negates.[6] A going beyond that is merely a going through, by contrast, might be likened to the nondialectical, strictly linear passage of the Roman legions of Titus, who, upon passing through the outer and inner courts of Herod's Temple, were amazed and bewildered, as Josephus describes it, at finding "nothing" in the Holy of Holies when "nothing" was, in fact, all they could find.[7]

Hegel was one of the first modern thinkers to query, in his *Differenzschrift*, why dialectic had come to be so spiritually and metaphysically impoverished. His searching questions point to a time in which dialectic would be reduced to an instrument of analysis and *praxis* as, for example, in the negative dialectics of Adorno and Habermas.[8] Was it inevitable that the Cosmic Temple be reduced to what Kazantzakis once termed "the space between the temples of the skull," as we find the spiritual vacuity of the cerebral cortex displayed in Beckett's *Endgame*?[9] What "eccentric" dialectical moves have brought about this "capital negation," in Wallace Stevens's words, voiding Transcendence of all traces of a "Julian thundercloud"[10] that might give rise to awe and wonder? What conversions of consciousness have led the postmodern world to resign itself to experience "no longer even faintly charged with the grandeur of God"?[11]

The stock answer, of course, is that the engodded world of the ancients broke apart irreparably in the Enlightenment and that, as a consequence, there has taken place a radical *démontage* or *déconstruction*, so to speak, of what Dante referred to as that "whole fashioned from a radiance shone from above the *Primum mobile*," which alone had the power "to draw vitality and virtue hence."[12] Only lately have we begun to comprehend the implications of the great post-Enlightenment deformation, and perhaps we, like the legions of Titus—and more to the point of postmodernity—have entered into a time when we cannot comprehend our loss being no longer conscious of what might have been lost. It is precisely the unconsciousness of our time that makes the present age of nihilism so perplexing in relation to all previous ages of cynicism and skepticism—and this, according to Theodore Roszak, is the meaning of the "totally secularized culture" in which one "can descend into the nihilist state without the conviction, without the experienced awareness, that any other possibility exists."[13]

One might argue, therefore, that the metaphysical potentiality of dialectic depends altogether on the extent to which Transcendence or Spirit is an experienced content or, more accurately, the extent to which it might become such. In the absence of compelling manifestations of Spirit, however, many conclude that Spirit is a mere chimera of the past—"our time of need," as Heidegger once called it, a time so destitute that all we can do is satisfy ourselves with Romantic, poetical longings for "the gods now departed," or simply forget such chimeras, resigning oneself to the final "consequence of pragmatism."[14]

If such words express with any accuracy the spirit of our time at the end of the twentieth century, it is amazing to discover that a similar mood captured Hegel at the end of the eighteenth century as he wrote "The Spirit of Christianity and Its Fate" (1797–98), and assessed how his own philosophy might make a difference in "The Difference between the Systems of Fichte, Jacobi, and Schelling" (1801) and explored the critical differences between Faith and Knowledge (1802). It may be the case that the difference between us and Hegel—that is to say, the difference between *early* and *post*modernity—lies precisely in the Derridian transfer to *différance*. But lest we resign ourselves to the "point of indifference," as Hegel described it, we must ask ourselves, before abandoning dialectic, whether we have really comprehended its power in matters religious and philosophical. For the *ontological* difference always needs to be radicalized, and this was precisely what concerned Hegel during his Frankfurt period between 1796 and 1800—the period that saw the composition of the critical essay "The Spirit of Christianity and Its Fate." This essay is propaedeutic to the development of his philosophy of Spirit in a critical way since, as the theological student Hegel knew well, Spirit has precisely to do with the essence of religion—if indeed, there be one, since, in the case of religion, we are speaking of an essence best likened to "the wind, coming and going where it will," as the biblical image suggests. Nevertheless it is formally given Spirit qua Absolute "to exist," as Anselm concluded, and "to exist" in such a way that it "cannot *not* exist." Thus it behooves us to ask whether we have exhausted our resources regarding the knowledge of its Being and whether Hegel might yet teach us something about it. Thus while the outcome of a given dialectical, metaphysical exercise may be highly dependent upon the antecedent experience of the dialectician, it is prudent to remind ourselves that the existence of Spirit qua Absolute is not contingent upon this or any other experience: "If the Absolute be anything," J. N. Findlay asserts, "it must be *id quo melius cogitari nequit*."[15]

In order to make this contention more specific, I examine here and in the chapter to follow some of the dialectical implications of Hegel's turn-of-the-century religious and intellectual conversion in Frankfurt. It was in that celebrated locale of dialecticians where the youthful Hegel and Hölderlin discovered the aesthetical and metaphysical power of dialectic as the means of going beyond the strictly *de jure* limitations of the Kantian transcendental dialectic of reflection. As we will see, it is a discovery that turns, to major degree, upon the meaning of negativity as an experienced content through renunciation. Hegel derives this experience, I contend, from Hölderlin, but its meaning becomes complete only as Hegel subsumes negativity in the logic of the concept; in other words, Transcendence as renunciation qua *Aufgebung*, becomes real through identity with *Aufhebung* as the means to Absolute Consciousness. But as it turns out for Hölderlin, the immediate pain of renunciation occasioned by personal loss was too deep, it seems, to provide an occasion for the intellectual conversion that would finally lay bare the meaning of Transcendence. As such, the dialectics of "detachment" (*Abgeschiedenheit*) did not finally lead Hölderlin into "serenification" (*Gelassenheit*), as in Eckhart or the *Sat-Chit-Ananda* of the Vedantic contemplative. It led rather, and in a more

Buddha-like way, to the renunciation of dialectic itself—even though, in Hölderlin's case, this renunciation is probably involuntary. In Hegel, however, the dialectic of renunciation is raised to philosophical perfection; that is, renunciation is understood as the means of moving from the lower emotive and representational stages of dialectic (and what later comes to be identified with the Schleiermacherian *Abhängigkeitsgefühl*), to the "flashing forth" of Absolute Consciousness. Indeed, the conceptual sublation of renunciation is, for Hegel, the way of transcending irrationalism altogether—whether "the night in which all cows are black," as he said sarcastically of Schelling, or the fate of being "swallowed up by the protective night of madness," as Heidegger mused regarding Hölderlin and Nietzsche. There is great cause for giving credence to the intellectual consequences of these potent existential factors, for in addition to the other dramatic events surrounding Hegel's publication of *The Phenomenology of Spirit* in 1807 (viz., the Battle of Jena and the birth of his illegitimate son, Ludwig), Hölderlin was, at that very time, being given over to the care of the psychiatric clinic at Tübingen, where, in the famous *Turm* in the house of the carpenter Zimmer, he would spend the final thirty-six years of his life.

In the remainder of this chapter we will address the general circumstances surrounding Hegel's intellectual conversion in Frankfurt and how what I call the transformation of dialectic comes about as the result not only of intense speculations regarding the nature and meaning of Transcendence but also of Hegel's concern for the romantic predicament of Hölderlin. This discussion will prepare the way, in the next chapter, for showing how the speculative transformation of dialectic gives rise to what Hamburger and others call the "transfigurational poetics" of Hölderlin. By this discussion we may better appreciate, I think, the extent to which Hölderlin and especially Hegel, during the Frankfurt period, stood at the meridian of the dialectical consciousness of Enlightenment. This discussion provides the basis for a deeper consideration of Madness and Enlightenment—or what some, including Hegel, consider to be the madness *of* the Enlightenment.

· 1 ·

Much has been written about the remarkable association of Hegel, Schelling, and Hölderlin at the *Tübinger Stift* during their divinity student years between 1788 and 1793. Few commentators have fully appreciated, however, the significance of this period to Hegel's development up to and including the turn of the century—especially the

Frankfurt years Hegel and Hölderlin shared between 1796 and 1801, and the bearing this period has on the thinking of the mature Hegel.[16] Schelling, at the time, was in transit from Tübingen to Jena, courting the famous circle of Romantics there—including Augustus Schlegel's beautiful wife, Carolina, who helped him to succeed and, by some estimates, surpass Fichte. Hegel and Hölderlin, on the other hand, were sustaining themselves as tutors to the children of the wealthy (forestalling, thereby, ordination into the parish ministry), writing to and being highly envious of Schelling, and above all thinking through the possibilities of developing their own "systems of philosophy" in order to begin, like Schelling, their assault on the mountain of critical Idealism.[17] The creative energies of Hegel and Hölderlin, both in the passion of their youth, thus converged and then separated in Frankfurt. Highly dissatisfied, as is well known, with the tutorial post he held in Bern, Hegel was happy to be extracted from it by Hölderlin in 1796. The personal as well as philosophical significance of their anticipated reunion is well documented in correspondence that includes the exchange of poetry, thus bearing witness to great friendship.[18]

Hegel and Hölderlin were infatuated with classical Greece during this period. Hölderlin had written his master's thesis on *Geschichte der schönen Künste unter den Griechen*, and he shared with Hegel the Romantic view that although the Greek *Sittlichkeit* was exemplary of creative aesthetic and political vitality, the prevailing Christian *Moralität* was identical to and chiefly responsible for the atrophy and ossification of German culture. Both were convinced that the future of Germany, especially its political unification, depended upon the generation of a common spiritual bond among its people—a *Volksreligion* wholly independent of the alien, imported Orientalism of Christianity. Hegel's views on the matter are brilliantly, albeit somewhat onerously, conveyed in the Bern essays.[19] For example, in the first parts of his essay "The Positivity of Christianity," the "Life of Jesus," and in the first part of the critical essay "The Spirit of Christianity and Its Fate," Hegel makes plain the quasi-Marcionite conviction (a conviction no doubt inspired by Schelling's thesis on Marcion and the Gnostics) that Christianity's salvation lies precisely in its encounter with, but as-yet incomplete transformation by, Greek culture, since so much Orientalism remained sedimented within it. In these essays Jesus is treated as the premature instantiation of the Spirit of Kant, Jesus being given the task of challenging the legalistic heteronomy of Mosaic Law because of his sense of the autonomy of moral truth.[20] But Jesus, for Hölderlin and the early Hegel, remains trapped with the remaining fragments of what they perceived as the cultic elements of an intractable Oriental extrinsicism. The subjective maxim of Jesus remained formally incomplete and he died, as he was later to die for Schweitzer,[21] not as a tragic figure in the Socratic sense but as one betrayed and confused by himself, by his friends, and by God (*ETW*, 81–83; *FS*, 118–20). It was inevitable, for Hegel, that this latent heteronomy would reappear as primitive Christianity passed from what Max Weber would later identify as its charismatic phase to its institutional phase. But contrary to Weber's sociological hypothesis, this inevitability consisted of the fact that, with the possible exception of Jesus himself, heteronomy was present in primitive Christianity from the outset since "the followers of Socrates," as he puts it in the "Spirit" essay, "loved him because of his virtue and his philosophy," whereas the disciples of Jesus, drawn to him by miracles and wonders, loved him without ever comprehending either his virtue or his philosophy. Thus the Church emerges, for Hegel, an even more insidious form of positivity by exemplifying, in its fully developed medieval Catholic form, what he comes to characterize as the "master-slave relation" (*die Herr-Knecht Beziehung*): "What deeper truth is there for slaves than that they have a master?" (*ETW*, 196; *FS*, 288). Indeed, slave morality is the inevitable consequence of the fact, in the early Hegel's view, that "the system of the Church [is synonymous with] a system of contempt for man" in encouraging people "to despise civil and political freedom as dung in comparison with the heavenly blessings and the enjoyment of eternal life" (*ETW*, 138; *FS*, 182).

In Part 3 of the "Spirit" essay, however, and as commentators have observed, one notes a rather abrupt break with Hegel's previous diatribe against positivity in religion, a break that evidences a dramatic change of perspective regarding Christianity through attaining a deeper conception of Spirit. Richard Kroner is correct, I think, in suggesting that these changes probably come about as the result of intense study whereby Hegel begins to discover (probably by way of Fichte) the creative and self-transcending dialectical potentiality of the Absolute Ego, the non-I and the I, presence and absence, infinitude and finitude—especially in the world-historical clash and contrast of Hellenism and Jewish Christianity as the foci of a self-transcending transformation leading to the historic European Enlightenment and the "world spirit on horseback," as exemplified by Napoleon. In any event, the *aufgehoben* of a strictly negative dialectic becomes, for Hegel after Frankfurt, the *Aufhebung* of a positive dialectic in which first love and then Spirit emerge as the definitive reconciling agencies of Transcendence and self-understanding. Thus released from the extrinsic bondage of duty and obligation, Hegel, according to Bernard Reardon, comes to an awareness of the necessity of developing a notion of Christianity informed not by the pietism of personality but by "love grounded in rationality."[22] In any event, Hegel, at least, moves from the adulation of the *Volkserzieher* (in the model of a Schiller or even a Goethe) to a position in which speculative metaphysics (as in the model of Schelling) becomes increasingly attractive as the way to make a difference in philosophy.[23]

Commentators are fairly well agreed, therefore, that something of momentous significance happens in Frankfurt—something that provides Hegel with the tremendous creative energy and restlessness so evident in the *Differenzschrift* (1801) and in *Glauben und Wissen* (1802). Indeed, it is precisely the Speculative Good Friday motif in the latter work that speeds him on his way to what Kroner has accurately termed the enigmatic *itinerarium ad mentis deum* represented by the *Phäno-menologie* (1807). But *why* did this happen at this precise moment in Hegel's life? Certainly a turn-of-the-century "spirit of the times" psychology plays an important role—especially given the chiliastic-eschatological element traditionally present in the Pietistic religious consciousness of Württemberg. What, after all, is Enlightenment self-realization but secularized eschatology? Something more materially specific may also be discerned, I think, by reading the "Spirit" essay (1798–99) against the romantic predicament of Hegel's friend Hölderlin. In other words, I suggest not only that the "Spirit" essay may be read for clues regarding Hegel's obviously changed attitude regarding Christianity, but that this change is also mirrored in an essay that functions as a kind of consolation for Hölderlin. By reading this essay from this double set of references, I think one may be in a better position to appreciate how the transformation of dialectic in Hegel is rooted in the exigencies of a concrete life situation.

· 2 ·

The spiritual transformation of dialectic in Hegel and Hölderlin consists in discovering the positive existential and speculative potentialities of dialectic as distinct from considering dialectic in its strictly transcendental-critical or analytical function. Here the key element, it seems to me, has to do with comprehending the performative role of renunciation in dialectic, a role immediately linked, as we will see, to Hegel's understanding of the nature of freedom and fate.

The beginnings of this transformation are already evidenced in "Eleusis," the poem sent to Hölderlin during the fall of 1796 just prior to joining him in Frankfurt. This poem is typically Romantic with respect to its lament of the passing glorious gods and traditions of Hellas, and its stinging critique of all superficial attempts to imitate or repristinate the past in the present by ordinary research. The traces of the fugitive gods, he says, have been utterly eclipsed and cannot be revived or retrieved: "The wisdom of your priests is silent, delivering not a / tone of the holy initiations to us." Then Hegel goes on to assert, anticipating Nietzsche's critique of Greek philology, that "the researcher's curiosity—more than love of wisdom—seeks in vain" for want of authentic motivation. Academic attempts to "master" the classic by "digging after the words / in which your higher meaning seems coined" is "vanity." At best philologists and doxographers may "catch some dust and ashes," he asserts in a sacramentalistic use of the image of Apollo's torso ground to dust, but "your life, your eternity, never returns" to the historicist. Neither is Romantic longing effective; far better to accept stoically the fact that "there remains no sign of your festive life, no trace of your image." This effacement of trace, parallel to the silence motif Heidegger later finds so compelling in Stefan George, is felt deeply by Hegel as he asserts, "He who would speak to another of this / though he spoke with angel tongues / would feel the poverty of words" (*FS*, 230–33).[24]

What is this something, this truth, now concealed from academicians and intellectuals? Is it akin to the apophatic essence of the Divine, as in pseudo-Dionysius—something necessarily "hidden" from the eyes of the "idly curious" contemplative? Clearly Hegel's allusions harbor nuances akin to Heidegger's regarding *Aletheia* when Heidegger suggests that for truth to appear out of its concealment, a kind of renunciation, whereby the attainment of an Eckhartian poverty is required as the precondition for disclosure. Whatever the case, such allusions to Transcendence and the role of renunciation in effecting its presence stand in considerable contrast to Hegel's previous assessments in which renunciation is viewed as something purely extrinsic—the heteronomous action of the self negating itself, as in the case of Jesus' disciples or even Jesus himself, in order to be unconditionally obedient to an "external lawgiver." Indeed, this is the difference between Jesus and Socrates, according to Hegel in the "Positivity" essay—that Jesus and his disciples "renounced" what they had already abandoned and had no stake in: nature and the state. But for Socrates and his followers, renunciation is pursued for the sake of moral authenticity as the object of knowledge is released or "let go," so to speak, so that it can "truly be" in order to bear witness to freedom in its highest form (*ETW*, 81; *FS*, 116). On this earlier view, therefore, it is impossible for a "virtue religion" to develop out of Christianity, since its notion of renunciation remains negative and extrinsic (*ETW*, 77; *FS*, 114).

In the "Spirit" essay, however, Hegel no longer views Jesus' capacity for renunciation as grounded in the heteronomy of the moral law—whether as derivative from the authority of the moral lawgiver or as entirely objective and formally universalizable maxim upon which moral action, as in Kant, can be based. Quite the contrary. Now we meet a Jesus who, by dint of his "spirit," has been "raised above morality," and therefore above Kant since Jesus has overcome the tension that remains in the Kantian universal due to the objective or positive nature of the universal. Against Kant's insistence on the formally universalizable objective category as the basis for a groundwork for moral theory, Hegel raises up as superior (by way of Jesus' Sermon on the Mount) the subjective power of love since, as he puts it, "in love all thought of duty vanishes" (*ETW*, 218; *FS, Grundkonzept*, 205ff.).

What occasioned this remarkable change in attitude? How is it that Hegel no longer views renunciation as the preemption of moral action, but as a subjective condition facilitating authentic moral self-transcendence? How do we account for this elevated understanding of subjectivity, and especially the power of love? Is this merely an indication of Hegel's Romantic phase, as many commentators have suggested? One may here also detect a similarity to Bonaventure's ideal of "affective rationality," and we know that the Spiritual Franciscans, especially Joachim of Fiore, were making an impression on Hegel and Hölderlin during this period.[25] And, of course, it is also true that Hegel and Hölderlin, at this point in their careers, were heavily under the influence of Romanticism and the philosophy of Nature. But Hegel, even during the Frankfurt period, does not long remain with the Nature philosophers and soon sides with Fichte over against Schelling with respect to the primacy of the transcendental ego and the necessary work of the concept—as evidenced by Part 3 of the "Spirit" essay.

Perhaps there may be other reasons for this remarkable interlude in which *Geist* is established as the *Grundkonzept* of Christianity. As suggested previously, it may be possible that Hegel's discoveries regarding the dialectic of love and Spirit came about indirectly as the result of his knowledge of Hölderlin's illicit love affair with Susette, the wife of Jacob Gontard, the wealthy Huguenot banker and employer of Hölderlin. There is no evidence, of course, that Hegel was directly involved, but it is fair to surmise that he was aware of Hölderlin's predicament and that he and his friend discussed the matter openly, perhaps with intensity, from time to time. Guided by this admittedly speculative assumption, it is instructive to read the "Spirit" essay as being informed by a double motive and intention that on the one hand, represents Hegel's continued attempt to come to terms with Christianity and, on the other hand, his attempt to provide a kind of consolation for Hölderlin, who, at the time, was suffering very directly the pains of Christian moral guilt. Thus I hypothesize that Hegel, erstwhile confidant of Hölderlin, was showing his friend how it might be possible to rise above Christian morality by coming directly to terms with it through the exigencies of a specific life situation and not merely through detached philosophical reflection. Morality, after all, as Hegel makes clear in the *Rechtsphilosophie*, is not an end in itself but a bridge between material existence and ethical life. Moreover, in addition to explaining the enigmatic discourse about Jesus and Maria Magdalena in the "Spirit" essay, the consolation approach helps to explain the motivation underlying some of Hölderlin's detailed but fragmentary letters and essays having to do with "freedom" and "punishment," written shortly after his arrival in Frankfurt—essays in which many of the concerns articulated by Hegel in the "Spirit" essay are thematic.[26] In any event, it is painfully clear in light of the Frankfurt aftermath that Hegel's *Aufhebung* qua *Übergang* turns out to be more successful for himself than for Hölderlin—the philosophical sublation that is a "lifting up" and a "going beyond," in this instance, being more convincing for the therapist than for the client.

Strength for this speculative double reading can be garnered by looking more closely at Hegel's discussion of infidelity and adultery in the context of Jesus' Sermon on the Mount in Matthew 5 (*ETW*, 214–18; *FS*, 312–16). Here, and in utmost tension with the conventional demands of Law and Right, Hegel develops the meaning of the higher claims of love between a man and a woman. In what otherwise is a somewhat confusing section (which has the quality of being a kind of evidential excursus filled with subordinate clauses and ambiguous references), Hegel's main point is clear, namely, that the internal contradiction in the demands of the moral law is never so obvious as in matters of love. On the one hand, the Law cannot be suspended, "cannot forego the punishment, cannot be merciful, or it would cancel itself" (*ETW*, 226; *FS*, 339). Thus the accusatorial aspect of the Law, as in Luther's *lex semper accusit*, is fundamental to Hegel's understanding. But it is just this existential experience of law that reveals another dimension, namely, that "when the lack of love causes love to sin," the letter of the Law's demand is abrogated by "bad conscience." In such a situation the importation of legal rights by the aggrieved party over against the accused simply adds insult to injury, and "the support which the husband draws from a law and a right through which he brings justice and propriety onto his side means adding to the outrage of his wife's love a contemptible harshness" (*ETW*, 217; *FS*, 329).

The "wife's love" for whom? The answer, of course, is indeterminate if we read this as merely a hypothetical case. But if it is an indirect allusion to Susette's love for Hölderlin, the remainder of Hegel's discourse takes on a more precise meaning. Indeed, it is precisely here that Hegel introduces a mysterious exception to the demands of the moral Law, the implications of which become clear in the context of Hegel's discussion in "Love as the Transcendence of Justice and the Reconciliation of Fate." The key players in this discourse are the world's most enigmatic lovers with respect to questions regarding religious and moral propriety—Jesus and the harlot Maria Magdalena. Hegel begins by expanding the contradiction between love and the demands of law through the Greek concept of fate. Given Hegel's largely Pauline understanding of law, there is, in this section, the attempt to surmount its heteronomous demands through a philosophical comprehension of fate and a sense of the tragic. In other words, the Gospel is here understood as the agency of a higher metaphysical reconciliation—for, as Hegel puts it, "if law and punishment cannot be reconciled, they can be transcended if fate can be reconciled" (*ETW*, 228; *FS*, 342). How is this possible? The answer, according to Hegel, is through renunciation grounded in love, whereby Spirit brings about a reconciliation of opposites—in other words, Spirit negates itself in order to be itself.

Not surprisingly, Hölderlin clearly believed the love he shared with Susette to be the work of fate. Susette, the young wife of his aging employer was, for Hölderlin, not only a woman of rare physical beauty but also his Diotima, his intellectual companion and poetical muse. It is in the fateful romance, Hegel reflects, where one meets "the most exalted form of guilt; the guilt of innocence" (*ETW*, 232; *FS*, 347: *die Schuld der Unschuld*). In such situations, one's only recourse, according to Hegel, is an act of renunciation that affirms and does not destroy the other, this renunciation being the mark of love's authenticity; for "to renounce one's relationships (*Diese Aufgebung seiner Beziehungen*) is to abstract from oneself, and this is a process with no fixed limits" (*ETW*, 235; *FS*, 349). The reason this is so, Hegel later asserts, is that "beauty of soul has as its negative attribute the highest freedom, i.e., the potentiality of renouncing everything in order to maintain one's self" (*ETW*, 236; *FS*, 350: *Die höchste Freiheit ist das negative Attribut der Schönheit der Seele, d.h. die Möglichkeit, auf alles Verzicht zu tun, um sich zu erhalten*). Through renunciation grounded in love, then, one touches or is touched by the true infinite and, as in the obvious case of Jesus, only the true infinite has the power to overcome the contradiction within law and fate. If one remains passive before the external demands of the Law, or if one remains active in a courageous confrontation of fate, contradiction remains one-sided and transcendence is impossible. But this contradiction can be overcome, according to Hegel, "by the man who *lets go* of what the other approaches with hostility, who ceases to call what the other assails." Such a man "escapes grief for loss, escapes handling by the other or by the judge, escapes the necessity of engaging with the other" (*ETW*, 235; *FS*, 349). The more vital and profound the relationship, in fact, the more vital and profound the possibility of transcendence through a sense of loss. Such intensity implies and, in fact, necessitates the movement of *Angst* into the very heart of the void as the precondition for reaffirming life once again (*ETW*, 236; *FS*, 350).

The moral extremities of reconciliation through a renunciation grounded in love are no better exemplified, for Hegel, than in the relationship between Jesus and Maria Magdalena—she who not only *has* but *is* a "beautiful consciousness." The scene Hegel recounts is unusually touching and, in many ways, unique in his entire work: Maria, the ritually unclean transgressor of Jewish ritual law, is depicted washing the feet of Jesus with her tears, drying them with her hair, and anointing them "with pure and costly spikenard." The offended disciples of Jesus, impervious to the significance of this act of devotion, voice their objections, convinced, on the one hand, that this action is a breach in ritual purity and, on the other, that such extravagance precludes the truth of what Hegel now views as the convoluted Kantian moralism of "giving to the poor." But it is utterly futile, Hegel concludes, for Jesus to attempt to explain this "beautiful thing" to such "coarse organs the fine fragrance of the Spirit whose breath they could not feel." However, for Jesus, "these floods of tears, these loving kisses extinguishing all guilt, this bliss of love drinking reconciliation from its effusion," is sufficient in and for itself. Hence Jesus' only possible rejoinder to the affronted disciples, according to Hegel, is the literally cryptic and fatefully ironic allusion that by this genuine religious action "she has anointed me for my burial" (*ETW*, 242–44; *FS*, 357–59).

Hegel does not expand here on the *Gott ist tot* motif implicit in this allusion; this comes three years later in his monograph *Glauben und Wissen*. Nevertheless this symbol—which becomes so central to his later reflections on the meaning of Christianity and Spirit, which become radically "determinate" (*bestimmt*) in its "particularity" (*Besonderheit*)—has its first appearance here. Indeed, what holds Hegel's attention is *Aufgebung cum Aufhebung*; that is, his attention is fixed upon the extent to which renunciation displays that "negative attribute" of the soul wherein its "greatest beauty" and "highest freedom" is fully manifest. It is precisely this discovery, of course, which eventually informs Hegel's choice of the *kenosis* christology of Saint Paul (Philippians 2.5–11) in the *Phänomenologie* (1807), as the theological theory best suited to describe the dynamic self-diremption of Absolute Spirit; indeed, the language of diremption (*die Trennung*) makes its initial appearance in this essay (*ETW*, 229; *FS*, 242). In the "Spirit" essay, however, Hegel focuses upon what has to be the most dramatic instance of the separation of intent and meaning in the ritual or cultic life of Christianity— the Eucharist or *Abendmahl*. And with this description, Hegel comes full circle, by way of the leading metaphors in the poem "Eleusis," to what constitutes for him in theory and, we may surmise, for Hölderlin in practice, the requirements of the "genuine religious action" that haunts Hegel throughout his life.

As in the case of Hegel's account of Maria Magdalena's devotional act of foot washing, the mystical significance of the simple sharing of bread and wine necessarily escapes comprehension by Jesus' disciples. To be sure, there is "the bond of friendship" among them during Seder, as Hegel points out, but nothing beyond conventional devotion. For the disciples do not understand that "virtue" (*Tugend*), when authentic, is "the modification of love" (*ETW*, 244; *FS*, 359–60). This general lack of understanding is the source of the disciples' confusion and perplexity in the aftermath of the Passover meal. Indeed, the various elements of this meal—the bread and wine, the "feeling" of the participants, and their consciousness or "intellect"—remain contradictory and "do not finally coalesce into one." For "when Apollo is ground to dust," Hegel says, picking up one of the strands in his "Eleusis" poem for Hölderlin, "devotion remains, but it cannot turn and worship the dust. The dust can remind us of the devotion but it cannot draw devotion to itself. Hence a regret arises, and this is the sensing of the separation, the contradiction, like the sadness accompanying the idea of living forces and the incompatibility between them and the corpse. After the supper the disciples began to be sorrowful because of the impending loss of their master, but after a genuinely religious action the soul is at peace. And after enjoying the supper, Christians today feel a reverent wonder either without sincerity or else with melancholy sincerity, because feeling's intensity was separate from the intellect and both were one-sided because worship was incomplete since something divine was promised and it melted away in the mouth" (*ETW*, 252–53; *FS*, 369).

Symbolical observances are not of themselves, therefore, identical to the "genuine religious action." But what is a genuine religious action? In many ways the whole of Hegel's philosophy may be seen as turning on finding the proper answer to this perplexing question— and this question, as mentioned previously, is another way of putting forth the question of "justification" (*Rechtfertigung*), the central problem in Lutheran theology. The truly genuine or authentic religious action—the "fulfilled" (*pleroma*) religious action—arises in Hegel's view out of neither obedience nor feeling, out of neither duty nor love.

To be sure, the subjective categories of feeling and love are superior to those that are merely positive validations, externally objective legitimations. But a contradiction (*Widerspruch*) remains; something remains external since it has to do with a contradiction in Subjectivity-itself yet to be reconciled in a true or actual (*wirklich*) form of objectivity (*ETW*, 253; *FS*, 370). Such reconciliation, for Hegel, is the proper work of the transcendental imagination wherein what was merely "symbolic" becomes "life in the Spirit" (*ETW*, 254; *FS*, 371), that is, "pure life" or "pure self-consciousness" (*FS*, 370: *Reines Leben oder reines Selbstbewußtsein*). For this to happen, however, memory's ability to represent images of the sense world (which is the literal meaning of *Einbildungskraft*) has to be transformed by the necessary work of the concept since the Concept-itself *is* the abstractive power of the soul in its negative beauty—the "source" (*die Quelle*), as it were, of the "pure life" that is "Being" (*ETW*, 254–55; *FS*, 371–72). Herein can be located what is truly "religious" as the "fulfillment (*pleroma*) of love," namely, "reflection and love united, bound together in thought" (*ETW*, 253; *FS*, 370: *Reflexion und Liebe vereint, beide verbunden gedacht*). By this consciousness life obtains a sense of Being precisely as "pure self-consciousness."[27] The genuine religious action for Hegel, then, requires a noetic reconciliation of opposites in Consciousness-itself, and it is through this unification that Being appears and Transcendence becomes real or actual. Apart from thought's ability to surmount this contradiction, one is forced to contend only with the "presence of absence," as evidenced by Hegel's comments on the Sacrament, with nihilism being one's ultimate philosophical fate. But when thought is performed by the dynamics of love-grounded renunciation, then it is possible, according to Hegel, to go beyond an uncritical affirmation of presence (Orthodoxy), or the lamentation of absence (Romantic Enlightenment), to a theonomous reconciliation of opposites in the pure or absolute self-consciousness. Such is the work of Spirit—the positive form of a negativity or renunciation that "lets go" of the Other for the sake of its affirmation since it is a letting-go and a letting-be that no longer attempt to force a unity with what is Other. Thus the ultimate gift of love-grounded renunciation (as in kenotic Christology) is the realization that nothing is foreign to oneself since what has been Other (as identical to its contradiction) is now reconciled as Being-in-and-for-itself. This is the Being of Eternal Presence, "the Spirit which grasps and comprehends Spirit" (*ETW*, 255; *FS*, 372: *Nur der Geist faßt und schließt den Geist in sich ein*).

Hegel's advice to Hölderlin, then, and in the estranged Romantic context of Frankfurt, is to "let go" of Susette through a renunciation that facilitates this higher presence—not a physical or a merely subjective presence, but the presence that transcends the categories of both law and fate. Hegel's counsel seems to be that by persisting in either of the former alternatives, Hölderlin will destroy both the object of love and himself. But by choosing the path of love-grounded renunciation—renunciation having become the movement of Spirit-itself—consciousness has already risen to a higher plane of Being. With this advice, if we can take it to be so, Hegel's nascent, speculative dialectic of Spirit prepares the way for the bold position he sets forth in the *Differenzschrift* just two years later: "When Reason recognizes itself as Absolute, philosophy begins where reflection and its style of thinking ends; that is, it begins with the identity of Idea and Being. Philosophy does not have to postulate one of its opposites, for in positing Absoluteness it immediately posits both Idea and Being, and the Absoluteness of Reason is nothing else than the identity of both" (*D*, 112; *JS*, 45).

For Hölderlin, the path of dialectic has a quite different outcome, as we shall see.

V

DIALECTIC

Die höchste Freiheit ist das negative Attribut der Schönheit
der Seele, d.h. die Möglichkeit, auf alles Verzicht
zu tun, um sich zu erhalten.
(Frühe Schriften)

DIALECTIC ABOUNDS in the poetry of Hölderlin, especially in the celebrated *Hymns* penned between 1799 and 1801, immediately following his Frankfurt period. But in the later poetry, the poetry of his breakdown written just prior to his madness, the dialectical mode disappears. In this chapter, we examine these two moments in the poetry of Hölderlin, the first in dialogue with Hegel, so to speak, and contiguous with the themes set forth in the previous chapter on the dialectics of self-transcendence. Following this, we again take up the dialetics of renunciation and what turns out for Hölderlin to be nothing less than the renunciation of dialectic itself. This is the path that eventually opens a new dialogue—this time with Heidegger—the prior dialogical path with Hegel having ended, as we will see in the next chapter, in one of the most famous silences in the history of philosophy.

· 1 ·

In Frankfurt, Hölderlin and Hegel discovered the metaphysical properties of a pneumatological dialectic based upon renunciation, a dialectical mode whereby reflection on the other is transformed through speculation and elevated to a higher plane of meaning and identity. Hölderlin's poem "Menon's Lament for Diotima" (1799) is illustrative of this elevation to a presence no longer encumbered by conventional space-time limitations, a presence that "is as having been" (*ist gewesen*), in the phrase of D. S. Carne-Ross,[1] which constitutes the linguistic heart of the dialectics of *aufgehoben*. In the previous year, Hölderlin had written an essay called "On the Difference between Poetic Modes," in which he set forth the structural formulas for a dialectical progression from lyric, to epic, and finally to tragic poetry. It is an essay that also contains a specific notation to "Diotima" and was written in 1798, the same year as Hegel's "The Spirit of Christianity and Its Fate." A poem of extraordinary emotional intensity, "Menon's Lament for Diotima" seems to be personally occasioned by the loss of Susette—she "who suffers and keeps silence." "Daily I search," he says, "now here, now there my wandering takes me / Countless times I have probed every highway's part." By the poem's end, however, Hölderlin begins to question whether, in fact, he is alone, since "something kind must be / Close to me from afar, so I smile as I wonder / How in the midst of my grief I can feel happy and blessed."[2]

This dialectical passage by way of renunciation to higher metaphysical presence and world-historical identity is even more pronounced formally in the hymn "Bread and Wine,"[3] where one encounters a precise structural, numerical, dialectical progression throughout the poem; whether within each set of six lines (2 × 2 × 2), within each stanza (6 × 6 × 6), within each tripartite section of stanzas (18 × 18 × 18), or within the poem as a whole (54 × 54 × 54). At each level Hölderlin posits a provocative phantasm, a contradictory phantasm, with heuristic movement toward the reconciliation of opposites. At the center of this immanent progression (a progression described in the essay on poetic modes as the successive metaphors of "feeling," "aspiration," and "intellectual intuition," or fantasy, sentiment and passion, respectively,[4]) are the images of a "wine god" who is at once Dionysus and Christ, the purpose of this juxtaposition being the reconciliation of opposites.[5] Like Hegel, Hölderlin is intent on the task of working toward the *Aufhebung* of Athens and Jerusalem in order to elucidate the *Sittlichkeit* appropriate to a Romantic Enlightenment conception of the *Heimat*.

Hölderlin begins "Bread and Wine" by confronting his reader with an apophatics of day's end, the appearance of the night and the potential transformation of diurnal law by the ecstasy of dreams. The first verse offers a tranquil and idyllic description of a village whose inhabitants are resting from the work of day in order to consider the "balance" of "gain and loss." But the night is "fantastical" (*schwärmerisches*) in its transformational power and possibility. These contrasts of day and night, reason and imagination, are intensified theologically in the second verse, where the poet suggests that even though God has willed that the "sunny day" (*der besonnene Tag*) should be "dearer" to mortals than the night, there are times "when even clear eyes love shadows." Thus something precious may be obtained from negativity—especially by the poet, since it is to "night" that "hymns are dedicated" and "to all those astray, the mad and the dead, she is sacred" (*sie geheiliget ist*). For the night, the all-comprehensive chthonic negation, "endures" by yielding its "holy intoxication" and "oblivion" to the poet seized by its power. Accepting the invitation to ecstasy, the aspiring poet-hero is "off to Olympian regions" there to dwell in the eschatological heights of the wine god who has been and who is yet to come.

These potent phenomena provide the setting for a series of first-level dialectical inquiries regarding the meaning of what appears. Hölderlin answers, in part, by way of a series of imagistic representations (*Vorstellungen*) and narrative allusions to the gods of Greece and to the God-man of Palestine. He recalls in verse 4 the "festive halls," the "thrones" and "temples" of ancient Greece—images most compelling during the "happy days of youth" since "carefree children" are the ones who "rush toward the gods" to receive their holy gifts unselfconsciously. Adults, constrained by diurnal law, are blinded and confused by direct confrontations with the high ones. To be sure, the "wealth" is there, but now the poet must "suffer" the condition of consciousness prior to "naming" these gifts—"words like flowers leaping alive" he must find (*Nun, nun, müssen dafür Worte, wie Blumen, entstehn*).

This, then, is the poet's sacred task: to raise up through language what has been received but also lost through language. Hölderlin feints before this challenge in "Bread and Wine," but not to the extent that he will in "Homecoming" or "As on a Holiday . . ." where this dialectical progression is interrupted through what is nothing less than the renunciation of dialectic itself. In "Bread and Wine" the poet's dread is manifest more as a lament regarding the failures of prior mediations, traditional mediations no longer deemed adequate to the new time of need: "Why no more," he implores, "does a god imprint on the brow of a mortal / Struck, as by lightning, the mark, brand him, as once he would do?" Is human consciousness now bereft of the ecstatic utterance? Must the god come again "assuming human shape" (*des Menschen Gestalt*) in order for the saving message to be conveyed? Surely such an event, he concludes in the sixth stanza, will fail as the assurance of living presence, a fate to be remembered only as a consolation of the past and nothing more.

But *why* this failure? With this question Hölderlin moves from the motifs of childhood and youth, maturity and old age, from the narrative images of Dionysus and Christ, toward the kind of conceptual resolution we find in Hegel—"the binding together of feeling's emotion and memory's reflection in thought." Such a resolution lies beyond the impasse of simple presence and absence (as evidenced by the lower stages of dialectic in the naive lyric and epic metaphor) in an aesthetic transposition of meaning through the tragic. Hölderlin begins by offering an answer both affirmative and negative in implication: *yes*, the gods have come, and *no*, we have come "too late" (*wir kommen zu späte*) to be any more in a position to receive what the gods have to give. The blazing presence that once was the case for prophets and poets, for Pindar and Homer, for Dante and Bonaventure, is no more and all that remains are the empty traces of the fugitive gods.

Is our fate then reduced to the task of ascertaining the meaning of the presence of absence? Hölderlin thinks not, at least at this point in his poetry, and like Hegel he concludes that nostalgic contemplation is an inadequate response to a sense of loss. Indeed, at the beginning of verse 7 Hölderlin explicitly states (as does Hegel in "Eleusis") that piously emotive, Romantic fixations on the traces of the fugitive gods will never suffice to make them present again. But although we may console ourselves through the wishful notion that the absent gods still somehow "care" about the human predicament, the poet is condemned to such cares—to "life become a dream about [the absent gods]" (*Traum von ihnen ist darauf das Leben*). But in the self-assured age of the Enlightenment, the poet's care seems strangely out of place, for "who wants poets at all in lean years" (*wozu Dichter in dürftiger Zeit*)?[6]

This heuristic negation, however, gives rise to an affirmative identification of the poet with the "holy priests of the wine god" (*des Weingottes heilige Priester*), and in the two final verses Hölderlin, like Hegel, raises the prospect of serenification through a genuine religious action. "Be time!" he says, for time is Transcendence. "Yes," the "genius" came, "proclaimed day's end, and then himself went away." "Yes," he has left his "gifts" of bread and wine, and "yes," we do remember having given "thanks" to "the heavenly ones who were once here." But presentiments cannot be authentic if, like bread and wine, they remain mere symbols. A true and authentic comprehension of the meaning of gifts exemplifying the "presence of absence" is possible *only* through the "reconciliation" (*Aussöhnung*) of opposites. And this reconciliation is taking place continuously in the "fruits of the earth" (*der Erde Frucht*), where the continuing consubstantial unity of earth and sky, men and gods, persists as it always has. Thus the "living boughs of the evergreen pine tree" (*wie das Laub der immergrünenden Fichte*) that "convey the trace of the gods now departed" (*die Spur der entflohenen Götter*)[7] are not merely symbolic and Romantic truths but living realities if one has the courage to affirm one's own historicity in the *Lebenswelt*: "We are it" (*Wir sind es*), that is, "we are *now* it"—"the children of God . . . foretold in the songs of the ancients" (*Was der Alten Gesang von Kindern Gottes geweissagt*). And with the exclamatory "See!" (*Siehe!*), Hölderlin conveys the conviction that only through the renunciation of the symbolical properties of these "traces" and "elements" can the Divine be affirmed in its living presence.

Thus the dialectics of renunciation for Hölderlin, as with Hegel's

"Speculative Good Friday," is the existential precondition for the reconciliation of feeling and reflection in thought. Hölderlin thus agrees with Hegel's conception of the "genuine religious action" in "Bread and Wine"—at least theoretically. But with the writing of *Heimkunft, Wie wenn am Feiertage . . .* , and other late poems we encounter nothing less than the renunciation of dialectic. The pain of personal loss, it would seem, leads Hölderlin into a night that cannot finally be surmounted by dialectic, renunciation remaining an in-and-for-itself and not the key to Transcendence. "The light," as Schelling reminds us, is "younger than the darkness," and it is to the darkness that Hölderlin returns.

· 2 ·

Hölderlin's great hymn "Homecoming," similar to "Menon's Lament for Diotima" and "Bread and Wine" in content and mood, does not complete the triadic *Aufhebung* of the lyric and the epic forms in the tragic. Rather, it ends abruptly with the sixth verse, upon a note of refusal. The lyric and the epic do not coalesce structurally in tragic resolution but remain in and for themselves, so to speak. The final word *nicht*, for Heidegger, is in fact the sign of a refusal of the dialectical *Aufhebung*. As such, it is the poem's single most important word symbolizing, he argues, what is most critical and most difficult in the vocation of the poet—the ability to "stand back" before the "unsaid" and the "unsayable" in honor of the "reserve" of Being's Truth.[8]

If Heidegger is correct in this reading,[9] is it possible to say what this refusal signifies? It is my contention that it signals the renunciation of dialectic, a refusal to go any longer the final step with Hegel in using dialectic as the philosophical-poetical means of effecting metaphysical resolution through the logic of the concept. If this is the case—that is, if this refusal represents an intentional aesthetical strategy on the part of Hölderlin—might his refusal or "turning back" be for personal as well as intellectual reasons? The highly enigmatic and disruptive "As on a Holiday . . ." (1803) (cited by Michael Hamburger for an innovative style that "anticipates both the Symbolist and Imagist revolutions in poetry"[10]) may reveal something about Hölderlin's *Kehre* regarding the role of dialectic in this instance. Indeed, the unexpected turn between the eighth and ninth verses seems to signal, even more dramatically than the *nicht* at the end of "Homecoming," not only the abandonment of dialectic but its utter condemnation.

Hölderlin also begins "Homecoming" by contemplating the interpenetrating forces of Nature and history, continuing the *Lebenswelt* motif introduced in "Bread and Wine." The notion of a "holiday" is therefore highly representative of the Romantic consciousness in which "nature and history meet and coincide," as Goethe says of the principle of identity. As in the case of Hölderlin's cryptic allusion to Saint John the Divine in "Patmos," the countryman-poet in "As on a Holiday . . ." echoes the conviction that even though "God is near but difficult to grasp" (*Nah ist / Und schwer zu fassen der Gott*), he is still intent on conveying "as much"[11] of the "Holy" as he has "seen" (*Und was / Ich sah, das Heilige sei mein Wort*). This "seer" (perhaps Schelling or even Hegel himself?) is portrayed as akin to the one who has a "fire in his eye," having once "conceived a lofty design" (*Und wie im Aug' ein Feuer dem Manne glänzt / Wenn Hohes er entwarf*). Such revelations can be received and conveyed, however, only by those who, like children, have "purity of heart" (*reinen Herzens*). For others, such revelational ecstasies are overwhelmed and interrupted by guilt and "shame": *Doch weh mir! wenn von / Weh mir!* he says, and with this disjunctive exclamation he ends the poem by confessing that he himself is among those "cast down" by the "Heavenly Ones" as a "false priest." Thus the song of a "free" and entirely "holy day" is not, after all, the song of ultimate revelation but that of warning: *Sie selbst, sie werfen mich tief unter die Lebenden / Den falschen Priester, ins Dunkel, dass ich / Das warnende Lied den Gelehrigen singe. / Dort.*

Does this dramatic "there," this location of the place of finitude, signal a refusal of speculative, metaphysical dialectic, and a return to the Kantian Cave?[12] Has the poet been pointed in a direction by his great friend Hegel that he either cannot or will not follow? There can be little doubt that Hölderlin stood in tremendous admiration of the ordered life of Hegel; and Hegel was of great consolation to him, no doubt, during this tempestuous Frankfurt period. Why then this break? Does it merely bear witness to Hölderlin's progressively deteriorating mental condition, as so many commentators have suggested, or does it tell us more? Does it suggest that Being's Truth will draw near to us only having renounced the speculative possibility of dialectic? To be sure, there are theological reasons for such a renunciation— conventional religious reasons with which Hölderlin was deeply familiar—in which case his final works might be measured against the more conventional theological horizon of Pietism.[13] For *Heimkunft*, as Heidegger reminds us, is not merely *about* a homecoming; it is quite literally Hölderlin's "coming home" to Nürtingen in 1802 after his restless wanderings in France.[14] As such, "Homecoming" seems to be a poem that has fundamentally to do with the rejection of speculative metaphysics and the reappropriation of the piety of the *Heimat*.[15]

Like Hegel's "Eleusis," written when he journeyed home from Bern to Stuttgart in 1796, Hölderlin's "Homecoming" clearly has much to say about the quest for Transcendence. But the *source* as well as the *meaning* of Transcendence for Hölderlin is now dramatically different. No longer is Transcendence viewed as identical to scaling the eidetic heights of consciousness; no longer is it identical to something he must resolutely attain by the consciousness that grasps. Transcendence for Hölderlin now has to do with an acceptance of the immanent truths "coming to meet him." Such a homecoming, then, is what Heidegger terms "a return to the proximity of the source."[16] The "dwelling" and the "serenification" (*Gelassenheit*), as Heidegger calls it, that ensues in "Homecoming" no longer has anything to do with the dialectical *Entschluß* of Hegel's Absolute Consciousness. What we meet is rather the transformation of dialectic into dialogue, as Gadamer puts it,[17] and what performs this transformation is no longer a conceptualized understanding of renunciation, but the disclosure of *grace*. And while the Catholic motif of a kind of *gratia praeveniens* in this work may, in fact, have much to do with Heidegger's attraction to it,[18] the most transparent theological images come directly from Lutheran Pietism—it being well understood by Hölderlin that for Luther an appropriation of saving truth is *not*, in the final analysis, the result of an exalted dialectical move, but the free gift of grace. Indeed, Luther also came to his spiritual discoveries upon rejecting dialectic in its medieval, Scholastic form, even though the precise character of this discovery is somewhat obscure. Nevertheless, as we have previously indicated, one of the most powerful examples of Luther's dialectical rejection of dialectic is to be found in the formula "I believe that I cannot believe." How, then, is salvation possible? Not through the mediation of an ecclesial hierarchy, and not through any mode of self-salvation effecting the *Einzelheit* of *Heiligung* through the logic of the concept. Personal salvation is possible, for Luther, *only* by the power of the Holy Spirit, which "calls, gathers, enlightens, and sanctifies," thereby rendering intelligible and accessible what is otherwise impossible to appropriate, whether emotionally or intellectually. Thus it is Spirit that "calls." But this pneumatological calling is not to be understood in the Rahnerian sense of being *Hörer des Wortes* by dint of a *potentia oboedentialis* intrinsic in the hearer. The proper work of the Holy Spirit is rather to make of this hearing a "word event," as Gerhard Ebeling has it out of Bultmann—a calling that happens "in spite of" one's capacity to understand it,[19] that is, in spite of dialectic.

The dynamics of Hölderlin's discovery can be elucidated more precisely, I believe, by reading "Homecoming" against the constitutive elements of Luther's crest, which seem embedded in the poem. To prepare for this quasi-allegorical reading, it may be helpful to recall Karl

Löwith's discussion of Luther's cross and rose in relation to the Hegel medallion presented to him by his students during the Berlin period. Löwith considers the symbol misapplied, even abominably so, whether as the attempt to place the seal of Lutheran Orthodoxy on the rationalism of Hegel or as an endorsement of the neo-Paganism of Goethe. The meaning of Luther's coat of arms (a black cross on a red heart against the field of a white rose) must be understood very strictly, he contends, by way of Luther's own explanation of its legend to Lazarus Spengler (1530): "The Christian's heart," Luther says, "walks upon roses when it stands beneath the cross" (*des Christen Herz auf Rosen geht, wenns mitten unterm Kreuze steht*). The blackness of the cross symbolizes mortification, and yet it is a mortification that "allows the heart to retain its natural color, that is, it does not destroy human nature, does not kill, but rather keeps alive—*Justus enim fide vivit, sed fide crucifixi.*" Moreover, this red, human heart stands "in the midst of a white rose to show that faith yields joy, comfort, and peace. . . . The rose is to be white, not red, for the color white is the color of the spirits and all angels. Such a rose stands in a field the color of heaven since joy in spirit and in faith is a beginning of the heavenly joy which is to be: now already comprehended within, held through hope, but not yet fully manifest."[20]

These elements are present in a subtle way throughout Hölderlin's *Heimkunft.* As in the case of "Bread and Wine," Hölderlin begins by confronting the reader with a phantasm of images appropriate to a journey "upward" and over a mountain range. It is here that one encounters, in Hölderlin's words, "the measureless workshop" (*die unermessliche Werkstatt*) of nature in a truly remarkable way, "chaos trembling with pleasure" and the "loving strife" of elements "youthful," "strong," and "nascent." For this is the place where nature and time are dynamically interfused as new days come thundering down from the mountain tops to awaken the "sleeping town below"—a town used to such dramatic presentiments, having received these "gifts" unselfconsciously down through the ages. It is the "work of Spirit," as Luther puts it, "to enlighten (*erleuchtet*) us with its gifts" and it is difficult to imagine a site where this "enlightening from above" might be more phenomenologically compelling than in the Swabian Alps.

In "Bread and Wine," by contrast, nature was viewed as being "little concerned about us" and a "stranger to all that is human" (*die Fremdlingin unter den Menschen*). But in "Homecoming" the situation is different, as Hölderlin lifts our attention to sensory phenomena above the mountain heights, to the dwelling place of God and the "holy beams of light" emanating from this ultimate source of life and hope. The God, the blessed heliotrope, is now viewed by the poet as the benevolent "renewer of seasons" and as gladdening, thereby, the souls of mortals who have "grown sad" and "numb with age." It is God himself, we can assume, who enters into and sustains time and the process of life; God himself who provides revelations and invitations, both natural and historical, to Transcendence—"unfurled wings to unfold." And it is here, in the second verse, where one first detects the base elements in Luther's crest. High above, he says, are the "silvery peaks" (*die silbernen Höhen*) of the Alps, where "roses" are blooming already against "the luminous snow" (*der leuchtende Schnee*). To the human sensibility such a juxtaposition of elements certainly seems a kind of miracle; but it is nothing unusual in the domain of the High One, for this is the realm of the pure, of "eternal Spirit" (*der Ätherische*) "giving life" (*Leben zu geben*) to creatures below. This dramatic image may be seen as the oblique inversion of Luther's seal, where the inner field of the mystic rose, as in Dante's Empyrean of the Divine, is white: "So now, displayed before me as a rose / Of snow-white purity, the sacred might / I saw, whom with his blood Christ made his spouse" (*Paradiso* 31.1–3). Such imagery is not lost in one of the hymns most cherished in German piety, *Es ist ein' Ros' entsprungen*:

> Lo, how a Rose e'er blooming, from tender stem hath sprung.
> Of Jesse's lineage coming, as men of old have sung.
> It came a floweret bright, amidst the cold of Winter,
> When halfspent was the night . . .[21]

"Much I said to him," Hölderlin begins his third verse, much I "besought" or petitioned on behalf of the "Fatherland" lest the "Spirit come" and we be "unprepared." Some commentators take this as a Jacobin allusion—Spirit here being identified with Napoleon. But this scarcely seems appropriate since the poet goes on to convey a sense of being completely overwhelmed by images of the "welcoming scene" of the valley and its lake as the poet descends from the heights: the "boatman," the "shore," the "path" and the "gardens," the "dew-laden buds" and the "bird's early song" all welcoming "the traveler home." Suddenly "everything seems familiar; even the word and the nod caught in passing / Seems like a friend's, and every face looks like a relative's face."

With this descent, Hölderlin no longer casts himself in the messianic role of the philosopher who might be the vehicle of Transcendent Truth, nor does he any more lament the "gods now departed" as in "Bread and Wine," or ponder as in *Wozu Dichter?* the indeterminacy of the poet's vocation. No longer is he perplexed by a strenuous contemplation of the meaning of the "presence of absence" as in "Menon's Lament for Diotima"; no longer is he obsessed by what is unreachable.

The final lines of the third stanza rather represent the epiphany of an extravagant series of "revelations" (*Offenbarungen*) of the type to which he alludes in "As on a Holiday . . ." But in contrast to "As on a Holiday . . ." Hölderlin's mood is different in "Homecoming," bliss now being complete in-and-for-itself quite apart from the work of the concept, conceptualization being an intrusion in a moment so rare. Thus he begins the fourth verse with a sense of "wonderment" (*Freilich wohl!*)—for how could it be otherwise? It is "the native land" (*das Geburtsland*), the land of origin and the ground to which he has now returned (*der Boden der Heimat*). It is precisely this kind of immediacy that informs the famous line "What thou seekest is near and already coming to greet thee" (*Was du suchest, es ist nahe, begegnet dir schon*). No longer are the gods the "fugitive ones." Far from it, for the poet now recognizes that he, like the Prodigal Son, has been fugitive from a source that endures, the source (*Quelle*) where "Being Abides," as Heidegger has it. No longer is the poet bewitched by "the lofty design" of Transcendence mirrored in the "fiery gleam" of the philosopher's eye, all questions regarding the conceptual mediation of the Absolute having vanished. Now, at least for this moment, he is the poet-priest—*care* being understood as the primary pastoral function. The answer to Being's call has been there all along, like the mighty "oak" (*die Eiche*) dwelling comfortably and unobtrusively in the "woods" (*die Wälder*) amid lesser "birches" and "beeches."

Is it forcing the work of interpretation to suggest that this "tree" of truth, the mighty oak, is a christological image bearing resemblance to the third element in Luther's crest, the cross? I do not think so—certainly not if one assumes Hölderlin to be familiar with and resonate deeply to the mediational power of a *theologia crucis*. Indeed, it is precisely the problem of mediation that is at issue in the fourth verse. How is it possible, Hölderlin asks, for the "wandering man" gone out to the "distant wonders" of "the godlike wild" (*das göttliche Wild*) to find the "words" capable of conveying the depth and meaning of this experience? In "Homecoming," Hölderlin no longer needs to search for the answer as in "Bread and Wine." Now "words like flowers" (*Worte, wie Blumen*) are already luminously present in the world below.

Hölderlin's awareness of nature as the form of *gratia preveniens* is reinforced in the fifth verse as the poet describes a return that is simultaneously a return to values: "There they receive me. Voice of my town, my mother!" This call is not merely the voice of the biological mother, but the larger communal, spiritual voice that stirs "old teachings" (*Langegelernter*) within him; it is the voice of *praxis pietatis*, of *sensus communis*. "Yes," he exclaims, "what used to be abides!" (*Ja! das Alte noch ist*), for this is the dwelling place of the faithful and the steadfast, of an *arche* that never changes and a "holy peace" (*des heiligen Friedens*) reserved for "the young and the old." No longer is there room for the egoic bliss of intellectual achievement. The relentless quest for Transcendence-itself is now strangely out of place: "Foolish is my speech," he confesses, but this "foolishness" is also his serenification: "It is my joy" (*Thörig red ich. Es ist die Freude*).[22]

Readers unfamiliar with the full range of the German word for "joy" (*Freude*) can scarcely appreciate its larger meaning and power, especially in Lutheran piety, where it finds one of its most powerful expressions in *Jesu, meine Freude*, the first line in the famous verse by the Pietist poet Johann Franke (1653), and is immortalized in the motet by Johann Sebastian Bach: *Jesu, meine Freude, meines Herzens Weide, meine Zier; Ach wie lang, ach lange ist dem Herzen verlangt nach dir!*[23] Does the poet have Christ as the object and source of this "joyous" reappropriation? Is this "holiday of springtime" (*den Feiertagen des Frühling*) synonymous with mere "understanding" as in the *Ich Siehe* of "Bread and Wine"? Or does it refer to the radiantly Christian "holiday of springtime," the *Auferstehung* of *Ostersonntag*?

The motet above, it will be recalled, is based on the eighth chapter of Saint Paul's Letter to the Romans, with its critical distinction between "the letter that kills" and "the Spirit that gives life." Obviously Hölderlin was highly familiar with this passage and also with what Luther drew out of it regarding the proper distinction between Law and Gospel, namely, that the saving truths are known and appropriated *not* by human effort but by the free gift of grace through the work of the Holy Spirit. One might be so bold as to conclude, then, that the poet's serenification here takes place *in spite of* and not *through* the dialectical mediation of the life of the concept and that, as such, the poem represents the transformation of dialectic into dialogue— whence, as Gadamer reminds us, it originally arose.

There is additional internal evidence, I think, to support this religious-theological interpretation. Verse 6 is expressly dialogical as the poet's words are words of invocation to the angels, the "heavenly" ones, to come and "reenter" the place of dwelling. They are words of "blessing," of prayer and devotion that do not finally presume even "to name" the one to whom they are addressed: "When we bless this meal, whose name may I speak and when late we / Rest from the life of each day, tell me; how do I give my thanks?" (*Wenn wir segnen das Mahl, wen darf ich nennen und wenn wir / Ruhn vom Leben des Tags, saget, wie bring' Ich den Dank?*). It is difficult to miss the eucharistic allusion of *das Mahl* as being also the *Abendmahl*, just as his previous identity as a "false priest" of Transcendence and the Holy is recalled by "standing back," in Heidegger's term, before what cannot be named, cannot be uttered:

"No god loves what is unseemly. / Him to grasp and to hold our joy is too small" (*Unschickliches liebet ein Gott nicht. / Ihn zu fassen ist fast unsere Freude zu klein*). Clearly *zu fassen* and *fast* must here be understood in the broader philosophical sense as meaning not only a human embrace or an intimate "holding" but also a conceptual location. For something that is *faßlich* is "conceivable" and may be appropriated by "resolution" (Hegel's *Entschluß* in "Eleusis") and a decisive "decision" (*Entschlossenheit*).[24] But Hölderlin here remains "silent" (*Schweigen*) where "holy names are lacking" (*es fehlen heilige Nahmen*)—and not only philosophically silent, but silent theologically and aesthetically in a manner defying even the piety of Luther, Franke, and Bach. For such names are not just "missing" in a way that they might again be found or simply recalled. Rather, language itself both participates in and is the sign of fault and contingency—a *Fehl* that is also *Schuld*. In other words, Hölderlin here brings out another aspect of the theoretical conviction he shared with Hegel and Schelling—that just as "the light is younger than the darkness," so also the *word* or language is younger than the *silence*. Only when the poet is fully aware of the primordiality of silence is it possible "to speak words like flowers." This, then, is the key to renunciation qua *Abgeschiedenheit*.

The depths of this conviction become evident as one considers the final poetry of Hölderlin before his madness—poetry that seems to be preparing itself for a final reappropriation by silence. In *Heimkunft* Hölderlin still conveys the mystic serenity prior to this final withdrawal—a serenity not unlike that of Plotinus, who said of his rapture, "to utter a word is to introduce a deficiency." So also in *Heimkunft*, Hölderlin remains content with the wordless sounds of the lyre "delighting the heavenly ones drawing near," for "Cares such as these, whether he likes it or not, in the soul / The singer must bear and often, but the others not" (*Sorgen, wie diese, muss, gern oder nicht, in der Seele / Tragen ein Sänger und oft, aber die anderen nicht*).

· 3 ·

"But the others *not*." What is the meaning of the negative at the end of "Homecoming"? A somewhat uncomplicated interpretation might be that "such are those of the poet" and not those of ordinary people—including philosophers and theologians. If so, this might suggest that such cares are present to the poet in privileged situations, in which case Hölderlin does not set himself apart as being in any way special or different. But it is Heidegger's view that true poets are in all ways unique, it being the poet's task, as he puts it, "to name the Holy," whereas it is merely the philosopher's task "to think Being." This distinction fits the later Hölderlin very well, especially if we take a more speculative reading of *nicht* as metaphor. In this case, *nicht* might be viewed as bearing witness to the always fragmentary nature of Enlightenment functioning as the apophatic mark of the *via negativa* in a very special way. If so, the *nicht* is not only the mark of negation, but the negation of negation—a negation encompassing the renunciation of dialectic and all speculation regarding the nature of "genuine religious actions." *Nicht* might therefore be viewed as the metaphoric refusal of a final dialectical move that, as in the "capital negation" of Wallace Stevens's *Aesthetic du Mal*, not only necessitates the cancellation of the Holy on the notion that the Holy has become a meaningless term, but that such meaninglessness is directly the result of attempting to determine its meaning as distinct from being content with the immediacy of *dwelling*.

Such a view is consistent with Ricoeur's suggestion that the vitality of the *living metaphor* depends upon its proximity to symbolical, prelinguistic realities and that, as such, metaphor remains hovering between *bios* and *logos* even though it is itself entirely the product of *logos*.[25] Thus the danger always present to metaphorical discourse (and hence the *care* of the poet's vocation) is that it will be reduced to mere metaphor, that is, to *la métaphor morte* as distinct from *la métaphor vivre*; for once metaphor is entirely subsumed by the logic of the concept, it no longer has the power to generate meanings that are ever new—the concept, in this instance, being the "continuous death of the representation." Hence the importance of recognizing, Ricoeur argues, that dialectic functions very differently for the poet and the philosopher. In poetry, dialectic is helpful only to the extent that it facilitates a faithful witness to what the poet has experienced and seen—witness being the form of the representation (*Vorstellung*). In philosophy, by contrast, it is entirely possible, if not inevitable, for dialectic to become its own object and end. Hence the poet recognizes intuitively and existentially the necessity, according to Ricoeur, following Jean Nabert, of the *dépouillement* or "divestment" as the personal act of "double humility" wherein reflective consciousness divests itself of its claim to absolute authority.[26] The French word *dépouillement* has, in fact, the force of "impoverishment" or "privative renunciation," which, at the formal level, is a divestment informed by an awareness of the tragic limitations of human understanding and that "all our knowledge of God," as in the *docta ignorantia* of Cusanus, "is the knowledge of our ignorance of God."

That Hölderlin was profoundly aware of the tragic limitations of knowledge, aware of the fragility of the Holy and its inability to withstand the assaults of dialectic, is clearly evident in the poems written immediately prior to his madness. This poetry signals the absence of anything that might be identified with serenity, the poet now hovering at the edge of the perilous abyss where the *deus absconditus* and the *deus revelatus* coincide. In his poem "The Rhine," for example, Hölderlin asks "why" the "sons of God" are no longer content "to dwell" in this the fairest of dwelling places, *An Neckars Weiden, am Rheine*. As in *Heimkunft*, the answer he provides has to do with a defect or "fault" (*der Fehl*), only this time it is a fault directly identified with something that persists in the human heart—a fault issuing from a fate so primordial that it cannot finally be surmounted by anything—including the "genuine religious action." Such individuals are consigned, like Hyperion, to the fate of perpetual restlessness: *Wie Wasser von Klippe / zu Klippe geworfen, / Jahr lang ins Ungewisse hinab*.

For Hölderlin, this restlessness (and in this instance perhaps in a way more akin to Schelling) can possibly be seen as originating in the undifferentiated *Ungrund* of Jacob Böhme—the power viewed as ultimately victorious over all forms of manifest Being, "chaotically coming back again / primordial confusion" (*Ist ordnungslos und wiederkehrt / Uralte Verwirrung*). Perhaps "Fernis and the Day of the Wolf," as in Norse legend, is Hölderlin's answer to Hegel's question regarding the proper meaning of the "Teuton's Fatherland." Whatever the case, Hölderlin desperately tries to assuage his apocalyptic apprehension in both drafts of "Celebration of Peace" (*Friedensfeier*) as if to capture once again the serenity of *Heimkunft*, but fails to do so. In a final poem, "The Single One" (*Der Einzige*), one finds the poet desperately clinging again to an image of the composite One, Dionysus and Christ, but concludes, as in *Wie wenn am Feriertage . . .* , that "a shame forbids me / to associate with you" (*Es hindert aber eine Scham / Mich dir zu vergleichen*).

What is the source of this "shame"? Is it unresolved romantic guilt having to do with the fate of Susette, his Diotima? Yet he was impassive, we are told, upon learning of her death in 1802. Or does his shame have to do with his unfulfilled religious vocation? In the first draft of "The Single One" the poet perhaps tells us as much as we can or need to know: "This time too much / From my own heart the song / Has come; if other songs follow / I'll make amends for the fault" (*Diesemal / Ist nämlich vom eigenen Herzen / Zu sehr gegangen der Gesang, / Gut machen will ich den Fehl / Wenn ich noch andere singe*).

In addition to raising personal doubts as to whether there would be new songs to sing, Hölderlin also raises the larger philosophical issue regarding the temporal contingency of all human life, the finitude that makes us all, sooner or later, prisoners of the cave. The final lines of this poem may be viewed accordingly, namely, as a "return to the cave," as J. N. Findlay has it,[27] or the necessary "dimming of reflection, the return to the tragic," as in Paul Ricoeur.[28] Did not the Son of God, Hölderlin asks, rise to "heaven in the winds" (*Himmel fuhr in den Lüften*) "sorely troubled" (*sehr betrübt*) by what was left behind unresolved? Must not the poet, like the God-man, also be "worldly," full of cares and ever human? In the second version of the same poem he provides a kind of answer: "Yes," he muses, some escape, some are saved from this fate, and perhaps "they are the learned" (*Gelehrt sind die*). But "one remains" (*dass eines bleibet*)—an isolated singularity amid the "countless fallen" (*Zahllose gefallen*) and this is in accord with the original divine intention and economy: "But that too is ended" (*Ist aber geendet*), and "ended," like *nicht* in "*Heimkunft*," is the final word of the poem.

VI

MADNESS

Der Geist ist die existierende Wahrheit der Materie, daß
die Materie selbst keine Wahrheit hat.
(Enzyklopädie)

THERE ARE over three hundred paginated references to
Kant in Hegel's *Werke*, and over two hundred references to
Fichte. Schelling and Jacobi each enjoy about a hundred en-
tries; even Schleiermacher has four. But there are no references to
Hölderlin.

The absence of any direct acknowledgment of Hölderlin, as Dieter
Henrich observes, certainly must be regarded as one of the most remarkable, even astonishing, aspects of Hegel's authorship. His only
references to Hölderlin are in his *Briefe*, the last being found in his
reply to a letter from Schelling in 1803 in which he seems to agree that
"something must be done" about the "sad condition" of their mutual
friend. Later, in 1807, Isaac von Sinclair replies to an apparent inquiry
by Hegel informing him that a physician by the name of Professor
Autenreith has been treating Hölderlin in the psychiatric clinic at
Tübingen but "with what success, I do not know." After this six-month
observation, Hölderlin would make his home in the now-famous *Turm*
of the carpenter Zimmer, on the banks of the Neckar just a few meters
from the Stift. There is no record that Hegel ever visited Hölderlin
during this long confinement.[1]

These perplexing facts and circumstances have caused much speculation among Hegel and especially Hölderlin scholars, the latter being
particularly interested in establishing the independent philosophical
autonomy of the poet with respect to Schelling and Hegel. It has been
argued, for example, that Hegel probably was not as close to his poet
friend as one might otherwise think. If he was—that is, if Hegel and
Hölderlin were as close as the Frankfurt materials suggest—then the
implication seems to be that Hegel's seemingly unsympathetic character permitted him to forget the plight of his poet friend rather quickly.
Among the rather more subversive theories recalled by Dieter Henrich is the suspicion that Hegel's silence is the product of having pi-
rated many of Hölderlin's ideas during the tempestuous Frankfurt
period. Hölderlin, it is argued, being otherwise preoccupied with per-

sonal matters during the beginning stages of his rapid mental deterioration, probably did not really care what became of his writings—especially the philosophical essays. Those supporting this notion would argue that the so-called *Systemprogramm* of 1796–97 (*FS*, 234–36) and especially the *Systemfragment* of 1800 (*FS*, 419–21) may have risen, therefore, from the hand of Hölderlin rather than that of Hegel or even Schelling.[2]

But Hegel's silence is deceptive since, as we have already noted, he tends to be obscure regarding matters of great personal importance. As a philosopher and a major critic of Romanticism, Hegel insisted that personal matters be rigorously excluded from *scientific* philosophy—even though it is patently obvious that when Hegel does "get personal," so to speak, as evidenced by the famous prefaces to several of his major works, one cannot escape the sense of existential urgency in what he says.

I contend, however, that Hölderlin played a profoundly formative role in Hegel's thought—not least, as I have argued in the previous chapter, in the pneumatological transformation of dialectic by way of the so-called Frankfurt conversion. I am further convinced that Hegel was so deeply disturbed by his friend's rapid emotional and mental deterioration that he repressed all reference. I believe, furthermore, that Hegel's silence is transparent to his own inordinate fear of madness—and reasonably so, owing to his sister Christiane's chronic mental depression. Prior to the rise of modern science (and especially prior to the recent success of psychopharmacology in treating various kinds of dementia) people had a tremendous fear of madness. It is reasonable to assume, therefore, that Hegel was not very much different from his nineteenth-century contemporaries on this matter.

In what follows I argue that Hegel's silence, far from providing evidence of his disinterest in the fate of his friend, rather bears testimony regarding the extent to which, so deeply moved and disturbed, he could only make indirect allusion to Hölderlin. I argue further that the indirectness of his references to Hölderlin are directly contained in his extensive, albeit somewhat odd, philosophical treatment of madness in the *Enzyklopädie*. By reading this section with a view to Hölderlin, one not only finds personal matters sublated, in the style so characteristic of Hegel, to the logic of the concept,[3] but that much of the "oddness" in his treatment of madness also disappears. Whether or not Hegel's treatment of madness is, in fact, an indirect commentary on Hölderlin, it provides a great deal of information on how Hegel might be read on the madness of the Enlightenment, as we will see in the next chapter.

· 1 ·

Hölderlin's dementia has been psychoanalyzed in retrospect by many scholars, the most frequent medical diagnosis being that he probably suffered from an acute form of melancholic schizophrenia. But such categories tell us little—even about a living analysand—and Hölderlin's case is particularly perplexing. One of the principal ironies associated with Hölderlin's confinement in Tübingen, in fact, is Dr. Alois Alzheimer's diagnosis, at the university's psychiatric clinic about a century later, of the mysterious degenerative mental disorder that now bears his name. As we know today, Alzheimer's disease is characterized by the rapid and as-yet irreversible onset of senility through a biochemical (probably viral) erosion of the higher functions of the cerebral cortex. Indeed, the degenerative progression of Alzheimer's disease is the inverse mirror image of Hegel's dynamic theory of consciousness since it begins with the loss of higher cognitive functions (*Vernunftsdenken*) and progresses to the loss of clear memory and the confused association of all manner of representations (*Vorstellungsdenken*). This second stage usually leads to the conclusion, by family and friends, that "something must be done" for the stricken individual—including confinement in an institution. Finally, the disease terminates in the destruction of the vital functions of the brain stem, bringing about the cessation of involuntary functions, sense intuitions (*Empfindungen*), and ultimately life itself.

Could one of the final ironies in the life of Hölderlin be that he had Alzheimer's disease? Medical science today considers the disease rare among individuals under fifty. But it can also strike the young; and the younger one is at the onset of this disease, the longer the victim lives.[4] Alzheimer's disease, no less than schizophrenia, would serve to explain many of the poet's strange behaviors, such as loss of memory, aimless wanderings, hypersensitivity, fragmentary poetical works, and so on. It would also explain the strange and perplexing behaviors of those close to him. Hölderlin's most intimate friends, children of the Enlightenment, thought reason capable of all things. Hence, the eventual abandonment of Hölderlin would be consistent with the inclination to abandon everything foreign to reason as some kind of strange deviation from what was otherwise the inevitable upward drift of matter into Spirit. Such a conclusion would also serve to explain the actions of the idly curious who, from time to time, visited the famous poet in the hopes of hearing a few lines of verse from an oracle otherwise "quite mad" (*verrückt*). It is interesting to note in passing that one of the prevailing hypotheses of the time regarding the causality of dementia was the moral degeneracy theory of Benjamin Franklin. At the commencement of Hölderlin's confinement in the Tübingen bastion of Pietism, his treatment was designed to reverse this condition by way of moral regeneration—only this time, as we are told by Sinclair, through the electrical charges of galvanometers and not the Holy Spirit![5]

But prior to dealing with Hegel's analysis of madness in the *Enzyklopädie*, let us recall again the principal issue driving Hegel's Frankfurt "Spirit" essay, since it is the issue with direct bearing on the personal fate of Hölderlin. Hegel begins the final section of his "Spirit" essay with the observation, as we saw earlier, that renunciation grounded in "love" has the power of transforming a heteronomous legal religious morality into something "autonomous," thereby "canceling its barrier in the sphere of morality" (*Liebe die Schranken der Kreise der Moralität aufhebt*) as well as in the sphere of "fate." Left to itself, however, "love is incomplete" (*die Liebe selbst ist noch unvollständig*), since it can be either "happy or unhappy" (*FS*, 370; *ETW*, 253).

Hegel thus settles on the more formal observation that love, forever captive to feeling's emotion, is unable "to rise above" itself and cannot be viewed as the answer to basic problems in ethics.[6] It is love's fate to be unable to pass from feeling's immediacy, and to remain trapped in its own emotion—emotion becoming the substitute for reality. Hegel illustrates this by way of comment on the disappearance of Jesus after his passion, resurrection, and ascension (*die Himmelfahrt*), by alluding to the presence of the absence of the beloved. But the more direct allusion to the absence of the beloved probably has to do with immediate romantic experience, whether Hölderlin's or even Hegel's. In this context, Hegel's choice of the name Maria may itself be viewed as a plurivocal metaphor with split references, whether to his own absent mother, the mother of Jesus qua *theotokos*, or, perhaps most dramatically, the friend of Jesus, Maria Magdalena, who, together with the other Marias, was eyewitness to the *presence of absence* in Saint Matthew's resurrection narrative. This, of course, is the Gospel account that concerns him in the "Spirit" essay inasmuch as it is Kant and the moral teachings of Jesus that are theoretically at issue.[7]

In any event, Hegel's main point has to do with the contradiction between immediate experience and subsequent reflections on the loving memory of this experience, the *an-sich* and the *für-sich* remaining separate from each other. Such a dichotomy, Hegel makes clear, can become the basis for sacramental delusion or, as Kierkegaard later observes, an "acoustic illusion."[8] The problem can only be overcome for Hegel at the point of the genuine religious action—the notion that "what is truly religious . . . is the fulfillment of love; reflection and love united, bound together in thought" (*ETW*, 253; *FS*, 370: *Religiöse ist also das pleroma der Liebe, Reflexion und Liebe vereint, beide verbunden gedacht*).

The reason this is the case, Hegel suggests (here certainly following Hölderlin), has to do with the fact that the ultimate meaning of love is infinite. However, the meaning of love, as infinite, cannot be captured in the "vessel" (*Gefäß*) of merely "intuitive" or "representational" thinking since these are, in fact, the appositional terms of its contradiction. It is precisely this point of contradiction and the necessity of surpassing it in thought, as we will see, which becomes explicit in Hegel's treatment of madness in the *Enzyklopädie*. Furthermore, we discover that it is not love in the ultimate or infinite sense that is really at issue. It is rather love reduced to and identified with feeling that robs love of its infinite philosophical potentiality and, in so doing, may provide warrants for personal degeneration and cultural deformation. In other words, Hegel is suspicious of a love ethic from the outset of his writings, being of the notion that such an ethic (as contrast to a faith ethic) cannot restrain itself from falling into subjectivism and, as we shall see, even madness.

· 2 ·

Hegel treats the subject of "madness" (*Verrücktheit*) in his anthropology of subjective Spirit or "Soul" under the heading *Die fühlende Seele* (*E*, §§403–12). Throughout this section it is particularly important to note the presence and function of *Geist* as a qualifier for all categories having to do with sanity and pure or absolute self-consciousness. Indeed, it is just this aspect of *Geist* that begs to be considered in its pneumatological aspect since the word Hegel uses for *healing* or *cure* is in all instances rooted in *Heil*, that is, the *whole* or the *holy*. To be mentally whole, then, seems to be directly analogous, for Hegel, to being sanctified—and sanctification (*Heiligung*), in the *ordo salutis* of Christian dogma, is the proper work of the Holy Spirit.

It is also important to note that Hegel, in this section of the *Enzyklopädie*, is not motived by the desire to define madness as a particular condition of consciousness. His fundamental concern is dynamic in the sense of trying to determine how it is the case that people ever become what we call *sane* in the first place.[9] In other words, Hegel seems interested in determining why sanity and mental health or, more precisely, spiritual well-being, should be considered the normative condition of consciousness, and how we come to this condition.

The fundamental task of a phenomenology of the experience of consciousness, therefore, is determining how consciousness is able to rise above the consciousness of the beasts through isolating the phenomenological particulars of this dynamic cognitive process. Only after accomplishing this, Hegel suggests—that is, only after establishing a philosophy of Spirit—will it be possible to understand how, given the alleged normalcy of the condition of sanity, certain unfortunate individuals suddenly lose control of their wits and become mad as if possessed by some external irrational agency. Needless to say, Hegel's attention to the retrograde devolution from sanity to insanity certainly calls to mind the condition of Hölderlin, and Hegel devotes the second section of the first part of his anthropology of subjective spirit to determining how something analogous to Hölderlin's condition happens, and why.

The location of Hegel's analysis of madness in the *Enzyklopädie* is itself extremely important (as is the structural location of everything Hegel writes) since his treatment of the "sensate soul" (*die fühlende Seele*) is developed dialectically between his treatment of "natural soul" and "actual soul,"—thereby providing symmetry to his treatment of "madness" after "normal self-feeling" but prior to "habituation." This importance consists of Hegel's belief that although feeling is important in the development of consciousness, it is not ultimately decisive as the Romantics and philosophers of Nature believed. For feeling is something that humans share with animals, especially domestic animals. But humans also have the ability to rise above mere feeling through understanding; that is, they have the power to move beyond feeling-in-itself to feeling-for-itself, and in so doing have the ability to move beyond being controlled by feeling to controlling feeling. This notion obviously plays an important role in Hegel's critique of Schleiermacher's emotivistic understanding of faith and in his critique of Pietist theology generally—especially Tholuck's, whose intuitivistic and pietistic mysticism, and whose antipathy for the Trinity, he attacks in the preface (*E*, 1, 25n). Thus, when Hegel ridicules Schleiermacher's canine conception of faith as "the feeling of absolute dependence" (*Abhängigkeitsgefühl*), it is his larger conception of *Selbstgefühl* and its cultural implications that must be kept clearly in mind.

Second, by this location (which follows his treatment of the classical understanding of the so-called lower appetites) Hegel clearly implies that "evil" (*Böse*) also originates in the complex of the feelings and ultimately in nature itself. For evil, he argues, is particularly manifest in crimes of passion where people act strictly in accord with the dictates of feeling and natural instinct. In such situations the beast in man comes out, so to speak, but not in the beast as such. For in the animal world, feeling does not hover between instinct and reason, as in the case of humans, but exists only at the top of instinct. What makes animals different from humans is that they do not have self-feeling but only feeling. Thus self-feeling, for Hegel, is a uniquely human trait making possible the critical transition between nature and reason, morality and ethics, since it is a precondition for the life of reason.[10] Nevertheless, the bottom or lower side of this transitional state is clearly at issue when it comes to determining the fullness of consciousness as Spirit. This is precisely the problem that concerns Hegel in his exposition of madness—namely, how it is possible for the person who has consciousness and even Spirit to revert back suddenly to the unmediated state of feeling. To understand this deformation or devolution of consciousness is to understand the nature of madness in the proper sense.

Finally, Hegel's submediate location of feeling in the structure of consciousness is important for understanding his critique of Pietism and Romanticism. Common to both movements is a denial or limitation of reason designed to elevate or intensify feeling (owing to its alleged immediacy, neutrality, and closer proximity to the object of pure subjectivity, i.e., the aesthetic object) in order to draw closer to reality. Such antirational, antiintellectualistic, but rationally postulated anthropological notions are absurd, for Hegel, since any conception of reality is first of all a conception that needs to be critically scrutinized and guided by logic. Indeed, precisely as the postulates of rationality, all quests for the immediate-immediate are the bane of philosophy and theology, the stuff of individual and collective disaster.[11]

But how is it, Hegel asks, that seemingly pure feelings, those feelings that have as their avowed purpose and intent the establishment of human justice and welfare, are so easily perverted into their opposite? How is it that movements of liberation are so easily transformed into wanton terror, as in the degeneration of the French Revolution after 1789? The answers, for Hegel, lie in the contradictions implicit in *Selbstgefühl*. Indeed, the contradiction Self-feeling–itself is, when unmediated by the concept, has no power to make objective and actual what remains and must forever remain merely subjective. Hegel in fact concludes that the reason feeling often desires to remain with feeling rather than subject itself to the critical mediations of the concept has to do with the fact that in such mediations feeling's intensity is necessarily adumbrated and even lost, since feeling qua feeling does not wish to relinquish the intensity that is its raison d'être.[12]

Hegel's discussion of feeling in Part 3 of the *Enzyklopädie* also parallels his treatment of judgment in the section on subjectivity in the *Logik* (Part 1), and his treatment of finite mechanics, especially gravity, in the

Naturphilosophie (Part 3). Thus his analysis of madness and derangement parallels his discussion of the particular in the *Logik* and, in his *Naturphilosophie*, the discussion of impact. The implication seems to be, then, that madness is somehow the consequence of "an unmediated impact of the particular," so to speak. Moreover, when viewed in relation to the preceding two sections of the *Naturphilosophie*, feeling receives attention through a consideration of "cohesion" in "the physics of specific individuality" and "the process of assimilation in plants and animals." When viewed in relation to the major sections that follow—"The Phenomenology of Consciousness" and "The Psychology of Spirit"—Hegel's treatment of feeling runs parallel to self-consciousness and practical spirit respectively, suggesting thereby that constructive *praxis* is precisely what is precluded by remaining within the unmediated domain of feeling. Indeed, madness and derangement are here schematically parallel to the master-slave relation under the recognitive self-consciousness—yet another indication of the psychological depth of Hegel's dialectic of explanation.[13] Finally, and perhaps most significantly for our purposes, the midpoint in Hegel's treatment of *Theoretical Spirit*, is to be located in representational thinking (*Vorstellungsdenken*)—and here especially in connection with the power of imagination (*Einbildungskraft qua Phantasie*). For it is precisely the hallucinatory or delusional states of madness that, for Hegel, are most manifest in nonmediated states of consciousness as distinct from the rationally mediated condition of self-possession in the nonderanged individual. In short, the power of imagination consists precisely in its linkage to the power of the concept and not in feeling as such, as the Romantics and Pietists had suggested.[14]

I make mention of these structural parallelisms not only to indicate the obvious fact that Hegel's dialectic unfolds everything schematically from its lowest to its highest manifestations but also to indicate clearly how Hegel views the feelings as being located on the "bottom side" of this process, so to speak—that is, below the middle point of the mediational nexus of what J. N. Findlay calls the "idea in its self-estranged state." As such, the human failure to move beyond or even to the *Mittelpunkt* of critical, ideational transformation—that is, to move from feeling's emotion and intensity through consciousness and reason, or, conversely, to be drawn back into it—may be seen as the precondition of delusion and even madness. Evidence for this conclusion may be found, for Hegel, in the case of individuals who, like Hölderlin, have moved through—or nearly through—the latter two stages and then suddenly revert back to the province of feeling exclusively. When this happens, as it clearly did to Hölderlin, the result, according to Hegel, is an especially egregious, perplexing, and degenerative form of madness. Moreover, this unusual retrogressive phenomenon, in contrast to "general dullness" and "idiocy," clearly interests Hegel the most, since the two latter forms of madness are largely involuntary and the result, he thinks, of some unfortunate biological inheritance. Indeed, the step back from reason into the abyss of the feelings seems also, for Hegel, to contain some strange and mysterious voluntary aspect, since the step back into madness implies that certain individuals actually *choose* insanity. Such a choice, for Hegel—especially as symbolized by Hölderlin—also points to the ultimate mystery underlying the dialectic of the voluntary and the involuntary, freedom and nature, the dialectic of Spirit.

· 3 ·

Hegel begins his discourse on feeling having already made it clear that nature is the raw material of Spirit. As such, Spirit is already *dirempted* or external to itself in nature but in such a way that it may also again rise to itself. Spirit thus extended and objectified or "sunk" (*versenkt*) into matter is manifest to us as "feeling" (*Gefühl*), where it remains until "volatilized" (*verflüchtigt*) into higher manifestations of subjectivity on the way to becoming objective (*an-und-für-sich*). Spirit is barely cognizable at this extreme level of external diremption since, as immediate "corporeality" (*Leiblichkeit*) and in the absence of any mediation, it is virtually impossible to detect its presence. This is why Hegel's category of *Empfindung*, as Findlay indicates, is not accurately translated as "sensation," since by this term we usually understand rather complex and sophisticated notions of what has already been or is being mediated. *Empfindung* for Hegel, as its verbal root *finden* suggests, has more to do with simple or brute "thereness" of Being (as in the Heideggerian sense of *Dasein* and, indeed, in Hegel's own development of *Dasein* in the *Logik*). It is precisely this radically material or "given" sense of nature qua matter that is "devoid" of truth according to Hegel (*E*, §389). This famous (and to many, infamous) proposition accurately contains Hegel's estimate of matter and, to the extent that Nature can be identified with the material order, it also provides an accurate sense of how Hegel views *Naturphilosophie* as "the study of the Idea in its self-estranged state" (*E*, §269).[15] As such, Nature is the raw material of Spirit for Hegel, Nature being the locus of Spirit freely extended and estranged from itself so that it might arise, out of this diremption, back to itself.[16]

Subjective Spirit, for Hegel, has similar properties, that is, Spirit in its mere subjectivity as soul is also sunk into matter. Far from being immortal in and of itself, soul is the physical side of Spirit, Spirit "outside of itself" (*Aussersichseyn*), until such time as it too is "volatilized" into "the subjective side of the notion" (*E*, §293). The soul is therefore viewed, as in Aristotle, as the source of energy or tendency inclining the motion of Spirit toward immanence or transcendence.[17] Thus he can say that while the British "soul of intellectual intuition" manifests itself most powerfully in poetry (since they are especially adept, he thinks, with respect to matters of "particularity" and "individuality"), they do not seem to have any great insight into the philosophical shape of things entire.[18] This conclusion follows, Hegel thinks, because the most important and prominent states of poetical consciousness are "waking and sleeping" and the region of "dreams." Such states, arising directly out of unmediated or only partially mediated empirical sensations are manifest as the soul's "confused corporeal memories and recollections" of itself (*Leiblichkeit*), with the emotions, both good and bad, pleasant and unpleasant, happy and sad, being identified as the empirical states of "self-feeling" (*E*, §§295, 296).[19]

Hegel's critique of empirical psychology follows the same path as his critique of conventional theology since both disciplines, he asserts, are hopelessly ensconced in the extrinsicism of *picture thinking*. In this regard, Hegel was perhaps prophetic in noting that therapeutic psychology would become the desacralized equivalent of religion in the post-Enlightenment world; that is, Hegel considered it likely, if not inevitable, that a new and, in fact, inferior form of extrinsicism would replace the older form—inferior in the self-assured deception that it was more scientific and therefore a superior kind of foundationalism. Indeed, his stinging criticism of the pseudomystical and vehemently anti-Catholic theologian Augustus Tholuck, focuses on the naiveté of accepting the data of "pictures" (*Bildern*) and representational thinking as absolute when this is but the middle ground of Spirit (*E*, §378). By positing the fundamentality of the middle or intermediate ground of experience, both theologian and psychologist succeed only in treating the subject as quasi-substantialistic "soul" but never as Spirit. It is only as Spirit, according to Hegel (and as Kierkegaard would also later argue), that the fundamental nature of man is freedom as transcendence and the ability to posit nature as Nature: "Truth makes Spirit free, but freedom makes it true," the truth of freedom, according to Hegel, "being attained by [the dialectical] overcoming of externality" (*E*, §382). Evil is identified by Hegel, following Kant, as precisely that which posits itself as "separate individuality before everything else," and it is precisely this *separateness* that informs his notion of "evil as the absence of thought." Thus conventional logic, which strives to be free of all contradictions, is not only an illusion but potentially evil since "as contrary, all consciousness contains a unity and a dividedness, hence a contradiction" that is fundamental to the maintenance of its unity in spite of pain and evil.

Hegel's dynamic notion of soul, by contrast, is based upon three divisions, modalities, or moments of Subjective Spirit: 1) Dirempted Spirit in nature as immediate or implied soul (anthropology); 2) Spirit become self-consciousness mediately and explicitly (phenomenology); and 3) Spirit become in-and-for-itself as Spirit (psychology in the classic philosophical sense of the term). The nodal point regarding sanity and insanity is between soul-in-itself and consciousness-for-itself as "soul moves out of this immediate oneness with its natural aspect, entering into opposition and conflict with it" (*E*, §387). At a strictly immediate or anthropological level, this means "the embracing of states of madness and somnambulism" (*dahin gehören die Zustände der Verrücktheit und des Somnambulismus*); but this transition, successfully made, brings one before the triumphant emergence of the miracle of consciousness, which is nothing less than "the victory of the soul over its corporeality," whereby corporeality or bodily being "is reduced to a sign or symbol." Thus soul becomes conscious being-for-itself, even though *das Ich* or Ego is still an empty abstraction since its subjectivity is not yet made object; that is, Ego has not yet become "reason objective to itself." The spiritual self-appropriation of *das Ich* objective to itself is the descriptive task of psychology. Indeed, such a psychology is, in fact, a *rational pneumatology*, since it is Spirit that makes "reason objective to itself," that is, in-and-for-itself. Spirit now posits itself in its unity as "intelligence" and "will" (the subjective and objective sides of Spirit respectively), and in so doing Spirit has returned to Spirit.

A central feature of Hegel's description has to do with his identification of the soul with the material or corporeal order. Hence questions regarding the soul's alleged immateriality are of no consequence for Hegel, this being an issue only for naive realists who view the soul as being a "mere thing"—albeit, in this case, an immaterial thing. Hegel thus develops his doctrine of the soul in an Aristotelian manner—that is, the soul is understood as "the form of the body" or as "passive *nous*," which has "the potentiality of all things" (*E*, §389). Spirit, on the other hand, is the actualizing power of the "intangible unity" of "absolute negativity" precisely as *energia* and *dunamis*. As such, Spirit is not an object alongside other objects but the truth "that matter has no truth" (*E*, §389: *daß die Materie selbst keine Wahrheit hat*). As such, the soul can complete itself in Spirit by participating in its presence, but is not itself Spirit.

Hegel's largely Aristotelian description of the development of soul runs as follows: First, the physical or natural soul (*die natürliche Seele*) is characterized, in a developmental context, by the intuitive and intense feelings of youth regarding a "world soul." Second, the feeling or sentient soul (*die fühlende Seele*), in and through which the contradictions of reflection first appear, also contains an inclination to dualism. Finally, the actual soul (*die wirkliche Seele*) is characterized by the capacity for Transcendence and is therefore the true or concrete universal encompassing all the formal particulars of soul in their original unity. This runs parallel, of course, to Hegel's conception of religion developing from its animistic or natural stage, through its subjective and artistic stage, to the stage of being revealed or critically self-conscious—the dynamics of sexuality being especially pronounced in the transition between the first two stages, and ethics between the latter two (*E*, §390, Z)—the structure, of course, repeated in his *Aesthetics* by way of the movement from architecture and sculpture, to painting and music, and finally to poetry.

By locating the possibility of madness in the semiextant "featureless abyss" of the "feeling soul," Hegel anticipated by a hundred years Freud's and Jung's theories of the unconscious. Of course, it may be objected that Hegel's theory is excessively metaphoric and not yet scientific in the clinical sense, even though such objections may not be easy to sustain given the current state of skepticism regarding the scientific status of psychoanalytic theory.[20] Moreover, Hegel's comparison of feeling's immediacy to the relationship between a mother and her unborn child has much to commend it strictly from the standpoint of coherence, and, on the rather more ominous side, his description of the rational subject sinking unalterably into the abyss of feeling and deranged madness (and what later comes to be identified as schizophrenia) resonates immediately to the case of Hölderlin.

In any event, it is clearly evident that Hegel has done his homework on psychological theory in order to amplify his analysis of feeling and madness. One might even think this research excessive since so much of his description makes reference to clinical matters. However, if Hegel is motivated to do so because of his abiding concern for the chronic mental condition of his sister, Christiane, and if it manifests his continuing interest in the fate of Hölderlin, then his empirically rich clinical observations and illustrations take on additional meaning and significance. It is interesting to note, with respect to Christiane, that Hegel makes no reference whatever to women in his survey of the French state-of-the-art clinical literature. The so-called problems of women, however, were a separate class of consideration in nineteenth-century psychological literature. Hence Hegel's references and examples follow this gender bias but do not, on that account, necessarily exclude indirect reference to his sister (in spite of the conventional attitude he advances in the *Rechtsphilosophie* concerning the role of women). The more one reads this section with an eye to Hölderlin, however, the more it appears that Hegel's attempt to elucidate systematically the experience of consciousness is also an attempt to come to terms somehow with the fate of the poetic genius sunk into the dark night of his emotions.

· 4 ·

"Self-feeling" (*Selbstgefühl*), Hegel asserts, has to do with an emergence of the latent subjectivity still buried or "sunk" (*versenkt*) in feeling. As such, *self-feeling* has much in common with *thumos* in Plato's doctrine of the soul as the existential matrix of contrary forces in dialectical opposition (*E*, §408). But because of the immediacy or corporeality (*Leiblichkeit*) of feeling at this level, subjectivity remains detached from its true or potential spirituality (*Geistigkeit*). As such, the individual is highly "susceptible" (*fähig*), as Hegel puts it, to "illness" in being unable or unwilling to "overcome" (*überwinden*) feeling through transforming it by way of the consciousness of ideality. It is almost as if the subject somehow *chooses*, as mentioned previously, to remain in the intermediate limbo of self-feeling's sense certainty.[21] What one encounters in many instances of this condition, according to Hegel, is the refusal to "subordinate" (*Unterordnung*) the feelings to an overall world-system of subjectivity—a refusal "to take the next step," as Kant put it, "into maturity" and Enlightenment. Failing to do so, the subject faces what seems to be an insurmountable contradiction (*Widerspruch*) represented, on the one hand, by the development of consciousness as a systematic totality (*Bewußtsein systematisierten Totalität*) and, on the other, to remain sunk in this particular obsessive feeling. To remain in this condition, that is, to be paralyzed by feeling, results in madness for Hegel (*E*, §408).[22]

Hegel seems to reject the view that obsessionally neurotic individuals become insane by way of having lost the abstract transcending power of reason. It is more likely the case, he believes, that such individuals still have rational powers but refuse to use them—and it is precisely this refusal that makes the contradictions in madness so strangely compelling. For Hegel takes special note of the fact that although such individuals seem perfectly capable of using their rational faculties, they refuse in one special case—the obsessional "special phase" of self-feeling. In such instances, "dreaming" seems to be more a part of waking than of sleeping, and because of this odd inversion "it is so difficult," Hegel muses, "to know when [this condition] becomes derangement." One thing is certain, however—that when the rational subject fails to become the dominant genius over his feelings, the feelings become "the evil genius" (*der böse Genius*) controlling the subject, and the subject may be identified as being possessed by an evil force. Hegel's use of the term *evil* is striking here in its agreement with the biblical maxim that the "heart," as the center of self-feeling, "is evil from its youth"—or at least potentially so, given the extent of its grounding in sense-certainty. For when reason cannot control the emotive realm, "unearthly elements are set free" in all their chaotic immediacy. What is indeterminate in immediacy, therefore, is the base element or chaos, which is evil precisely to the extent it bears witness, in Hegel's view, to the absence of thought.

The weightiness of Hegel's comments on the proximity of evil and feeling, however, are placed into sharp contrast by way of a series of humorous illustrations, especially in the *Zusätze*, regarding various remedies for insanity. Perhaps in reflection Hegel wished "to lighten up a bit," as one would say nowadays. In any event, he makes clear his incredulity regarding the instrumentally manipulative, empirically based remedies being used as early nineteenth-century therapies or cures for madness. He suggests, for example, that a sure and certain cure for alleged clairvoyant states of consciousness (in and through which otherwise entirely dull and prosaic individuals are allegedly transformed into poetic and artistic visionaries) is the "application of leeches to the rectum" (*E*, §406, Z, 2). It goes without saying that such a treatment would be an efficient means, especially today, of inducing many self-identified prophets and visionaries to seek different vocations! But since Hegel also recognized that such therapies were cruel and utterly ridiculous when applied to the demented but otherwise authentic poetic genius, it is reasonable to assume he might have known that such altogether crude remedies were being prescribed and probably used in the case of Hölderlin.

On the other hand, Hegel's description of melancholic depressive regressions into the abyss of self-feeling are entirely serious, and it is here he invokes what was the state-of-the-art French scientific literature. Indeed, the French, he notes, are infinitely superior to the Germans in the diagnosis and treatment of mental disorders—especially as evidenced by Philippe Pinel's work entitled *Traité médico-philosophique sur l'aliénation mentale ou la manie* (Paris, 1801), from which he draws much of his information. While it is impossible to tell when this work first came to Hegel's attention, it is intructive to note that its publication date coincides with the beginning of Hölderlin's breakdown. Of even greater interest, from a theoretical standpoint, is Pinel's insistence that an effective treatment of mental disorders must

presuppose, as in the case of physical disorders, the antecedent, normative presence of health, which has somehow been overwhelmed or
displaced by disease.

Obviously such a view is entirely consistent with Hegel's theory of
consciousness. For in the degenerative state, Hegel argues, reason
must still be assumed to exist—albeit in a deranged and distorted way
since reason is in the grip, as he puts it, of "particular, unmediated
feelings or emotions" (E, §408). It is only through the effective rational mediation of these "particular feelings" that sanity can be re-
stored. With this strategy Hegel, by way of Pinel, anticipates basic
methods in psychoanalysis and depth psychology—especially the notion of transference. In other words, Hegel justifies his attention to
madness by viewing it as a latent stage through which the soul must
pass on the way to consciousness or Spirit in the proper sense.[23]

Fortunately most consciousnesses do not experience the extremities
of such radical negation, and if they do (especially in Hegel's day) they
are not likely to come out of it very quickly. Hegel admits as much in
a statement that his discussion has been concerned with an "extreme"
case (E, §408, Z); hence it should not be taken that every individual
must experience madness to know sanity any more than one must experience crime in order to understand justice. Nonetheless, if madness represents, at least theoretically, one of the itinerant stages of
consciousness, it is important to know the structural role it plays.

To this end, Hegel describes three basic types or degrees of madness: 1) Idiocy, Absentmindedness, and Frenetic-Mindedness (der
Blödsinn, die Zerstreutheit und die Faselei); 2) Madness proper (eigentliche
Narrheit); and 3) Mania or Frenzy (die Tollheit oder der Wahnsinn). Idiocy, the first type, holds little interest for Hegel since it is the most
involuntary form of madness. Such individuals, being the "victims of
nature," as he puts it, have frequently come into the world as the unhappy products of inbreeding and cultural isolation that is characteristic of life in "narrow valleys and marshy districts." The "blood-deter-
mined" idiot cannot help his or her condition any more than the
person thrust into idiocy as the result of some external trauma, such as
a blow on the head. Nevertheless, acute mental distraction, forgetfulness, and hyperactive behaviors are borderline conditions that, for
Hegel, may or may not be related to madness proper. These symp-
toms are, therefore, to be carefully distinguished from "profound"
forms of idiocy achieved through meditation and contemplation (as in
Cusanus's Idiota, for example), whereby one's consciousness is abstracted from everything but the intentional object of nonbeing. This
focus on the "single one," he says (using the phrase made famous by
Hölderlin), "is a lofty distractedness and far removed from insanity"

since it is the result of the most intense form of mental concentration. Moreover, in the pathologic instance, such phenomena may be further complicated by parallel manifestations of forgetfulness regarding the mundane details of life, such as one's personal appearance, while the rest of one's creative life remains lucid. It was precisely this kind of discontinuity in the personality of Hölderlin, of course, that so astonished his friends—that while he "pays no attention anymore to how he looks" his poetry nevertheless remains "incomparable."[24]

It is in the second or "proper" state of madness, Hegel asserts, where derangement becomes clearly evident since the "fixed idea" of obsession has now acquired a specific "content." Such individuals have slipped over into "the abyss of indeterminateness"—a psychical state, he suggests, most likely to happen to individuals deeply "dissatisfied with the actual world" who prefer to remain "shut up in their own subjectivity." Nevertheless, such individuals may still retain profound creative powers in relation to the expression of this "fixed idea" or obsession—so much so, in fact, that it is frequently difficult to ascertain where madness begins and ends and whether cures have been or can ever be effective. Again, in the *Zuzätze*, Hegel provides the humorous image of the depressed Englishman who tried to hang himself ("being a nation of poets," he says, "the English are subject to such afflictions") but repented of his death wish when his servant cut him down, and proceeded "to deduct two pence from his [servant's] wages for acting without orders." In such a case, Hegel muses, madness has been replaced "with the disease of avarice!" (*E*, §408, Z).

The third kind of mania or frenzy described by Hegel—*die Tollheit oder der Wahnsinn*—probably comes closest to our biographical-historical point of reference in Hölderlin. Being the most conscious, rationally calculated form of madness, mania or frenzy is also the most ambiguous since it is a form of derangement in which, as Hegel puts it, "the maniac himself has a vivid feeling of the contradiction between his merely subjective idea and the objective world, and cannot rid himself of this idea but is fully intent on making it an actuality at the expense of destroying what is actual. Implied in this notion of mania is the fact that it need not spring from an empty conceit, but can be brought about by a stroke of great misfortune, by a derangement of a person's individual world" (*E*, §408, Z). Manifestations of mania may be either tranquil or violent, this alternation being the feature that characterizes the acute instability of such persons since, as Hegel observes, "in his distress he is mastered by the unmediated oppositions" (*unvermittelten Gegensatzes*) in addition to having obsessions with the past accompanied by complex "moral and ethical feelings" (*E*, §408, Z).

Mania or *die Tollheit* (which takes the feminine article) also indicates a mental pathology that, like rabies, seems to have causality based in some kind of chemical malfunction. Frenzy or *der Wahnsinn*, on the other hand (which takes the masculine article), has primarily to do with "delusion." While both forms are mental aberrations, it may be important to note that the former kind of irrationality is more likely to be associated with "the problems of women" (*hysterikos*) since women are by nature subject, as was common in the nineteenth century, to a kind of lunacy that men simply do not comprehend—the moodiness of women during their menstrual periods, for example, being directly associated with the impact of lunar periodicity and chronometrics. This instinctive or animalistic elemental connaturality, according to Hegel, is particularly the lot of poets "sunk," as he thinks they tend to be, in their "feelings." As such, women, for Hegel (as he makes clear in his discussion of the sexes in the *Rechtsphilosophie*, §§164, 165) and by implication, poets, are by nature less responsive to the powers of reason and analysis than are men.

Finally, near the end of his lengthy *Zuzatz* on *Frenzy* (*E*, §408), Hegel observes that in addition to having something to do with abrupt changes in meteorological conditions, frenzied conditions rarely take place before age fifteen, and that "big muscular men with black hair" seem to be the most susceptible. While Hegel himself seems willing to qualify such incidental empirical facts as being merely external to a philosophical account of the meaning of madness, the fact remains that he saw fit to allude to these alleged empirical facts in passing. That being the case, and also in passing, as it were, it is fascinating to note that Hölderlin fits the above physical description precisely, his 1802 passport (*Reisepaß*) stating, among other things, that he is "a large, muscular man of six feet" (*6 Fuß*), and a "fair-skinned, brown-eyed brunette."[25]

· 5 ·

Because madness, for Hegel, is a structural deformation of consciousness, the ultimate treatment or cure must be discernible at the roots of consciousness, that is, it must be intrinsic in the root of the *heilig*—the "whole" or the "holy" as manifest in the life of Spirit. Hegel's ultimate point of theological reference, then, is the Holy Spirit and the work of "sanctification" (*Heiligung*), the process become articulate in a philosophically grounded rational pneumatology. It is precisely here, then, that we identify a direct convergence of a theological phenomenology of Spirit and a rational pneumatology, since it is Spirit and Spirit alone, according to Hegel, that can overcome the contradiction between abstract universality and concrete particularity—universality and particularity being the operative modes of Spirit.

This spiritual overcoming, of course, becomes much more explicit in the final sections of the *Enzyklopädie*, especially in the transition to *Objective Spirit* (§§481, 482) where Hegel clarifies how the general idea of freedom becomes actual in the "moral, legal, religious, and scientific" institutions that arise out of subjective Spirit "true to its concept." Hegel's larger argument, however, is present in outline in the section on Habit, and is important for at least two reasons: First, the work of the Holy Spirit and sanctification, for Hegel, is accomplished and understood within the province of organized, institutional religion (especially Pietism) largely at the level of feeling and representational thinking. Hegel takes very seriously, as he makes clear in his *Rechtsphilosophie*, the fundamental structures of the work of the Spirit in the Trinity for the consolidation of belief in the life of the individual and the community. Second, this conviction is foreshadowed in the final two sections of his analysis of physical Spirit (*die fühlende Seele*), where he treats "habit" and "habituation", (*die Gewohnheit*) and the "actual soul" (*E*, §§409–12)—and it is especially cogent when viewed against his answer in the section on Free Spirit (*E*, §482).

The English word *habit*, however—even in archaic usage—does not convey the full force of Hegel's *Gewohnheit* for several reasons. First, the word *habit*, in ordinary usage, tends to suggest something rather dour, mundane, and downright pejorative—such as in doing something "out of the force of habit," automatically and unself-consciously, or worse, as in "having a habit," as with substance abuse. To get at the full sense of Hegel's usage, one has to go back to the semiarchaic ecclesial meaning of *habit*, the discipline of habituation that leads to virtue. Just as nuns and monks put on the garments of habit as the visible symbols of having entered into a special, cloistered life under the guidance of a specific rule or discipline, so also habit for Hegel has more to do with what Webster identifies as the *obsolete* form of habit— an abode or dwelling.

Hegel's use of *Gewohnheit* presupposes this archaic English meaning, since *Gewohnheit* is intended to convey the explicit sense of "living" (*wohnen*) with the *Wohnheim* or *Heimat* being the place of dwelling and *pietas* being what is or should be manifest in the family dwelling (*R*, §163). This is the meaning, of course, implicit in the medieval Scholastic notion of *habitus* or "habituation" qua *habito*, whereby one makes something one's own through a "being-with" for an extended length of time—that is, knowledge by connaturality.

Obviously, this connotation stands in sharp contrast to the pejorative nuance of *habituation*, understood as a form of bondage or enslavement. *Dwelling-within-and-being-comfortable-with-what-is-one's-own* is what

Hegel has in mind with respect to *Gewohnheit*—to be so accommodated to one's self or soul that one is *selig* or "blessed" in a state of *Seligkeit* or "serene joy." Such a state of actual blessedness presupposes that the so-called passions of the soul, or the soul in its corporeal element, have been converted into an actualized ideality within which one is at peace. Having achieved this state, one is no longer victimized by the passions, the demons of the soul having been exorcised through disciplined habituation. And while the subject, in this pious state, has not as yet risen to self-consciousness and Spirit, the way to this *Aufhebung* qua *Erhebung* is now open since the particular contents of feeling are ordered in such a way that sublation is possible: "Habit is the [ordering] mechanism of feeling . . . [just as] memory is the [ordering] mechanism of intelligence" (*E*, §410). Thus there are only "good" and not "bad" habits, for Hegel, "the main point about habit [being] that by its means one gets emancipated from the feelings even while being affected by them" (*E*, §410). A so-called bad habit is therefore an oxymoron in the sense of suggesting that one is really not emancipated at all but still within the grip of the feelings. Thus it is *habitus*, in Hegel's view (as in Aristotle's), that determines character—the lack of which signals, conversely, the absence of *habitus*, in which case one is no longer at home in the world.

This kind of constructive habituation, so frequently "overlooked" by empirical psychology, according to Hegel (*E*, §410), is the critical element with respect to the development of an "actually" healthy consciousness. The critical element of "habituation" is, in fact, precisely the counterpoint to madness in the dialectic of consciousness.[26] One is not *at home* in one's madness; indeed, it is precisely *not-being-at-home* that makes the condition of madness the deformed, visible sign that something is wrong.[27] Thus madness is the extreme contradiction of the truth process since it is a destruction of habituation that makes possible the negation of value. It is the primary function of soul to overcome, as in Aristotle, the conflicts and the contradictions in its existence—this overcoming being possible commensurate with the character of the soul's body. And since character is the product of one's habits, contradictions in character are especially manifest when the emotions have "free reign" whereby, as in Plato's *Phaedrus*, one is drawn now here, now there, in disordered confusion. Thus moral and existential malfunction can be minimized, for Hegel, only through the power of "habituation" and "being at home with one's self" (*Dies Beisichselbersein nennen wir die Gewohnheit*) whereby "the soul is no longer confined to a merely subjective particular idea by which it is displaced from the centre of its concrete actuality, [but] has so completely received into its ideality the immediate and particularized content presented to it, has come to feel so at home in it, that it moves about in its freedom" (*E*, §410, Z).

Constructive habituation, then, is the soul's means of detaching itself from itself, the corporeality with which "it was [previously] identical," in order to become identical with itself *in* its ideality over and against feeling's emotion and possession. Only then is soul in a position to be *for itself* in self-consciousness. Destructive forms of habituation are, in fact, visible signs of the soul's inability to rise above its corporeality, signs that the soul is content to remain within the limitations of sense-certainty. As such, the ensouled body is the representational middle term for Hegel in and through which one "comes together with the external world" as a possible self-consciousness or *Existenz* with the potentiality of absolute consciousness. Only by this dialectic does the soul become real or actual (*wirklich*), constructive and productive, as distinct from being merely an abstract or idealized unity (i.e., what one thinks one *might* be) or remaining merely a material diversity in the sensations and passions alone (i.e., "spaced out" as distinct from "being together," in colloquial usage). For the soul is Spirit's initial instantiation, a diremption that initially is nearly identical, as Hegel indicates, with its physical Other in the womb of one's mother. Nevertheless the soul also has the neo-Platonic destiny, as in Augustine's *cor inequietum*, precisely as Spirit, to reach out beyond itself to the self that is its Absolute Other (Transcendence or God) in the realization of absolute self-consciousness.

Therefore, and in contrast to this Platonic aspect, Spirit becomes truly "free" only as it becomes "true" (*E*, 481), a point made against the so-called free spirits who live out the mere appearance of freedom through the emotions and caprice. True freedom rather has to do with the unity of the theoretical and the practical. The full implication of this unity, of course, only becomes clear at the end of his *Psychologie* in Part 3 of the *Enzyklopädie*, while being clearly foreshadowed in a transitional way through Hegel's highly illustrative anthropological treatment of madness. Indeed, freedom, as it is usually construed in various subjectivisms including neo-Pietism and Romanticism, is an altogether illusory and contradictory notion if it is not actualized and made objective in the manner analogous to the soul becoming freely at home in its body. It is precisely in this sense that conventional Pietism is viewed, by Hegel, as infinitely superior to its secularized counterparts insofar as it has the ability to actualize itself in the *sensus communis* of a coherently moral community.[28]

Hegel's development of the dialectical, processual nature of the soul, therefore, follows from his triadic understanding of how Spirit functions in the *ordo salutis* of orthodox Christian theology. For Christianity, he says in his "answer" (*E*, §482), provides the historical context in which human destiny as "free" is made fully explicit by the free movement of Absolute Spirit into the world. Human freedom is not realized, he insists, by "impulsive" speculation regarding its realities and possibilities, but only through speculation made "objective" in "legal, moral, religious, and scientific actuality" (*E*, §482, Z), such objective actuality being made possible by "the great Protestant principle of the North."

If Christianity provides the theoretical-historical model for Hegel's treatment of madness, it is Hölderlin who provides, as I have argued, the existential occasion. This is not to suggest, of course, that Hegel's treatment of madness in the *Enzyklopädie* is simply a kind of philosophical allegory on the fate of Hölderlin. But since the very notion of an *encyklos* is to "circle round,"[29] it is not at all unreasonable, I think, to suggest that Hölderlin provides Hegel with the exigent question for a detailed analysis of this topic. If I am correct in this assumption, then it becomes readily apparent that Hegel is not the cold, unfeeling and hyperrationalistic thinker so many of his detractors have made him out to be. It means rather that his existential concerns, true to his system, are sublimated within the higher life of the concept that, for Hegel, is philosophy's raison d'être.

The only way to determine Hegel's position with respect to Hölderlin, therefore, is to adduce what he might have thought from the system itself. Such a strategy, obviously, is far less necessary in the case of Schelling and the other contemporaries of Hegel who play a role in the development of his thought. Indeed, it is the hybrid character of Schelling's thought that probably provided impetus for Hegel's rather abrupt break with him after the *Phänomenologie*. But Hegel's silence on Hölderlin is quite another matter. While Hölderlin wrote philosophical essays, he was a poet through and through. Hegel probably realized this more than the rest of his Romantic contemporaries. In fact, Hölderlin's poetry, as E. M. Butler rightly observes, was of such a sublime quality that he probably constituted something of a threat to the established Romantics of the Jena circle.[30] I believe that Hegel also knew this and, as a consequence, Hölderlin remained Hegel's *daimon*, his existential Other, and this concerned, even frightened, Hegel deeply throughout his life. After all, Hölderlin was the embodiment of what Schelling talked about, soul deeply interfused with matter. Hegel acknowledged this during the Frankfurt period in the image of the beautiful consciousness. But this beautiful soul, this sublime consciousness, this flower blooming in water, to use Heideggerian images, when wrested like the lotus blossom from its purity and innocence, withers and dies the moment the world intrudes on its being. As a consequence, Hölderlin must also exemplify for Hegel one of the most extreme and tragic examples of the "unhappy consciousness"— only in this case unable to resign itself in *apathia*. It would be strange indeed if Hegel did not see these associations and also be deeply troubled by them as, in fact, I contend he was. For Hölderlin was not merely pure innocence, this beautiful soul, this occasion of *Gelassenheit*. Hölderlin's choice was also seemingly one of a "step backward" culminating in madness—a choice facilitated by his obsessional fixation on the past and its loss. This choice of the immediacy of absence and vacuity therefore provides—indeed, compels—Hegel, as I have argued, to the "step forward" as the only means possible of becoming and hence preserving the self. Indeed, this is precisely what the pneumatological transformation of dialectic is about in Hegel.

The fate of Hölderlin, I think, was an event that also greatly facilitates for Hegel the preservation of the idea of a transformed Christianity in the life of the state. Thus while Schelling attempts to bring about this transformation by way of the step backward into the theoretical *Abgrund* of the Böhmean beginnings, it was Hölderlin's existential exemplification of this choice that greatly jolted the consciousness of Hegel in precisely the opposite direction. While Hölderlin's step was occasioned by romantic love, Hegel could also see that love was experienced not as the "true" but as the "bad" or "evil" infinite because it was, in the final analysis, mediated only by feeling and not by Spirit qua *Begriff*, since it is Spirit and Spirit alone that provides the way beyond the manifest contradictions of feeling. This is why Hegel's critique of Enlightenment, as we will see in the next chapter, is so strongly determined by what he believes to be the necessary work of the concept. But the concept can accomplish this only because the concept as Spirit, as we will see in our concluding chapter, is essentially *Prozeß*, this process being nothing less than the continuous life and work of the concept. Thus the work of the concept turns out to be the work of the Holy Spirit understood as Absolute Spirit.

Is it possible to choose madness? Psychiatrists, I suspect, are still somewhat divided on this matter. But we know for a fact that many choose death, either by suicide or even by natural means. We also know that apart from the will to live, sound health is nearly impossible. Certainly it must have seemed to the youthful friends of Hölderlin, and especially to Hegel, that the poet had chosen madness as the dark refuge for his infinite anguish. How else can it be explained that one so talented, one so smitten by the gods and Transcendence, should abandon his genius and his destiny? But as Hegel says of the *talent* of genius, "talent alone is not to be esteemed higher than Reason, which by its own activity has come to a knowledge of its Notion as an absolutely free thinking and willing. In philosophy, genius by itself does not go very far; it must subject itself to the strict discipline of logical thinking; it is only by this subjection that genius succeeds in achieving its perfect freedom" (*E*, §395).

VII

ENLIGHTENMENT

Diese reine Einsicht ist also der Geist, der allem Bewußtsein
zuruft: seid für euch selbst, was ihr alle an euch
selbst seid, vernünftig.
(Phänomenology des Geistes)

ONE OF the more provocative theses on the meaning of the historic European Enlightenment has been posed by Alasdair MacIntyre: "Let us suppose," he speculates, "that the eighteenth and nineteenth centuries, brilliant and creative as they were, were in fact centuries not as we and they take them to be of Enlightenment, but of a peculiar kind of darkness in which men so dazzled themselves that they could no longer see."[1] MacIntyre's critique is aimed not at Enlightenment-as-such but at pseudo-Enlightenment. It is a critique bearing close resemblance, in both shape and content, as we will see, to Hegel's.

MacIntyre's specific target is one of the Enlightenment's most prodigious offspring—social science—since it was and in many cases still is the claim of late nineteenth- and early twentieth-century social science to be able to provide wholly objective, value-free, empirically based analyses and explanations of human behavior. Of course, "value-free" in this instance does not mean free of all value, least of all what Gadamer terms the "Enlightenment prejudice against prejudice." Indeed, this is just the *blind spot* of Enlightenment rationality—the assumption that once it is possible to conduct and present social scientific researches free of presuppositions and other external constraints imposed by religious traditions and beliefs, "progress" will inevitably follow, and with it "agreement among all rational persons as to what the rationally justified conclusions of such enquiry are."[2] But far from providing enlightened new world direction, the social sciences, driven by this assumption, are in fact a major contributing cause of the moral and ethical malaise of our time, according to MacIntyre—not only locally but globally since the far-reaching influence of American enterprise provides the opportunity for the benevolent extension of social scientific expertise to the rest of the world, especially the developing world. With the wider world of human subjects at its disposal, social science now entertains the prospect of becoming universal, hence realizing, in essence, the progressive, evolutionary expectations of the Enlightenment.

It is not that MacIntyre finds particular successes and failures of social-scientific enterprise particularly disturbing; like all projects in engineering, some work, others do not. Unlike conventional projects in engineering, however, it is vastly more difficult to correct the damages caused by mistakes in social engineering. What is particularly disturbing at the theoretical level, therefore, is the elevation of instrumentalist rationality to the status of an a priori principle universally valid in all the numberless projects of social science irrespective of regional and contextual consequences. Such an elevation became possible once the secularized "knowledge elite," in Peter Berger's phrase, adopted wholesale the positivistic values of nineteenth-century natural science: "analysis, prediction, and probability." By this wager "hope" was turned into the "safe bet," but by this emulation the social sciences have also demonstrated, according to MacIntyre, the absence of anything in common with true science. And the reason this is the case derives from the progressive abandonment of the traditional virtues and transcendental values that made science possible in the first instance. By its devaluation of history and tradition, social science no longer comprehends the social and cultural contexts out of and within which its own enterprise developed and to which it was initially responsive. With the loss of historical memory "rational justification" therefore becomes limited to matters of technique and expertise, matters of moral substance and implication being bracketed as having the odor of prior "external constraints."[3] Following Spengler's observation, by way of Voltaire, that the Holy Roman Empire was "neither Holy, nor Roman, nor an Empire," MacIntyre charges that the positivistic social sciences are neither "social" nor "scientific," and least of all "positive" in terms of value implication, thus "remaining mere deceptions of what they pretend to be."[4]

But the tables are being turned, as it were, since social science is lately finding itself suspect through the very instrumentalist rationality it previously sanctified. This suspicion is generated by the empirical realization that many if not most of the projects produced by social-scientific expertise fail to work or work only at the expense of the well-being of the community.[5] Guided from their inception by what Ricoeur terms "the hermeneutics of suspicion," the social sciences have systematically undermined traditional values only to find themselves, and their sustaining institutions, the new objects of suspicion and even scorn.[6] Historically identified with the post-Enlightenment masters of demystification—Marx, Nietzsche, and Freud—the hermeneutics of suspicion attempts to demonstrate, in pseudoscientific ways, how traditional religious and conventional capitalist values are the products of false consciousness and how this condition can be overcome, both individually and collectively, through the proper diagnosis and emancipatory *praxis*.[7] While it may no longer be possible to ground one's beliefs and values in a theoretical consciousness transparent to the Divine, it is possible nevertheless, they argue, to arrive at rationally justified legitimation through the proper kind of *praxis*. But emancipatory *praxis*, according to MacIntyre, requires moral agency grounded in values that are not ephemeral; and the Achilles' heel of the denizens of late modernity, as defined by social science, is the inability to define the Good apart from the immediate goods of personal preferences and consumer rights.[8]

By its tacit and sometimes overt acceptance of the ideological commitments peculiar to the hermeneutics of suspicion, philosophy itself, in MacIntyre's view, has greatly contributed to what we might here cautiously describe as the postmodern condition.[9] Of course, much contemporary philosophy, especially analytic philosophy, tends to be too aloof to be guilty of explicit ideological avowals that have the potentiality of turning out to be false. Philosophy's culpability lies rather in its devotion to formalist-instrumentalist rationality—precisely the kind of thinking, MacIntyre argues, that is the bastard offspring of the historic European Enlightenment. Nevertheless, the formalist-instrumentalist collusion between philosophy and social science is proof-positive, according to MacIntyre, that many of its modern and postmodern devotees are necessarily "alienated from virtue" altogether.

That such alienation is very much a post-Enlightenment phenomenon is demonstrated by the fact that traditional (classical) societies, as MacIntyre reminds us, have no formally abstract term for virtue at all. The same situation obviously obtains with respect to the designator religion since, in the traditional religious society, there is no way to identify religion as some separate kind of activity or behavior that can be abstracted from all other activities and behaviors.[10] Religion is simply the time-honored way of being-in-the-world as the classical terms *Tao* and *Torah* both suggest. So also the heroic (Greek) society regards morality and society as being synonymous—*arete* ("virtue" or "excellence"), according to MacIntyre, being unintelligible apart from *action*. How one lives one's life in a given role and situation, therefore, is identical with one's virtue or the lack thereof. One simply cannot abstract from the living content within which virtue becomes determinate in order to have a better understanding of what it is. The plot or narrative structure of the life of the hero and his or her virtue are isomorphic to each other.[11]

MacIntyre's critique is much informed by Gadamer's observation that meaningful discussions of ethics are inseparable from the ethos and ethnos of a given polis or community within which they arise. Like Gadamer, MacIntyre argues that critical, formalist approaches to ethics (such as Kant's) must be combined with Aristotelian *phronesis* in order to determine implication in the actual practice of life (*Lebenspraxis*). Purely formal or instrumental approaches to moral philosophy empty ethics of its living content, this content being the embodiment of the values and virtues in the life of the community or tradition for which they are important. Hence, the list of virtues prominent in a given age is inextricably bound up with the definition a particular age gives to its common-life. Preoccupation with the analysis of purely abstract, transcendental or formal virtues and values has never been characteristic of a virtuous age. Such activities (including the development of programmatic lists of values and virtues) indicate, according to MacIntyre, that a given culture, having cast aside the normativity of once-traditional virtues and values, "is unsure of itself," as Hegel puts it in the *Phänomenologie*, no longer capable of providing itself with a coherent definition of virtue.

MacIntyre's argument shares with Hegel the observation that as the West rejected the classically Aristotelian or biblical virtues, its moral consciousness became necessarily "unhappy" and "stoical" (*PS*, 217). The unhappy consciousness is in fact the direct consequence of value deformation and the loss of *subtilitas applicandi*, as Gadamer puts it, with respect to effecting constructive moral action through subtle interpretations and applications of the moral law.[12] It has sometimes been argued, for example, that imperial host societies, initially welcoming immigrant populations willing to assume the tasks established classes identify with drudgery, live to regret this openness as foreign or alien ways begin to infiltrate and even supplant so-called traditional values. Cultural pluralism, once celebrated as the source of enlightened aesthetic enrichment, becomes identified as a primary cause of moral relativism and general confusion regarding previously canonical versions of emplotment.[13] The onset of radical heterogeneity with respect to the incoherence of a radically pluralistic communal narrative generates the suspicion that young people are growing up *scriptless*, devoid of any clear notion as to who they are, where they are going, or what they might become.[14]

But the primary source of cultural deformation in today's post-industrial societies (as Nietzsche, perhaps, was the first to understand) is not some external or alien deconstructive agency; it is rather the quasi-enlightened Establishment-Knowledge-Elite itself. This is precisely what makes the postmodern predicament so perplexing since, as

MacIntyre and others have pointed out, the cultural barbarians are already "within the gates" and have been for some time. Since the identity of the Knowledge-elite is ideological rather than ethnic, an identity consisting of a quasi-Enlightenment stance that has forfeited its own traditions for the sake of some marginalized but largely imaginary perspective, there is little if any willingness on the part of the power classes to acknowledge moral accountability regarding the purveyance of its deformative, corrosive influence (especially in education and the media) and the negative effect this has on the rest of society.[15]

The dominant pattern of most immigrant groups, in fact, is to emulate and identify actively with the perceived so-called traditional values of the host society in order to cultivate citizenship.[16] In the case of America, such values have traditionally been identified with the so-called Protestant work ethic—hard work, enterprise, and the accumulation of property such industry affords. Immigrant groups, through the first and second generations, are therefore the most likely to acknowledge the truth of an Aristotelian conception of virtue as exemplified in the lives of the local cultural heroes. In other words, it is a sense of the *lived and commonly shared past* that usually provides the baseline for self-definition and consensus regarding matters of virtue since the lived past of a common mythic fund is necessary for the ongoing task of moral emplotment and the well-being of society. Such funds are part and parcel of the "tradition constituted, tradition constitutive" community of discourse and only in such communities, according to MacIntyre, is rational debate regarding values possible since it is only in such contexts where values are of more than merely academic interest. But in the prevailing post-Enlightenment, post-traditional, post-Nietzschean, postmodern age, there is, according to MacIntyre, a diminished sense of any kind of intelligible emplotment whatever, the salient feature of all *post* epochs being the loss of any commonly shared sense of a redemptive past.[17] Thus in contrast to the heroes of antiquity or the saints in medieval times, where virtue was understood in terms of the common good, the consumer society's popular heroes are the mindless, amoral instantiations of altogether secularized individuals completely disconnected from any conception of the good other than what is good for them. If it is therefore the case today that immigrants seem "different" from their predecessors, this difference may be attributed to the breakdown of a *sensus communis* in which virtuous models of emulation are no longer identifiable.

While MacIntyre thus seems to share with Lyotard the view that metanarratives have disappeared for a great many people in our time,[18] especially the highly educated, he certainly does not share the view that metanarratives are to be shunned as some kind of devious metaphysical intrusions on personal freedom. The common abhorrence of the postmodern critic regarding any proposed solutions by way of metanarrative arises from the notion that such proposals presuppose a grasp of totality arising from fraudulent strategies of universalization and the "privileging" of certain solutions over others. Hence the cynical postmodern critic tends to offer no answers beyond deconstructive moves that further facilitate a continued dismantling of what remains of tradition—a tradition no longer lived but still artificially venerated, they believe, by certain academics.[19]

Obviously this is a red herring, however, since it is the primary function of academics to instruct students who, for the most part, will not become members of the teaching establishment but rather, one hopes, productive members of society! Hence deconstructive discourse is truncated in the sense that is very largely the intermural activity of critics who view *anomie* as an *ordo salutis, sui generis*. But MacIntyre has lately come to recognize that the liberal democratic, post-Enlightenment tradition, while it may be defective in many ways, is the tradition responsible for generating the structures of moral critique whereby dynamic, progressive, liberal societies became possible in the first instance. As such, liberalism is, in fact, the prevailing metanarrative of our time since it is the narrative by which all others are measured. This is nothing less than what Hegel considered to be the superiority of *revealed* religion; that is, religion *true to its concept* comprehended itself in-and-for-itself provides the occasion for comparative studies in religion. Sensing that we are somehow stuck *between* Aristotle and Nietzsche with respect to foundational and antifoundational approaches to moral theory and ethics, MacIntyre initially recommended "a new, doubtless very different Saint Benedict, at the end of *After Virtue*, as the shock treatment necessary to jolt modern liberal society out of its moral lethargy. More recently, however, he has delineated the means of engaging liberal tradition dialectically and constructively—the reason being that mature moral, liberal traditions provide us with a context and a content whereby it is possible to discern "the range of conditions in which incoherence would become inescapable and to explain how these conditions come about."[20]

By this commendation—namely, recovering the metanarrative of liberal democratic institutions as the only way to save them—MacIntyre picks up on another aspect of Hegel's critique of Enlightenment. For Hegel clearly recognized the preconditions for the kind of moral conversion MacIntyre commends, the truth of which is contained in the old Pietist maxim that "religion is better caught than taught." In other words, the "betwixt and between" MacIntyre describes as the moral condition of most individuals is a *metaxy* within which it is extremely difficult to "catch anything" whatever of substance so long as people remain uncommitted to anything other than the *metaxy* of noncommitment. Thus if it is the case that few if any alternative visions of reality and value exist anymore, there is little of moral substance that can be effectively taught by way of programs of moral education and ethical application in the absence of teachers committed to this enterprise in both theory and practice.[21] Education in the classical sense of *edoceo*, after all, means "to elicit" (*educo*) and bring to light the truth of what is already there, what is present in a given life-world. This kind of "recognition" (as in Hegel's *Anerkennung* as well as in the Platonic doctrine of *anamnesis*) presupposes not only the history of a redemptive past but a redemptive present; and redemptive pasts and presents are cognizable if and only if a society can break from its legacy of individualistic noncommitment thereby providing the young with something "to catch" through an imitation of its own activities.

Whatever the eventual outcome of MacIntyre's "traditions" approach to moral theory—that is, moral theory developed from within a "tradition constituted, tradition constituted" frame of reference—he has already very effectively alerted us to the obvious but frequently overlooked fact that the social sciences, especially in their establishment forms, are not the extensions of the "dazzling light" we take to be synonymous with the historical European Enlightenment in any sense whatever. They are rather the extension of a certain kind of reasoning ("instrumentalist rationality" or *Zweckrationalität*) that has been identified with Enlightenment and the peculiar, hypnotic power by which its devotees and clients are sustained and maintained in a perpetual state of moral hovering. And while instrumentalist rationality has come to be identified with the historical epoch known as the Enlightenment, it is important to note that this kind of rationality is far from being identical with Enlightenment-as-such. Indeed, the kind of Enlightenment rationality articulated by MacIntyre can more properly be viewed, as Hegel saw, in terms of *anti*-Enlightenment since true Enlightenment has the power to make actual what it knows and commends. It is precisely in this sense that MacIntyre makes abundantly clear the need to clarify and elucidate the term *Enlightenment* itself far more than we have previously if we are to speak meaningfully about its various implications and applications to the postmodern condition.

In order to do so, it is important to note from the outset the obvious fact that far from having a univocal meaning, the term *Enlightenment* is a polyvalent metaphor with multiple reference. On the one hand it refers to the historic European Enlightenment (1775–1800) and the emergence of modern liberal democratic institutions; but on the other hand, it refers to the transcendental, experiential, existentially luminous state in which one is said to have become critically wise or intelligent in an authentic, life-giving way—to have attained "autonomous moral self-understanding" or *Selbstbewußtsein*, as German Idealism has it, in the most complete possible way.

In Hegel's case, as Stanley Rosen has argued,[22] *Selbstbewußtsein* takes on the meaning of *Wisdom*. Moreover, the wisdom of true Enlightenment, as Hegel understands it, is in many ways similar to what the biblical proverb commends—the moral wisdom that "makes one's face shine" with cognitive luminosity and radiance, *wisdom* being that enlightened condition that is the outcome of authentic intellectual, moral, and religious conversion, as Lonergan reminds us.[23] It was Hegel, I contend, who first caught these multiple nuances of Enlightenment with greater depth and intensity than any other single thinker. Hegel and Schelling, in fact, were among the first to identify the *Aufklärerei* with the *Ausklärerei*,[24] the "enlighteners" with the "disenlighteners," and it was Hegel, of course, who equated pseudo-Enlightenment with the "unhappy consciousness," especially in matters of morality and religion. But far from being the *end* of Enlightenment, the consciousness unhappy with itself is a necessary stage in the ongoing project of true or authentic Enlightenment. Hence, the truly critical response to the various problems of Enlightenment is not *less* but *more* Enlightenment—providing one has seen clearly into the spiritual foundations *of* Enlightenment.

It is not surprising, then, that Hegel's interest in the spiritual foundations of Enlightenment compelled him, during the Berlin period, to the development of what can only be described as a *comparative* approach to the philosophy of religion. In other words, Hegel seemed to be of the view that mere formalism in the philosophy of religion is no more adequate than formalism in ethics (formalism here being identical with the philosophy of reflection). Philosophy worth its salt has to be concerned with and mediated by the material consistency of world; in other words, Enlightenment, like Spirit, must become actual (*wirklich*) and not remain subjective. Moreover, when one considers the meaning of Enlightenment from the standpoint of the history of religions, one has to face up to the highly textured and nuanced conceptions of its meaning, for in the history of religions Enlightenment is not limited to the internal or autonomous operations of consciousness: Enlightenment is also something that *happens* to the subject—something given in revelation as the work of Spirit.

Because Hegel understands both the internal and the external textures of the dialectic of Spirit so well, one must begin, as Habermas rightly insists, with Hegel as the philosophical baseline, as it were, for understanding the philosophy of the Enlightenment.[25] In so doing, one also begins to discover that the rational grounds for MacIntyre's indictment of late modernity and postmodernity (which may sound new and even astonishing to many enlightened liberal-progressive thinkers) were was first noted by Hegel in ways that remain unsurpassed even today. The reason Hegel still commands this lofty position, I contend, has much to do with the fact that his lucidity on Enlightenment is informed, like MacIntyre's, by the ability to comprehend the religious, or spiritual meaning of Enlightenment—in Hegel's case, a critique of Enlightenment grounded in speculative pneumatology.

Prior to discussing Hegel's critique of Enlightenment, it may be helpful, for purposes of contexualization, to begin with a brief look at Kant. Enlightenment philosophy is synonymous with Kant insofar as the Age of Enlightenment has to do with the rise of critical philosophical and moral consciousness. As such, Kant represents, as Jaspers once put it, the nodal point of transformation in modern philosophy; and it is through careful scrutiny of Kant's transcendental-critical insight regarding Enlightenment that Hegel comprehends the historical dimensions and future implications of the Enlightenment.

· 1 ·

Kant was sixty when he published the celebrated essay *Beantwortung der Frage: Was ist Aufklärung?* in the 30 September 1784 issue of the *Berlinische Monatsschrift*. Two months later Hegel would celebrate his fourteenth birthday and, shortly thereafter, begin to record his own philosophical reflections on the meaning of Enlightenment in his *Tagebuch*—reflections that would also culminate a half-century later, as fate would have it, in learned presentations before the court of the king of Prussia.

It will be recalled that while Kant's brief essay on Enlightenment was written for a general audience, it was also written for the king. Following the death of Frederick the Great two years later, Kant was increasingly caught up in political controversies regarding censorship. Frederick the Great, in Kant's estimate, was truly *aufgeklärt* in his ability to permit freedom in matters of religion and personal conscience while remaining constant with respect to the necessity of maintaining a sense of duty and obedience among his subjects regarding matters of social and cultural order. As such, Frederick the Great exemplified, for Kant, the responsible freedom he believed to be synonymous with the spirit of true Enlightenment.

But this situation changed dramatically with the succession of Frederick William II in 1786. Consistent with the Prussian tendency toward political conservatism and religious orthodoxism, the *Neue Fritz* appointed the reactionary Wollner as his Minister of Church and Education, thereby displacing the liberal legacy of Baron von Zedlitz, to whom Kant had dedicated his *Critique of Pure Reason* in 1781. With these repressive changes, Kant himself came under the threat of censure—the king in fact commanded Kant, in 1794, to desist from further undermining orthodox Christian doctrine. Owing to these historical circumstances, Kant's brief essay is magnified in significance as an index of what Kant thought with respect to the meaning of Enlightenment for society generally.[26]

Kant begins by reminding his readers that Enlightenment most assuredly is not a collective, historical reality. Ages are *not* enlightened. There are only ages or epochs during which there is greater probability that individuals might "become enlightened." It is far more accurate, in Kant's view, to speak of "Ages of Ignorance" since only stupidity, in the current idiom, seems to be truly nondiscriminatory irrespective of time and place. Having successfully "domesticated the animals," Kant says sarcastically but also prophetically, we are now "domesticating ourselves" (and here especially "the entire fair sex") into a "blissful ignorance" whereby one both discourages and prevents "the dangerous and difficult step into maturity."[27]

Maturity qua *autonomie* is Kant's synonym for Enlightenment since it requires Enlightenment "to leave self-caused immaturity." The meaning of *self-caused* is extremely important here owing to Kant's voluntarism and the view that one's fate in life is very largely the product of one's choices and actions. Consistent with the Kantian-inspired formulation in Kierkegaard and Schopenhauer out of Kant, "the more will, the more self," *immaturity* is understood as the "unwillingness to use one's intelligence without the guidance of another"; to be immature and unenlightened is to remain permanently within the heteronomous constraints of what society provides without ever making an attempt to ascertain whether the grounds of authority presupposed by the provider are legitimate or rationally justifiable. It is within this dialectical configuration of forces that one should understand Kant's symbol of enlightened autonomy, *sapere aude*—"Have the courage to use your own intelligence"—and it is precisely this nuance that drives the meaning of *Selbstbewußtsein* in German Idealism.

Having this kind of courage presupposes the stoical strength of individual will; but in order "to will," there must be freedom to do so, that is, freedom must be understood as real. Freedom, for Kant, is the precondition for any possible enlightenment—freedom being, as Karl

Jaspers asserts out of Kant, "the preeminent cipher of *Transzendenz* and *mögliche Existenz*."[28] Clearly Kant does not here have in mind the "open society" in a Popperian sense (even though Popper seems to think so),[29] and he certainly does not equate freedom with inalienable "consumer rights" and "freedom of preference" as MacIntyre comments regarding its meaning nowadays. Mature, autonomous self-consciousness, for Kant, means rather freedom of conscience with respect to matters speculative and theoretical, and duty with respect to social obligations. These two, freedom of conscience and a sense of duty, constitute the dialectic implicit in Kant's ethics—both being grounded in a subjective maxim that presupposes the ability of consciousness to comprehend the meaning of an unconditionally "good will" in-and-for-itself. Kant's belief is historically informed by Luther's *Freiheits-Prinzip*, to wit, that the Christian person is the "free lord of all subject to none" while also remaining at the same time a "perfectly dutiful servant of all, subject to all."[30] This is why Kant, out of this "two spheres" notion of social ethics, can praise Frederick the Great for insisting, on the one hand, that Word and Sacrament be properly administered, while also providing speculative-hermeneutical space regarding the theological meaning of Word and Sacrament.[31] But it is only in the ordered society that such freedom is possible, and apart from this subtle but necessary condition[32] one faces the prospect and even the inevitability of totalitarianism in one form or another. Consequently, totalitarianism, according to Kant, is not really an external determination but an internal one.[33] One can have freedom in absolutism and bondage in democracy depending on the particular conditions of each. Totalitarianism therefore really has to do with what is *Widervernunft*,[34] that is, with the posture of "antireason" or "anti-intellectualism" that suffocates altogether the free exercise of reason and is therefore immoral.[35] Had Kant written this essay 150 years later, he might have substituted the term *ideology* for the kind of spiritual despotism to which he refers here since it is the ideologue who imposes and instantiates policies, which minimize or prevent, whether directly or indirectly, the possibility of critical thinking and the free expression of its findings.

· 2 ·

Child of the Enlightenment, Hegel was both deeply fascinated with and deeply troubled by its problematic throughout his life. And as in the case of Kant, Pietism provides the religious background against which Hegel attempts to come to terms with Enlightenment. The outcome of this religious mediation, however, is quite different, since it is the expressly metaphysical dimension of religion, and not the moral, which provides Hegel with the motivation of attending to religion in order to come to terms with the Enlightenment. Hegel's theological training at Tübingen also makes a difference, for while Hegel was a student he had no clearly defined school of philosophy and theology, in contrast to Kant, against which to measure himself. Neo-Pietism had already abandoned clear-headed traditional theology—turning to biblicism, as mentioned earlier, in the attempt to refute Kantianism. But Kant had Wolffian rationalism with which to contend. This rationalism, as strongly represented by his teachers at Königsberg, Schultz and Knutzen, was also combined with traditional Pietism whereas, in the case of Hegel's teachers, these elements were disconjunctive. As a consequence, Hegel measured himself against his contemporaries and peers, especially Fichte and Schelling, and not against his teachers. After extrapolating from Pietism what Kant believed to be its most important feature, a sense of the moral *ought*, and after destroying Wolffian metaphysics, he seemed quite content to leave religion (or what was left of it) to the theologians. Hegel, by contrast, always provides the sense that he believes religion much too important to be left to the theologians and evidences throughout his works the attempt to recover the truth of religion—especially the metaphysical aspect and implication of religious insight. Second, and in contrast to the provincialism of Kant, Hegel's Württemberg background, combined with his Nürnberg experience, provided more diverse cultural settings whereby his Lutheranism combined with Catholic sentiments, as evidenced by his lifelong interest in the meaning of the Sacraments and in medieval philosophy, especially the mystics. Thus when T. M. Greene reports that Kant, prior to writing *Religion Within the Limits of Reason Alone*, refreshed himself by turning once again to his "old catechism," it seems to me that Hegel never left the catechism, that is, never left the dialectic of faith and knowledge, belief and pure insight implicit in Luther's explanation of *der heilige Geist*. For these are the categories through which Hegel comes to terms with Enlightenment whether as a datum or condition of consciousness or as the power or condition underlying the growth and development of the historical epoch we now call modernity.[36]

These, then, are the categories that concern us here: Hegel's critique of Kant in *Glauben und Wissen* (1802–03) combined with the meaning of negation as the deep structure of Enlightenment or, more precisely, the enlightened self-consciousness. In addressing these issues, we focus on the *Phänomenologie*, Section B, Part 4, "Spirit Estranged from Itself," where Hegel treats "Faith and Pure Insight,"

"The Truth of Enlightenment," and "Absolute Freedom and Terror," and we do so by recontextualizing these views against his earlier critique of Kant in *Glauben und Wissen* and his initial reflections on the nature and meaning of Enlightenment in the *Frühe Schriften* of the Bern and Frankfurt periods. By this strategy we intend to indicate the extent to which Hegel's understanding of Enlightenment is grounded in a concept of negation that parallels the concept of Enlightenment we find prominently displayed in speculative mysticism and in his later writings on the comparative philosophy of religion. This will place us in a position whereby we can access Hegel's concept of Absolute Spirit in the final chapters as the pneumatological transformation of dialectic completes itself in Free Spirit.[37]

Hegel makes it clear that the historic European Enlightenment and the German thinkers with which it is most directly associated—Kant, Fichte, and Jacobi—cannot be taken as synonymous with Enlightenment-as-such. In fact, the philosophers of the so-called Enlightenment "being conscious of nothingness [i.e., the power of negation], have merely turned this nothingness into a system" (*JS*, 289; *FK*, 56). This consciousness is not Enlightenment but rather the prelude to nihilism since it is an approach that succeeds only in banishing the external or extrinsic (positive) side of religion without ever touching its essence, which is an essence grounded in the mystery of freedom. Having absolutized the infinity of the concept, Enlightenment philosophy succeeds only in setting the finite and the infinite at odds and in absolute contradiction to each other, and winds up substituting this opposition for reality. The negative consequence of placing philosophy and religion into an absolute opposition is that Enlightenment philosophy falls prey to the very eudaemonism it finds so objectionable in the simple life of faith, and the older "dogmatism of being is translated into the dogmatism of thinking" (*JS*, 430; *FK*, 189). This dogmatism consists in the exchange of object for subject, the outer for the inner, the soul for the Ego, with philosophy reduced, as in Locke, "to empirical psychology" (*JS* 297; *FK*, 63). With the reduction of philosophy to utility and instrumentality, so-called Enlightenment reason becomes identical with *Zweckrationalität*.

Kant showed decisively, according to Hegel, that "the beginning of the Ideal of Reason" is to be found "in the intellect itself" (*JS*, 316; *FK*, 79). Kant also demonstrated convincingly for Hegel the inherent dialectical *triplicity* of the intellect; that a priori formality and the a posteriori practicality are linked together by *judgment* (*JS*, 317; *FK*, 80). But Kant fell short, according to Hegel, in limiting the transcendental imagination to a faculty of representation whereby the *productive* imagination is reduced to *reproductive* functions. It is precisely the philosophy of pure representationalism (*Darstellungs-Philosophie*) that makes Kant, in Findlay's words, "the purest representation of cave philosophy." For Hegel (and, of course, for Findlay) the true destiny of philosophy is the "transcendence of the cave."[38] For this to happen, the imagination must also be understood as "primary and originary" and not merely reproductive—that is, imagination must be understood as self-transcending, its power originating in the unitive ground of Reason-itself or Absolute Spirit (*JS*, 308; *FK*, 73).

Hegel's comments on the "intuitive intellect" or productive imagination in this work, of course, bear the heavy trace of Schelling, with whom he was collaborating during the time. But even here it is important to note that Hegel, by his use of the term *intuitive*, is not referring to some kind of immediate-immediate whereby one might penetrate "the intelligible substratum of nature" and establish [thereby] the universal "laws of [cosmic] mechanism." Kant is entirely correct, he says, in rejecting such a notion as "transcending our capacity altogether," such laws pertaining only to the realm of phenomena (*JS*, 327; *FK*, 91). Instead of being preoccupied, as was Schelling, with a Romantic theosophy of nature or an archaeological alchemy of reason, Hegel seeks to establish the basis for a dialectic of imagination within Reason-itself in order that this dialectic might culminate in Absolute Consciousness. The trajectory of his analysis, then, is teleological and eschatological rather than primordialistic and archaic. This motif is established as early as the opening lines of his essay "On the Life of Jesus" (1795), where, in a prologue paralleling that of John the Evangelist in the Fourth Gospel, he asserts the following principles from which he never departs: "Pure reason, transcending all limits, is divinity itself . . . Through reason [i.e., through God] man learns of his destiny, the unconditional purpose of his life." And further, "The cultivation of reason is the sole source of truth and tranquility since John, never pretending to possess reason exclusively or as something rare, insisted that all men could uncover it in themselves" [viz., the Johannine saying that it is "God's will that all men shall be saved by coming to a knowledge of the truth"] (*LJ*, 75). The serenification or *Seligkeit* that results from this *unio mystica* is for Hegel attainable only by way of the progressive dialectic of consciousness wherein the authentically speculative side of Reason-itself is recovered as the means to the Absolute. This absolute goal of the thinking consciousness is one and the same, Hegel believes, with the truth implicit in Parmenidean assertion that "to think and to be are the same"—or to speak more religiously, one's eternal reward is identical with the highest state of consciousness one has attained in this life.

It is virtually impossible to miss the theological motive in Hegel's critique of Kant, Jacobi, and Fichte, since by this critique Hegel intends to bring about a rebirth of consciousness through what he calls both literally and figuratively "the Speculative Good Friday." One must not make the fatal mistake, Hegel asserts, of simply resigning oneself to the Death of God implied in the *der Dogmatismus des Seins* and substitute for speculative theology the rehabilitation of moral value, as was the case, he believed, with Kant in *Religion Within the Limits of Reason Alone* (1793). There are two reasons for this, one existential and the other formal: First, in order to comprehend the existential depth of Christian tradition, one must be willing truly to enter "the abyss of infinitude" as dramatically represented in Luther's famous Good Friday hymn, "God Himself is Dead," remembering that this too is but a "moment" in the life of the "Supreme Idea" or Spirit. But this is the absolutely essential moment if reconciliation is to be viewed as an ontological fact and not merely a chimera of wishful thinking. Therefore, one can only discover the meaning of a "religion within the limits of reason (*Vernunft*)" by descending completely into the ontological abyss of negativity as encompassed by Christianity's deepest insight. Kant, in Hegel's view, does not do this since such a descent is impossible if one continues to cling to some "empirical being" shored up by "moral precepts" or the "formal abstractions" in ethics. Only when religion reestablishes itself in "Absolute Freedom" and the "harsh truth of God-forsakenness," Hegel asserts, anticipating Nietzsche, will philosophy again rise up to its speculative, metaphysical possibility (*JS*, 432; *FK*, 191). This God-forsaken Abyss, for Hegel, is the primary vortex of freedom, the innermost matrix of the dialectic of finitude and infinitude, and it only manifests itself in a secondary way in a philosophy of the will. Christianity, in Hegel's view, has the unique opportunity of making this insight concrete owing to the nature of its concept, this concept being the self-negation of the Absolute as the essential moment in the comprehension of itself. This ontological mystery, underlying what Ricoeur identifies as being at the center of that "most primordial, most enigmatic dialectic"—the metaphoric "is–is not" predicate[39]—provides the basis for the pneumatological transformation of dialectic since it is a transformation made materially explicit in the Incarnation, which lies at the heart of the Christian *mythos*. Only when philosophy comprehends the depths of negation within religious consciousness and not in spite of it, only when it "dies to the world" of *Verstehen*, so to speak, will philosophy be able to "rise up to the Supreme Idea" in the *Vernünftigkeit*, which is nothing less than Absolute Spirit. The truly enlightened philosophical and religious self-consciousness, then, is the consciousness transformed by an absolute negation and renunciation through which it is given to itself as Absolute Consciousness.

· 3 ·

What is the *truth* of Enlightenment for Hegel? It is the truth of *pure, critical insight*. With this conviction, Hegel is at one with Kant. But what is pure, critical insight and what does it affect—that is, what does one accomplish with it once one has it? This is the decisive question, since the mere *having* of pure, critical insight is not sufficient for Hegel.

Marx believed he found the answer in the famous passage where Hegel speaks of the "reconciliation" of the heretofore disparate worlds of Spirit and matter, Being and existence. With this *Aufhebung*, therefore, "Heaven is transplanted to earth below" (*PS*, §581; *PG*, 431: *Beide Welten sind versöhnt und der Himmel auf die Erde herunter verpflanzt*). But the truth of Enlightenment is completely misunderstood if this passage is taken to mean a final or ultimate demystification of Being through the reduction of Transcendence to immanence. It was never Hegel's intention to exchange the Divine for the human, as so many critics have charged.

The deeper truth of enlightened "pure" critical insight has rather to do with comprehending the truth of Spirit through Absolute Negativity, a negativity that lies at the heart of the "is–is not" dialectic of the copula of pure consciousness. Only having understood this do we begin to recognize Consciousness-itself as our only access to Being or, more accurately, that consciousness and Being are identical by dint of the encompassing power of Spirit. It is just this awareness of the deep ground of consciousness in Spirit that is missing from Enlightenment philosophy, according to Hegel, since "Enlightenment does not recognize the content of its negation as the negative of itself—the negative of its Other." When Enlightenment philosophy condemns the extrinsic symbols of conventional religious piety as the productions or projections of a naive or *false* consciousness, the so-called Enlightenment is, in fact, condemning its own consciousness by failing to acknowledge the implicit dialectic of negation whereby it has arrived at its judgment. Failing to do so, Enlightenment falsifies itself by the very means it has negated religion and metaphysics. Enlightenment philosophy thus forgets that it too is mediated knowledge or, more accurately, forgets the extent of its dependence on mediation. Thus the naive reduction of the objects of faith into mere *sense objects* bespeaks Enlightenment's blind spot with respect to the meaning of the dialectics of a mediation of meaning already present in religion. Hence Enlightenment is not *enlightened* precisely because it further extends the very extrinsicism it finds objectionable in religion. This extrinsicism consists of self-legitimation through positive grounding—not anymore in the external grounding of metaphysics, to be sure, but now through the internal grounding of the reflective consciousness. Moreover, the alleged externality (*Positivität*) in popular religion is not really the result of a superficial union of the symbols of faith with the Absolute; it is an apparent unity caused only by the limitations of representational thinking. The "self-mediating, self-relating ground" of religious consciousness has rather to do with "Spirit-itself bearing witness to itself in the inner heart of the individual consciousness as well as through the universal presence everywhere of belief in it" (*PS*, §572). In other words, the moral strength of *subtilitas applicandi* derivative of the *sensus communis* is the true witness to the authenticity of religious consciousness, and this insight Hegel clearly derives from Pietism. Thus the conventional life of religious faith, for Hegel, is far superior to Enlightenment faith (or faith *in* the Enlightenment) because it is a faith with a *content* that enables it to become *wirklich* or "objectively real," where it counts, in the moral life of the community. Enlightenment, by contrast, "having once emptied the wineskins of belief," no longer has the ability to provide the basis for any new communal solidarity. The objectivity of the object has simply been exchanged for the subjectivity of the subject, community is sacrificed on the high altar of individualism, and Enlightenment is left with the privatized anthropocentrism of "feeling" disguised as thought, and idealized intentions become the substitute for moral action.

True religion, therefore, does not have to resign itself to this unhappy exchange and should not, he warns, "be led astray and corrupted by the [false] insinuations of Enlightenment" (*PS*, §§554, 572, 573). Furthermore, there is no cause for knee-jerk biblicist and dogmatical reactions by Pietists and Orthodoxists to Enlightenment criticisms regarding the alleged heteronomy of the contents of its faith since Enlightenment faith is itself devoid of content. Indeed, the worst possible response by the faithful religious is to be led down the path of subjectivism (as Hegel believed to be the case with Schleiermacher) as a way of compensatory compromise with Enlightenment critics regarding alleged losses of authoritative external grounding. Lessing's "broad ugly ditch" is not broached by either subjective historicism or the so-called necessary proofs of reason, for Lessing, like Kant, has an extrinsic conception of necessity. Indeed, both of these posed alternatives of subjectivism and historicism are different aspects of the quest for legitimation that drives *Verstehensphilosophie*. Religious consciousness must rather understand that far from being structurally different from Enlightenment consciousness, it has the same cognitive features and potentialities: 1) a concept of Absolute Being; 2) this concept made subjective in the believing relation; and, most important, 3) the development of culture whereby the subject's relation to the Absolute is made determinate and actual (*wirklich*) in ethical life. Indeed, when religious consciousness understands itself structurally, it will also understand that it is with respect to 3) that Enlightenment faces its most serious defect—moral actualization in *Lebenspraxis*. For if it is the case that absolute sacrifice as exemplified in the divine drama of self-diremption is the focal point of the Christian cultus, and if it is the case that Christianity qua cultus draws its moral strength from this symbol, how does Enlightenment, Hegel asks, make explicit its "collective bond to the Great Void of the Absolute?" (*PS*, §586).[40]

The stark implication of this searching question, of course, is that the Enlightenment cannot provide this since there is nothing to provide. Indeed, the only possible response by the Enlightenment is its argument for the quasi-warrant of continuous deconstruction by the critic who, while marginalized by Enlightenment, nevertheless remains parasitically within society—there being, as MacIntyre observes, no viable "outside" context for rational, moral discourse.[41] But there is no need for the deconstructive move, in Hegel's view, since it is already provided, at a metaphysical level, by what the Absolute Self-Diremption encompasses in the "Speculative Good Friday," an Absolute Self-Diremption that, as Saint Paul observes, has *ta panta* implications beyond all possible replications. Hence Hegel shares with Kierkegaard the view that the Absolute Self-Diremption represents a *skandalon* completely and totally beyond the rational purview of the conventional Enlightenment philosophy of reflection. Contrary to Kierkegaard, the scandal of the offended consciousness, according to Hegel, is not "beyond reason." It is a *skandalon* that points rather to the mystery of Spirit transparent to the power of Reason understood as Absolute Consciousness. The truth of Enlightenment is therefore nothing less than the truth perceived through the pneumatological transformation of dialectic.[42]

With these metaphysically speculative reflections on the meaning of Enlightenment, Hegel obviously evidences a much greater degree of existential grounding in Pietism than one finds in the case of Kant. In other words, Hegel's critique of Kant's "religion within the limits of reason alone" is more than merely academic since Kant touched a vital nerve in Hegel's religious sensibility. This is why Hegel concludes that reason qua *Verstand* in the Kantian instance will not suffice to overcome the loss of the primary or first-level religious naivete that it un-

dermines. Unconditional acceptance of the primacy of the critical philosophy of reflection will only make matters worse since the pseudoen-
lightened now conclude there is a rational basis for the rejection of
religion even though this rejection is superficial, and have nothing
to substitute for it. *Verstand* vis-à-vis religious consciousness or *faith*
therefore functions, for Hegel, in the "accusatorial" sense of Luther's
second use of the Law (*lex semper accusit*)—critical reflection being
identified with *why* it is the case that the things previously believed are
no longer true and cannot therefore be salutary. But this rational self-
justification or self-legitimation is rational only in the weak sense for
Hegel. For if intellectual conversions by way of the Kantian critical
philosophy may be shown to be one-sided and therefore superficial, it
may also be shown that this one-sidedness arises from the fact that
Kant's critique is insufficiently rational; Kant does not go far enough
with respect to recognizing the ultimate identity of reason and Spirit.
This does not mean, however, that an absolutizing of the transcendental Ego, as in Fichte, is the answer. The Fichtean move only makes
matters worse—though it is better than the quasi-Romantic move of
Schelling. Hegel rather looks to renunciation and negation for the
answer and in so doing follows a path closer to Hölderlin and, of
course, Augustine and Luther: "True Enlightenment has within it this
stain of unsatisfied longing, and in its empty Absolute we find this in
the form of the pure abstract object; in passing beyond its individual
nature to an unfulfilled beyond, the stain appears as an act and a process; and in the selfishness of what is *useful* it is seen in the form of the
sensuous object." True or authentic Enlightenment, however, continues the task of attempting "to remove this stain . . . [and] by considering more closely the positive result of what constitutes the truth for
it, we shall find that the stain is implicitly removed already" (*PS*, §589).

Hegel's choice of defilement imagery to account for this feeling of
"unsatisfied longing" is extremely thought-provoking since it alludes
not only to the primordial instance of what Ricoeur identifies as a *Fall*
or *fault*—a defilement that can be removed only by some sacred ablu-
tion—but also to Hölderlin's sense of *Fehl* in "The Single One." What
then is the *implicit* removal of this stain? Hegel's transcendental answer, from the Tübingen essay through his mature works, remains
constant: Enlightenment must become Enlightened, must become
wisdom (*TE*, 15–16).

How this process of Enlightenment unfolds becomes evident as one
considers the manner in which Hegel reformulates Kant's *sapere aude*
motif. At the end of the section on "Faith and Pure Insight" in the
Phenomenology and just prior to his treatment of Enlightenment as
such, Hegel asserts: "This pure insight, then, is the Spirit that calls to

every consciousness: be for yourselves what you essentially are in yourselves, *rational*." (*PS*, §537; *PG*, 398: *Diese reine Einsicht ist also der Geist, der allem Bewußtsein zuruft*; seid für euch selbst, *was ihr alle* an euch selbst seid, vernünftig). Here it must be noted, and in some contrast to Kant, that Hegel's call to rational autonomy or Enlightenment is not the call of the self to the self but the "call of Spirit" to the self. But how does the Spirit *call*? Is this mere metaphoric usage? Many readers might see it this way. On the other hand it may be that Hegel can say what he means regarding true Enlightenment (and in a manner that parallels precisely Luther's exposition of Spirit) only by way of metaphoric predication. We conclude this chapter by indicating how this seems to be the case.

First, it is important to note that Hegel's treatment of Enlightenment comes precisely at that stage in the *Phenomenology* where Spirit in culture is most estranged from itself. In other words, only at the radical end-point of absolute negation and estrangement does Spirit becomes "sure of itself" in morality. This end point of absolute negation culminates in the consciousness of what he terms "absolute freedom and terror." But "absolute freedom and terror" should not here simply be identified with the antinomianism that culminates in the French "reign of terror" as some commentators have suggested. Like Kant, Hegel consistently identifies freedom with the *mystery* of freedom he finds implicit in the Protestant Principle—something Enlightenment philosophy in its superficial critique of religion has not, he believes, even begun to fathom.[43] The "reign of terror" is itself, in fact, the historic sign that the so-called Enlightenment's comprehension of the Protestant Principle is superficial since it concludes, on the basis of its critique of the alleged externality of religion, that it is now "free" of responsible freedom.[44] The fact of the matter is that Enlightenment confuses freedom with nothingness and, by identifying "being conscious of the power of nothingness" with "the power of negation," it has "made this nothingness into a system" thereby substituting for the old religion the bleak prospect of nihilism. To be sure, Enlightenment does not itself recognize that this is the case, does not recognize its complicity in this reduction, and the reason that it does not have this awareness is that it is not really enlightened. This deficiency, in fact, is proof-positive of the Enlightenment's nonenlightenment.

With this observation we come full circle to MacIntyre's thesis regarding the Enlightenment as a "peculiar kind of darkness in which men so dazzled themselves, they could no longer see." Hegel's insight regarding the origins of this darkness, namely, "that we have done it to ourselves," finds full negative expression in the *cor requiem deo* of Nietzsche's madman a half-century later. But the "negative-negative," if we may call it that, is not sufficient for Hegel. And the reason this is the case is that Enlightenment does not recognize the positive-con-structive element concealed under the form of its opposite, namely, negation as a positive-negative. For Hegel, the positive-constructive ground of negation is nothing less than the true infinite or the Eternal, as he makes clear from the outset of *Glauben und Wissen*. Indeed, the *Phenomenology* makes clear Hegel's intention of extending and refin-ing the mystery of negation and negativity in what is, in fact, a new science of logic. This *Logik* is the direct continuation and systematic elucidation of the early Hegel's Eckhartian observation in the "Spirit" essay that "beauty of soul has as its negative attribute the highest free-dom, namely, the potentiality of *renouncing everything* in order to main-tain one's self. For he who seeks to save his life will lose it" (*FS*, 350).

At the level of *intentio recta*, Hegel is referring, of course, to Jesus, who, through the exercise of absolute freedom manifest as disinterest or detachment, is able to surmount the demands of law and fate and be open, thereby, to authentic reconciliation. For it is here in absolute negativity that Spirit is fully manifest as a moral and christological category consistent with the Protestant Principle. However, negativity ultimately takes on its positive implication only as a pneumatological category. Here I come back to the Enlightenment credo of Hegel: "This pure insight [the truth of Enlightenment] is nothing less than the Spirit that calls to every consciousness: Be for yourselves what you essentially are in yourselves—*rational*." For Hegel, as for Luther, it is Spirit that "calls, gathers, enlightens, and sanctifies" (*sondern der heilige Geist hat mich durchs Evangelium berufen, mit seinen Gaben erleuchtet, im rechten Glauben geheiliget und erhalten*), Spirit alone that overcomes the absolute paradox of the two worlds of universal and particular, whether in their formal or their material aspects. While the Incarna-tion is the concrete, representational symbol of this overcoming, it is Spirit that makes it actual and Spirit alone that makes it intelligible in the spiritual community.

It seems evident, then, that Hegel recognized very clearly the extent to which Christian theology had trivialized the doctrine of the Holy Spirit by failing to explicate fully the *truth of Enlightenment* present to its own confession. Hegel's deep dissatisfaction with Kant's doctrine of the transcendental imagination, and with the reverse sides of Kant's doctrine of the Ego in Jacobi and Fichte respectively, ultimately stems, I believe, from Hegel's disappointment with Kant's failure to compre-hend fully the *triplicity* of the trinitarian confession, what it implied for his critique of reason, and what it meant for the life of the soul and for the community. In other words, having abandoned the traditional doctrine of the soul qua Spirit, the productive imagination in Kant turns out to be reproductive, and philosophy is left with the two irreconcilable elements of the sensuous and the supersensuous, the empirical and the transcendental, without understanding that both are the posits of Spirit and can only be understood by Spirit.

Far from being static or a merely formal resolution of the problem of Enlightenment, the pneumatological transformation of dialectic is faced with the continuous task of reconciling the truths of morality and religion—or, if one prefers the categories of Nietzsche, Spirit has to do with the open-ended project of reconciling the *will to power* with the *eternal recurrence of the same*, Spirit being the bond of Being, as it were, between freedom and nature. Nietzsche's observation that this reconciliation may not take place for a millennium, or ever, for that matter, and that the on-project of *humanitas* may be "endlessly on the open sea," does not falsify Hegel's position. The dialectic of Spirit is no external thing, nor is it merely internal. Spirit rather provides the encompassing conceptual ground for all such distinctions without being reducible to any. Thus the dialectic of determinacy and indeterminacy, hovering at the boundary of theism and atheism, joy and anguish, is the necessary precondition for the true project of authentic Enlightenment precisely because Enlightenment is an ongoing *Prozeß*. This process, which is nothing less than the process of faith as consciousness (*Glauben als Bewußtsein*) does not make Enlightenment the "darkness" of human understanding except in the restricted sense of something already completed. The progressive, prosessual, self-transcending character of Spirit-itself rather bears witness (*sola fides*) to the truth that "Enlightenment must become enlightened" and true to itself as conscience. Indeed, this is the meaning and implication present to Luther's comments regarding the "enlightening gifts" of the Spirit, namely, that Enlightenment is not an end in itself but the means of actualizing more effectively and historically the moral life of the spiritual community. Moral self-actualization therefore requires a social context of mediation in order to be effective as an ongoing process.[45] That context is the ethical life (*Sittlichkeit*) afforded by the spiritual community because virtue, like religion, according to the Pietist maxim, "is better caught than taught."

We turn now, in the final chapters, to further consideration as to how this may to be accomplished by recapitulating the movement of Hegel's grand philosophical category from Holy Spirit to Absolute Spirit and Free Spirit.

VIII

ABSOLUTE SPIRIT

Das Absolute ist der Geist; dies ist die höchste
Definition des Absoluten.
(*Enzyklopädie*)

I N THESE FINAL CHAPTERS, we seek to demonstrate further
the validity of our pneumatological thesis by reading Hegel's doctrine of Spirit against his doctrine of Being in the *Logic*. Both
doctrines are heavily informed, I argue, by Hegel's interpretation of
the pre-Socratics and his studies in the comparative philosophy of religion. We will, therefore, simultaneously be considering Hegel's doctrine of Absolute Spirit against the *history* of Spirit, as it were, or, more
precisely, some of Hegel's readings of interpretations of Spirit in the
history of philosophy and religion. After this discussion we will be able
to appreciate more fully how Hegel comes to his assertion that "the
Spirit is the highest definition of the Absolute" (*E*, §384) and how
Hegel's *logic* of Spirit (the fusion of *pneuma* and *nous*), far from being
the secular profanization of Spirit, as Berdyaev calls it,[1] is the primary
mark of its *resacralization*.[2]

· 1 ·

Hegel's concept of Spirit follows directly from his doctrine of Being.
But because Hegel's doctrine of Being is relatively unintelligible apart
from his concept of Spirit it can be argued that a pneumatological a
priori, so to speak, undergirds his concept of Being and that this pneumatological a priori provides it with the religious and metaphysical
energy that makes it in all ways unique. Few individuals in the history
of philosophy have thought through the problem of Being so intensely, and fewer still have provided, at the same time, such noetically
cogent yet mystically sublime explanations of Being. It is the pneumatological dimension of Hegel's logic, I argue, that interfuses his doctrine of Being with these qualities, making it a living thing.[3]

Hegel commences his *Logic* (in both its *Greater* and *Lesser* forms)
with a fundamental but nonfoundational ontological inquiry:[4] Hegel's
inquiry is fundamental in the sense that he views Being qua Being as

"immediate and indeterminate" (*WL*, 82; *E*, §86) on the notion that the question of *beginning* itself has to be the absolutely necessary starting point for any logic that has the attainment of Absolute Consciousness as its stated goal as distinct from the goal of mere formal clarity and coherence. On the other hand, the question of fundamentality is non-foundational since Hegel is not here attempting to ground extant beings upon some essentialistic notion of Being. Hegel's question of Being is antecedent to the question of both beings and Being in the conventional sense. Hence the founding of Hegel's *Logic* has nothing whatever to do with the establishment of conceptual correspondence to something external; its founding and grounding rests entirely upon a logical articulation of "the experience of consciousness," as he asserts from the outset in the *Phenomenology* (1807), and upon what can be adduced dialectically from this experience with respect to the nature of Being.

At the most primordial level of consideration, therefore, the question of Being, for Hegel, is akin to what Eckhart asserts regarding the experience of the Divine "in the desert of its loneliness and solitude" whereby one is forced to utilize images of depravation in order to differentiate the Godhead (*die Gottheit*) from the attributes or hypostases of the Divine or any other determinate form of Being that might erroneously, on the basis of this determination, be concluded to be foundational. Thus Being, in its isolated abstraction, is Pure Nothing (*das reine Nichts*) since it is Being of which absolutely nothing determinate can or should be said. The scholastic formulation *ex nihilo, nihil fit* therefore errs by assuming that becoming is already a property of nothing (*WL*, 85). Such claims can be made only by modes of thinking that presuppose, but do not acknowledge, the *process* of becoming underlying the subject-object structure of experience. But one cannot make such assumptions when considering Being qua Being since the naming of Being, in this instance, is akin to hurling objectified determinations into the void—"words in the silence which will not break," as Plotinus once put it eloquently. Thus Hegel makes it explicitly clear that he is not speaking of Being in relation to its Other, to non-Being or Nothingness. It is rather the case that to speak of Being at the basic level of nonfoundational *in-sich* abstracted isolation and purity is to speak of Being and Nothingness as two aspects of the same unnameable genus. Distinctions regarding genera and subgenera are not only irrelevant but impossible since, "in the case of Being and Nothing, there can be no distinction, such a distinction [in this instance] being without a bottom upon which to stand" (*E*, §87, Z).

To consider Being and Nothing as separate realities therefore requires a groundwork for determination. But because this groundwork, for Hegel, as for Heraclitus, is the flux of *becoming*, it does not provide the groundwork of stability upon which foundationalistic determinations can be made. In accounting for the being of becoming, Hegel cannot improve on the descriptions of Primordial Spirit one finds, for example, in the *Rig Veda* (to which, apart from mood, his account is strikingly similar).[5] As the poet ponders the primal unity of Being and Nothing, in the *Rig Veda*, an undulation or unrest first marks the source of Becoming, the "breathless breathing of its own accord," and prior to this initial ground of determinacy, nothing whatever can be said of the nature of reality. Least of all can intracosmic deities provide answers to the Leibnizean ontological riddle "why something and not nothing?" since, at the foundational level of determinacy, the terms upon which such questions are posed collapse in the void of indeterminacy.[6] Hegel's position is therefore something of a combination of Heraclitus (vis-à-vis the Eleatics, as we will see), Genesis 1.1–2, and Eastern philosophy:[7] "Becoming is therefore the first concrete thought and therefore the first notion of which Being and Nothing are mere abstractions" (E, §88, Z).

One cannot underestimate the significance of Hegel's *Arche-Begriff* since it is what ultimately grounds his logic in life. *Werden* or *Prozeß* is the first break in the nondifferentiated unity of Being and non-Being; and *becoming*, as in the dialectic of the true and false vacuum in contemporary astrophysical speculation, provides the basis for not only initial determinacy but all subsequent determinations of Being. It is not surprising, therefore, that Hegel should take very seriously prephilosophical, prescientific, cosmogonic notions of Being and Becoming—whether the aforementioned Vedic and Hebraic sources or, for that matter, the preface to *Saint John's Gospel*, where the still-silent Voice of Being or *logos* speaks the "light which is younger than the darkness" as groundwork for subsequent cosmic determinacy. Hegel was wise in attending to these archaic sources since modern science has not really improved on the imaginative metaphoric reconstructions of the ancients—the "lighting of Being out of the night of its concealment," as Heidegger puts it, being similarly inspired. Indeed, by its sophisticated instrumentations and perhaps to its own surprise, modern science seems to have drawn nearer to archaic intuitions of the primal indeterminacy.[8]

Hegel's *Logic* therefore seems to owe more to the history of philosophy and religion than it does to conventional logic. Indeed, because Hegel's ultimate philosophical goal is nothing short of overcoming in an absolute way, as Franz Rosenzweig later observed,[9] the traditional hiatus between Athens and Jerusalem, the *me ontic* and the *ouk ontic* notions of Being, he turned to nonconventional sources. As his *Lec-*

tures on the History of Philosophy bear witness, Hegel was particularly taken with the pre-Socratics in the development of his doctrine of Being—about 30 percent of these lectures being devoted to them. Throughout this instruction Hegel's primary purpose, as in the case of his *Lectures on the Philosophy of Religion*, is one of determining precisely how philosophy and religion "come into the fullness of [their] notion or concept." Indeed, as the general trajectory of the *Lectures on the Philosophy of Religion* indicates quite clearly (1821, 1824, 1827, 1831), Hegel was both increasingly drawn toward and perplexed by Buddhist and Vedantic philosophy—Benares beginning to serve, in addition to Athens and Jerusalem, as an additional point of dialectical reference in the movement of Spirit.[10] But in the case of Western philosophy, Hegel is quite clear that the first decisive transformation of consciousness takes place in the transition from the Miletians to the Eleatics, Pythagoras being viewed as the *methexis* of this turning point;[11] and with respect to the question of Spirit, Hegel focuses his attention upon Anaximander and Anaximenes, for it is here that *Geist* qua *pneuma* finds its first cogent philosophical articulation.

It may be helpful here, prior to considering Hegel's views on the pre-Socratics more fully, to note that the German word *Geist*, according to the philologist Walter Wili, "goes back to the Indo-Iranian *gheizd* whose root *ghei* means 'to move powerfully.'"[12] The original meaning of *Geist*, therefore, has to do with both "motive" and "vital force." In fact it may be that this substantival nuance of *Geist* (the protogrammatical collapse of verbs and nouns in primal speech, as Cassirer once observed[13]) is captured by the Old German brewing terms *Gischt* and *Gäscht*, which have to do with "foam" and "yeast" respectively—*Geist* being the active result of fermentation, as C. G. Jung suggests with reference to alcoholic spirits.[14] This indigenous philosophical etymology seems subsumed in Hegel's reflections on *pneuma* from the pre-Socratics through Middle Platonism and into Early Christianity,[15] for in these reflections one finds a rich and imaginative association of Spirit with a notion of *psyche* that conveys the meaning of the Latin terms *animus* and *spiritus* as the embedded experiences of *Atem* and *Luft*, *breath* and *wind* or *air*—precisely those sensory manifestations in and through which *pneuma* and *Geist* become initially manifest (*VGP* 1, 213–19). Hence it is not surprising to Hegel that the Miletian materialists, in their quest for the *Urstoff* of reality, and drawn, as they were, to the power of the wind, should eventually conclude, as does Heraclitus, that although *aer* may be a subtle element, *logos* is subtler still. Moreover, this subtlety consists in its being a structural feature of the active power of process that, like "fire," underlies the becoming of all things (*VGP* 1, 328). Thus Walter Wili concludes in a quasi-Hegelian way: "The parallels of the cosmological and the psychological, of fire and spirit, meet in the metaphysical: Fire is the original [underlying] substance of the cosmos [in Heraclitus] and spirit is its helmsman. But through breathing the inward lives in the outward, and participates in the outward; through the breath, vehicle of the *logos*, the microcosm is joined to the macrocosm; the *logos* in us and the *logos* in the universe are one and the same."[16]

Obviously no single pre-Socratic thinker provides the definitive key for Hegel with respect to the meaning of Spirit (even though Parmenides and Heraclitus hold a special place regarding the form of Hegel's *Logic*). Hegel's position is based rather upon a composite of pre-Socratic insights—a composite within which *Geist* or *pneuma* becomes the symbol that encompasses all of its manifest expressions, whether *aether*, *logos*, or *nous*, and also the gods, whether the celestial deities of the fixed stars, the planets, or the terrestrial deities of the earthen elements. It is this primal triad (*VGP* 1, 252) that obviously underlies and informs the notion for Hegel, as for Plato, that the soul is somehow the "between" (*metaxy*) or *Anknüpfungspunkt* of heaven and earth. Moreover, it is this triad that provides, in Hegel's view, the structural properties of the Holy Trinity in Christianity whereby the God of Abraham and Isaac becomes identical with the formal immateriality (and for Hegel, the "universality" [*Allgemeinheit*]) of the Father; where Jesus as the incarnate *logos* is the God become fully determinate or "particular" (*Besonderheit*); and where God as Spirit becomes identical with *nous* or "reason" as the agency whereby one becomes fully aware, in both theory and practice, of the "unity" (*Einzelheit*) of the Father and the Son, universal and particular, whether in the individual consciousness or the collective consciousness of the "spiritual community" (*die geistliche Gemeinde*).[17] Hegel's *Trinitätslehre*, in fact, is nothing less than the refined and highly differentiated articulation of these historical, cultural, and noetic elements. As such, the Trinity is true *not* because it is posited in dogmatic isolation as a discrete series of hypostases or instantiations; it is true because it is the supreme historical revelation of what is universally true as a structural feature of consciousness.[18]

Although Thales of Miletus is not viewed by Hegel as a particularly profound thinker (in keeping with the doxographic caricatures of Thales "falling into his well," which were popular at the time), he is nevertheless fascinated with Thales' determination of *water* as the ground (*to hupokeimenon*) of reality (*VGP* 1, 198; *HP* 1, 175). For Thales' observation, as Hegel points out, was not the product of theistic speculation, since there was no precedent for this kind of thinking in the sixth century B.C.E. Thales' reasoned vitalistic conclusions rather followed from observing the necessity of water for organic growth. As such, his views represent a demythologization of the older myths informing Hesiod's *Theogony*—the origin of all things in the primal liquidity of Oceanus and Tethys (*VGP* 1, 200; *HP* 1, 177). Moreover, Thales' speculations provide the first and necessary material element underlying the Stoical and Gnostic notion of the *logos spermatikos*, which, in the case of Heraclitus, is presupposed in the "vaporous" or processual nature of the Soul.

The primal element of water (conceived as the formless-form or essence not unlike the conception of *Tao* in Chinese philosophy),[19] is further abstracted from matter in Anaximander's conception of *to apeiron*, the "boundless indefinite," which contains all definites within it by the principle of *energeia* (*VGP* 1, 211; *HP* 1, 186). It is this "absolute continuity" between the indefinite and the definite, so central to Heraclitus's active notion of *logos*, which fascinates Hegel even though Anaximenes, the contemporary of Anaximander, reconnects this boundless indefinite with "air" (*aer*) or *Luft* as the primal material element necessary to account for the nature of the "soul" (*psyche*). This anthropological composite of reality as a definite-indefinite, as infinity, represents, for Hegel, the first decisive movement from "natural philosophy to a philosophy of consciousness" in pre-Socratic philosophy (*VGP* 1, 214; *HP* 1, 189). Moreover, these pre-Socratic elements are explicit in Hegel's *First Philosophy of Spirit* (218ff.), the obvious importance of which cannot be underestimated to the extent that his *Phenomenology*, as he puts it, is a "phenomenology of the experience of consciousness."[20]

While Anaximenes viewed the soul as being, in some sense, the aggregate of composite *chthon* and simple *aei*, the chthonic and the uranic, the terrestrial and the celestial, it is Pythagoras who, according to Hegel, "breaks free" of the sensuous element in thinking. In so doing, Pythagoras becomes a philosopher in the proper sense, this transition marking nothing less than the shift from a naive realism to Idealism and the philosophy of Spirit or mind. And while Hegel has little regard for the "brotherhood" and the mythological hagiography that accumulates around *Father Pythagoras*, he notes that this kind of iconization can be helpful when it comes to preserving the history of ideas—even though the transmission may be inaccurate. Nevertheless, the chief thing is the movement from realism to the philosophy of mind (*VGP* 1, 234–35; *HP* 1, 210–11: *Intellektualphilosophie*), a transition made possible by the mathematical "sensuous-nonsensuous" Pythagorean agency of mediation—or what Plotinus eventually comes to term the definitive movement from the *acousmatici* to the *mathematici* in speculative religious and philosophical consciousness.[21] Not least, for

Hegel, among the accomplishments of the Pythagoreans is the full development of a numerical dialectic of triplicity and tetrarchy. For while Pythagorean number theory becomes mechanistic and superficial in its various applications, the structural features of this kind of thinking play a critical role in the history of dialectic and, in Hegel's estimate, provide a legitimate conceptual basis for the Christian understanding of the Trinity (*VGP* 1, 252–53; *HP* 1, 221–22: *Dreiheit*).[22]

With Xenophanes and Parmenides the first transition is complete; philosophy becomes entirely notional and disconnected from all extrinsicism, even "numbers,"—and now concerned, as he puts it, with "the pure movement of thought in the concept . . . the beginning of dialectic in the true sense." Hegel continues: "When we reflect in anticipation of how the course of pure thought must be formed, we find that (a) pure thought (pure Being, the One, as *noumenon*) manifests itself immediately in its rigid isolation and self-identity, and everything else as null; (b) the hitherto timid thought—which, after it is strengthened, ascribes value to the Other and constitutes itself therefrom—shows that it then grasps the other in its simplicity and even in so doing shows its nullity; and finally (c) thought manifests the Other in the manifold nature of its determinations" (*VGP* 1, 275; *HP* 1, 240). The two successive moments in Eleatic philosophy, appearing in Xenophanes, Parmenides, Melissus, Zeno, and Heraclitus respectively, are summarized as follows: first, in the notion of Xenophanes where God is known as the highest Being as Spirit, that is, as the pure "spherical" unity of itself as "is-ness," neither limited nor unlimited, determined or undetermined, but as Eternal Being; and second, in the discovery of Parmenides regarding the equivalence of "thinking and Being" (as in Hegel's own doctrine of Being in the *Logic*) as the insight undergirding the Spinozistic maxim, *determinatio est negatio*, that all a posteriori determinations of being are negations of Being. Indeed, "this is the principal thought (*Hauptgedanke*)," Hegel asserts emphatically; "thought produces itself and what is produced is a Thought. Thought is thus identical with its Being, because it is nothing outside of its Being"—and this is the "great affirmation" acknowledged by Plotinus (*VGP* 1, 289–90; *HP* 1, 253).

Only at the next stage of the Greek philosophical development, that is, only with Zeno's antinomies and the Heraclitian conception of *logos* as "becoming," do we enter, according to Hegel, the definitive arena for the determination of Being and non-Being, existence and nonexistence, in the proper sense. For in the primal apprehension of Being whereby thought thinks itself, as Hegel asserts in his *Logic*, we simultaneously have the apprehension of thinking-Being as akin to thinking-Nothing. It is precisely an appreciation of the comprehension of non-determinate rather than determinate Being that informs Aristotle's admiration of Parmenides in the *Metaphysics* and, a fortiori, Hegel's admiration of Aristotle, to wit, that Spirit is the unity of thought and Being in and through the life of the concept.

What emerges in Zeno and Heraclitus, then, in contrast to previous Greek philosophical attempts to establish the base element or foundational dimension of reality, is an awareness of the *fundamental* but *non-foundational* nature of dialectic in its immanent mode. For dialectic, in Hegel's view, is not to be understood as a mechanistic means of determining the existence or nonexistence, primacy or derivative status, of any particular entity. Rather, dialectic is the process through which the *mystery of Consciousness-itself* comes into focus (*VGP* 1, 301; *HP* 1, 265). This is the great and all-important discovery of the pre-Socratics according to Hegel. Thus Zeno's denial of motion and Heraclitus's affirmation of motion are the opposite sides of the same dialectical process—the internal and the external, the formal and the material dimensions of *logos*, now become transparent to the mystery that dialectic, as a transcendental-relational *complexio oppositorum*, encompasses all possible relations and relata and, in so doing, renders both intelligible. It is Heraclitus who first comprehends this distinction, Heraclitus who, according to Hegel, takes the "second step" from Being to Becoming as the means of seeing that dialectic is itself the *process* of Spirit—and the process of Spirit, as we have argued throughout, is identical with the *pneumatological transformation of dialectic* in the philosophy of Hegel: "Here we see land," he asserts emphatically, and "there is no proposition in Heraclitus which I have not adopted in my own Logic" (*VGP* 1, 329; *HP* 1, 279).

· 2 ·

Being determinate in its first form, according to Hegel's *Logic*, is *Dasein*. Absorbed isomorphically in Becoming (*das Werden*), Being and Nothing are negated in the unity of their contradiction and the result is the determinacy of *there-being* (*WL*, 115; *E*, §89). "Being determinate" may in fact be too strong a translation of *Dasein* since we are not, in this instance, speaking about determinate being in any particular sense. We are speaking rather of the ontological precondition of determinate being. Hegel's use of *Dasein* thus functions as a designator obviating the necessity of having to choose between Being and non-Being as the base, constitutive condition of the reality or nonreality of beings. *Dasein* thus functions primordially without making Hegel a primordialist; in other words, *Dasein* is "inclusive of its negation" (*E*,

§89, Z) and is not something to which negation must be added as a property.[23]

By Hegel's qualitative determination of *Dasein's* immediacy, it seems that he also wishes to rescue Anselm's ontological argument from the scrap heap of its Kantian fate.[24] For Quality, he says, is not a determinate but an immediate mode of *Dasein*. Therefore, the notion of *quality*, in this instance, is grasped immediately as an *intellectus archetypus* prior to any mediated mode or instantiation of what is qualitatively determinate. In Anselmian terms, one has an immediate notion of "the greatest beyond which nothing greater can exist" in the same manner that one has an immediate notion of Being as *Dasein* prior to the determinacy of beings.[25] Like Anselm's *greatest*, this quality is characterized as being "being for another" while still "being in itself." *Dasein's* self-negation as *Dasein* is therefore immediate and does not introduce something foreign to itself—does not introduce an Other beyond this negation. *Dasein* rather indicates the limit proper to its being since "a thing is what it is only by virtue of its limit" (*E*, §90, 91; 92 Z; *WL*, 131–32; *SL*, 122–23). As such, the sheer "thatness" of *Dasein* is synonymous with the *quantum* and *mass* by which everything else is measured from points external to itself. Nevertheless, it is only because Being qua *Dasein* also has the potential attribute of being *Fürsichsein* that it is possible to take the next step to a consideration of *essence* or, as Hegel calls it, Being-in-its-externality.

The step to a "doctrine of Essence," Hegel insists, is the "most difficult" in philosophy and logic. Most of the traditional difficulties associated with this doctrine are obviated, however, by Hegel's unique prior development of the doctrine of Being; in other words, lack of clarity regarding *beginnings* (which are, in fact, the derivative product of a lack of clarity regarding Being as *Dasein*) tends to make most doctrines of essence seem rather arbitrary. But Hegel is no longer attempting to arrive at a doctrine of essence through pure negation in the abstract sense of *Dasein*. He is speaking rather of "Being gone into itself in immanent self-mediation"; in other words, Hegel is identifying a process synonymous with Becoming since, having once acknowledged the fundamentality of process, it is now possible to *reflect* on the meaning of essence without becoming an essentialist. Moreover, negativity, considered in the context of Being as Becoming, is already a *mediated* negativity since questions of essence are possible only as truth determinations by way of reflection. The German verb *wesen*, Hegel points out, is particularly well suited to bring out this distinction where, as in the use of *ist gewesen*, something is said *to be as having been*—precisely what Heidegger develops as the *Gewesenheit* of Being. Thus determinations of identity and difference have meaning only within the dialectic of "reflected essence" with *Grund* understood as the fundamental but nonfoundational unitive basis of the dialectic of determinacy or meaning (*E*, §116). Out of this reflective grounding what we term *existence* arises, "existence [being] the immediate unity of reflection-into-self and reflection-into-another" (E, §123). This tensive dialectic is what makes something a *phenomenon* or a "shining forth" (*Erscheinung*) in its appearance; for the essence of a thing is identical with the mode of its appearing, whether to itself or to another. Thus *appearance* is not, as Kant contended, merely a subjective factor (*E*, §131). It is rather an essential part of the phenomenon's identity as it presents itself to us. This is precisely the mystery, of course, picked up and expanded upon by Heidegger with respect to *legein ta phainomena*, namely, the *apophainesthai ta phainomena* or what he calls the "letting what shows itself be seen from itself just as it shows itself from itself."[26]

The *truth* of the *showing forth* of Being and Essence or, in Heideggerian terms, the truth of the showing forth that is the ownmost dialectic of Being and Essence manifest as *phenomena*, is what one comprehends and can only comprehend, for Hegel, in and through the logic of the *concept*—"in and through" because Hegel's logic of the concept is not of something static but something dynamic, as the linguistic embodiment of *das Werden*. The theological analogue of this notion (certainly known to Hegel) is the *communicatio idiomatum* in christology as the logical feature necessary to convey a dynamic sense of divine energy while also avoiding a static and tritheistic *Trinitätslehre*. For what Christianity espouses, according to Hegel, is a God "who has not only created a world which confronts him as his other, but has also from all eternity begotten a Son in whom he, as Spirit, is at home with himself." It is precisely this dynamism that makes Christianity, in Hegel's view, the religion of freedom (*E*, §§159, 161, 162, Z, 163) since the reality of *freedom* is presupposed in the philosophy of its concept—the freedom to be Other while still remaining oneself.

Accordingly and in keeping with the trinitarian conception, Hegel's doctrine of the concept has three modalities and moments: 1) the purely subjective and formal mode of universality (*Allgemeinheit*); 2) the objective and immediately material mode of particularity (*Besonderheit*); and 3) the unity of both subject and object (*Einzelheit*) in the Absolute Idea (*E*, §§162, 163). The primary function of the concept, therefore, is the synthetic reconciliation and realization made manifest in Spirit as Idea for "the Idea is True in and for itself, the absolute unity of concept and objectivity" (*E*, §213: *Die Idee ist das Wahre an und für sich, die absolute Einheit des Begriffs und der Objektivität*). Indeed, because of this triplicity, eidetic unity is not static but dynamic both ontologically and existentially; in other words, it is dynamic at both the theoretical and the practical level. On the one hand, "The Idea is essentially a *process* because its identity is the absolute and free identity of the concept, only insofar as it is absolute negativity and for that reason dialectical" (*E*, §215). On the other hand, eidetic unity through the logic of Spirit can be likened to the process of making the known-unknown into the known-known as one discovers the truth of the logic inherent thereto. This integrative hermeneutical process of appropriation is nothing less than the continuous mediation of the Holy Spirit for, as Hegel puts it, "In this respect the Absolute Idea may be likened to the old man who utters the same Creed as the child, but for whom it now has the meaning of an entire lifetime. Indeed, even if the child understands the religious content, he cannot but still conclude that all of life and the entire world lies beyond it . . . Such is life . . . what matters is the entire movement. . . . Thus we have had the content already, and what we have now is the knowledge that the content is the living development of the Idea. This simple retrospect is contained in the form of the Idea. Each of the stages . . . is an image of the Absolute, but at first in a limited mode, and thus it is forced onward to the whole." (*E*, §237, Z).

This *Zusatz* can be overlooked as being merely a quasi-homiletical allusion, only if the Pietistic underpinnings of Hegel's philosophy remain unappreciated. The goal of philosophy for Hegel, however, is not just knowledge but saving or absolute knowledge; and absolute knowledge can only be said to be absolute if it is saving knowledge. Herein lies the conjunction of Holy Spirit and Absolute Spirit—namely, speculative pneumatology as the means of eternalization since the true infinite, for Hegel, is nothing less than the Eternal-itself. Indeed, the soteriological dimension of Hegel's philosophical project is evident in Hegel's earliest work where, as we have seen in the "Spirit" essay (1797/1989), he concerns himself with defining the "genuine religious action" in a way that is nothing less than the philosophical analogue of comprehending the meaning of justification by grace through faith.[27]

· 3 ·

Hegel's lifelong concerns regarding the "genuine religious action" carry over into the opening argument in Part 3 of the *Enzyklopädie*—an argument that happens to parallel, structurally, the organization of F. C. Sartorius's *Compendium Theologiae Dogmaticae* (1782), the standard dogmatics *Lehrbuch* at the beginning of Hegel's Tübingen period.[28] As such, Hegel's *Enzyklopädie* is the philosophical equivalent of a compendium—in this case, a compendium inclusive of the method whereby it sets forth its claims through the logic of the concept (as distinct from the manner in which the dogmatic claims of some of his contemporaries are set forth through biblicism). Hegel's mature philosophy of Spirit can be viewed, therefore, as the existential and metaphysical appropriation and transformation of conventional pneumatology whereby Holy Spirit becomes identical with Absolute Spirit.

Absolute Spirit is nothing less than the *Aufhebung* of human spirit and Divine Spirit for the following reasons: First, Hegel is clearly of the notion that *Geist* cannot merely be identified with mind or rationality—at least not mind or reason in the sense that Hegel's contemporaries understood it, whether the "philosophy of reflection" (*Verstehensphilosophie*) or the "instrumentalist rationality" (*Zweckrationalität*) that dominates the philosophy of mind after the Enlightenment. However, when reason is understood as being inclusive of these two factors, namely, *intellectus* in its formal-transcendental aspect, and *ratio* in its material-analytical aspect, one begins to obtain a sense of the role played by Spirit in Hegel's understanding of rational self-autonomy (*Selbstbewußtseins*) qua thinking-faith (*fides intelligens*). For Hegel, however, the experience of consciousness or mind is not exhausted by this synthetic association since Spirit-itself provides the ground for this synthesis while always surpassing it. For example, when Hegel asserts (freely interpolating on the biblical utterances of Jesus and Saint Paul) that "truth makes Spirit free and freedom makes it true" (*E*, §382, Z), this is not hyperbole. The attributes of *truth* and *freedom* are precisely what make Spirit what it is in terms of the range and power of reason. But the dialectical self-realization of Spirit is not possible in isolation but only through the Other as perceived in Spirit's mode of manifestation—a mode of manifestation that is one with the mode of its Being: *Die Bestimmtheit des Geistes ist daher die Manifestation* (*E*, §383). This manifestation does not have to do with any particular empirical thing about Spirit become manifest; *manifestation is rather Spirit's proper mode of Being*. Hegel's choice of the term *Manifestation*, as distinct from *Offenbarung* or "revelation," provides him with the basis for placing emphasis upon the *act* of revealing rather than *what* is revealed. Nevertheless, Hegel makes his point by way of the revealed Christian doctrine of Incarnation in which *Geist* (as in his reflections on *kenosis* in the *Phänomenologie*) chooses to become particular and concrete, positing and dirempting itself accordingly, in order to reconcile the Other while maintaining and, in fact, preserving the integrity of the Other (*E*, §383, Z). It is precisely because of this reconciling, preserving activity of Spirit that Hegel concludes (in a Paulinian way): "The Absolute is Spirit; the supreme definition of the Absolute [is Spirit]" (*E*, §384:

Das Absolute ist der Geist; dies ist die höchste Definition des Absoluten). This being the case, the supreme task of philosophy is comprehending the process of Spirit in its freedom and in its truth.

Second, the goal of comprehension is never finished. Absolute Consciousness is ever-developmental—a project, as in the case of Jaspers's philosophizing on the grounds of *mögliche Existenz*, but without being limiting this project to existential self-understanding. In other words, philosophy, for Hegel, is not merely an immanent project as existentialists such as Sartre or even Jaspers would have it; nor is it radically transcendental as in the sense of Maritain or even Lonergan.[29] Hegel's logic of Spirit is precisely his means of overcoming the abyss between the logic of *Existenz* and *Transzendenz*. The conceptual-categorical articulation of this abyss is what makes it Absolute Knowledge. As such, the philosophical effects of this dialectical overcoming are akin to the salutary effects Luther specifies with respect to the necessity of daily dying and rising in the Divine Spirit as intrinsic to the meaning of Life-itself. Indeed, apart from the reality of Spirit, this dialectic would be impossible—would lead only to the "unhappy consciousness" and even madness, as in the case of Hölderlin. Here again the catechetical analogy of Hegel is cogent since we have, in the childhood of our thinking, a vague, subjective conception of *Geist* in its abstract indeterminateness. In adulthood, this conception becomes increasingly objective as *Geist* becomes "actual" in the process of going-out-from-oneself-to-the-Other. But late maturity, as in Vedantic philosophy, affords the ultimate opportunity for the reconciliation and completion of objective and subjective Spirit through the in-and-for-itself of Absolute Consciousness. Wisdom is nothing less than being fully conscious of being-given-to-oneself-by-the-other just as, in the catechetical formula, one now comprehends *how* and *why*, in fact, *what* was asserted to be the case is *true* (*E*, §384, Z). In such a manner the quite ordinary religious background of Hegel provides impetus to the dialectical *process* implicit in Hegel's *Science of Logic*—including the desire "to comprehend the mind of the Creator prior to the creation." As such, Spirit's development is to be understood first in the form of its "relation to itself . . . as an ideal totality . . . and as subjective Spirit"; second, in the form of "reality . . . in the world produced and to be produced by it . . . with freedom understood as necessity . . . as objective Spirit"; and, third, "as being in and for itself in its ideality and concept" where Spirit is "in its absolute Truth as absolute Spirit" (*E*, §385).

Third, this self-transcending, self-reconciling, self-realizing philosophy of Spirit, Hegel argues, follows from a philosophy of *limits* (*Grenzen*) properly conceived. This is the mystical dimension of Hegel that so greatly impressed Franz van Baader during the Berlin period, for Hegel argues that the awareness and acknowledgment of limits, far from limiting the possibility of metaphysics, as in Kant, is the manifest sign that the fundamental nature of Spirit is to be beyond itself as limit. The speculative moment in metaphysics therefore consists of the awareness that finitude is but a moment in the life of *Geist*. Spirit, by definition, is unlimited but chooses, by its act of creation, to limit itself and become God—and not only in the abstract formal sense, but *materially*, through incarnation. This does not imply a *limited* deity or *demiurge*; it is rather an elucidation of the *Prozeß* of diremption that identifies God's fundamental nature as Spirit encompassing both the limited and the unlimited, the intracosmic and the extracosmic. Without these properties and attributes, Spirit would not be Absolute Spirit. The task, then, is not to decide whether *Geist* is finite or infinite, limited or unlimited, human or divine, but rather to recognize how these foci are contained within divinity but also surpassed and encompassed by *Geist* as the moving ground of rational self-consciousness.

Finally, Hegel's analysis of the modalities of Spirit, in each and every instance, parallels topics that are the proper domain of a theological pneumatology. The critical difference, of course, is that in theology these modalities are formally obscured by the substance ontology implicit in conventional theological discussions concerned with the proper relations of the *hypostases* or *persons* within the Trinity. But these extrinsic problems of identity and relation are dissolved in Hegel's logic of Spirit; and this nonreductionistic dissolution provides Hegel's speculative pneumatology with the basis for a nondisconjunctive consideration of justice and injustice, good and evil, society and the state, morality and the ethical life in the *Rechtsphilosophie* (1821), which immediately follows the first edition of the *Enzyklopädie* (1817). The philosophy of Right, in fact, is the culmination of his philosophy of Spirit—its logical and practical extension. Basic questions in moral, social, and political philosophy are theologically implicit in the doctrine of the Trinity but do not—indeed, cannot—come to adequate expression when the substance ontology upon which they are frequently based is overturned by critical, transcendental philosophy. Conversely, such questions tend to be trivialized in the personalistic reactions to substance ontology so characteristic of Protestantism. But Hegel's philosophy of Spirit overcomes the logical incompatiblism within representational thinking, which is nothing less than the incompatibility between Orthodoxy and Pietism. Hegel accomplishes this by treating, very strictly, Spirit qua Spirit in his speculative pneumatology and providing, thereby, the formal groundwork for these practical matters.[30]

As we indicated at the beginning of this study, theologians after the fourth century paid little attention to the phenomenology of *pneuma*, focusing rather on the institutional-sacramental mediation of Spirit's authority. This neglect led to the replacement or, more accurately, the displacement of pneumatology by ecclesiology. In Hegel, however, these moments are formally separate. Hegel does not wish to confuse his pneumatology by wedding it to an outmoded doctrine of the Church. The political and social philosophy of the Church rather is now replaced, in the *Rechtsphilosophie*, by a far more encompassing post-Enlightenment conception of society and the state—a conception within which art, religion, and philosophy each play integral but not exclusive roles. The final section of the *Enzyklopädie* prepares the reader for precisely this transition. Here again, Hegel's distinction between pneumatology and ecclesiology is consistent with Luther's view that the sanctifying work of the Holy Spirit has preeminently to do with understanding the *enlightening gifts* or manifestations of Spirit (*mit seinen Gaben erleuchtet*) and with making actual one's comprehension of the meaning of creation and redemption in the *communio sanctorum*—what Hegel calls the *spiritual community*.

Luther, it will be recalled, radically adumbrated the apostolic authority of the Church by way of the *Freiheits-Prinzip*, which informs his doctrine of the "universal priesthood of all believers." With this elevation of the worth of the individual subject and the drastic limitation of the sacradotal authority of the professional clergy, the institutional shape and character of the *communio sanctorum* could no longer be based upon the authority of the sacramental system and an external hierarchy of mediators. Thus shape of the society, its conception of authority and its system of governance, could no longer be viewed as given a priori in religion or the pneumatology deemed proper to it. Such structural actualities must rather develop from within and be consistent with the process of Spirit's self-actualization in the consciousness of the individual subject. This is precisely how Hegel's *Rechtsphilosophie* is to be understood—as the theory of Right, which *follows from* as distinct from being antecedent to pneumatology. Hegel's immediate concern in the *Enzyklopädie*, therefore, is to indicate how his system could respond to and surmount the *philosophy of limits* that had become synonymous with the new critical philosophy while also being consistent with the values implicit in the older *Trinitätslehre*. For the very awareness of limits is the sign that Spirit is beyond itself as a finite limit; in fact, the philosophy of limits properly understood should indicate that both finitude and infinity are mere moments within the life of Eternal Spirit just as, from a more conventional theological view, they are moments within the life of God. Being by definition *infinite* and *unlimited*, God chooses, both by his act of creation and by that of redemption, to limit himself *not* because he is *limited* (as in some process conceptions of deity) but because God, as the true infinite or Absolute Spirit, encompasses the ideas of limit and the unlimited, finitude and infinitude. The dialectic of Spirit therefore contains within itself the terms of its own process and self-development precisely because it is a pneumatological and not a conventional dialectic.

In the final chapter, we will delineate the implication of Hegel's doctrine of Absolute Spirit for Free Spirit, giving special attention to his doctrine of the soul, and recapitulating where we have been in this study.

IX

FREE SPIRIT

Die Freiheit ist die höchste Bestimmung des Geistes.
(*Ästhetik*)

Der freie Geist ist der wirkliche Geist.
(*Enzyklopädie*)

HEGEL'S sense of the past and its loss,[1] as we have noted, is far more searching and intense than Kant's, and his faith in the prospects of Enlightenment, as a consequence, far more measured. Had Kant lived to reflect upon the implications of Prussia's defeat by Napoleon at the Battle of Jena (1806), his optimism, no doubt, would have been tempered considerably.[2] To a far greater degree, however, the difference between Hegel and Kant (or, for that matter, the difference between Hegel and many of his contemporaries) is informed by the extent of his devotion to the grand, classical, European tradition and its dialectical transformation by the cataclysmic series of intellectual, cultural, and political upheavals leading to the so-called historic European Enlightenment. During such a time, "one thing remains," Hegel reflects ponderously in his *Lecture Manuscript*: "finitude turned in upon itself, arrogant barrenness and lack of content, the extremity of self-satisfied disenlightenment" (*Ausklärung*) (*LPR* 3, §96).

Hegel's sense of loss, however, does not drift into an archaic romantic primordialism as it did with so many of his contemporaries. One does not compensate cultural loss through the invention of a mythical past, nor counterbalance it, as in the case of Marx, with the promise of a utopian future. Hegel's reflection on "the shape of things grown old" is rather tempered (even in the famous preface to his *Rechtsphilosophie*) by the dialectics of renunciation and the expectation of a new transcendental creativity rising out of the ruins of the past: the prospect of unified science, humane government, and authentic self-Being. Between this sense of the past and prudential hope regarding the future, Hegel carries out the only "satisfaction of self-consciousness" available to that "isolated order of priests" (*RP*, 162; *LPR* 3, §97) known as philosophers, namely, "comprehending one's own time in thought" (*RP*, 26). In Hegel's case, the mode and substance of this comprehension, as we have argued throughout, is deeply religious—a contemplative comprehension of "the shape of things grown old," as it were, deeply interfused with the social values of the Pietist tradition within which he was nurtured.

For Hegel the attainment of self-consciousness has two historical foci: the Renaissance and the Reformation. In isolation, one from the other, the meaning of these epochs is incomplete. But as the symbolical terms of a self-transcending dialectic, the Renaissance and the Reformation are Spirit's historic bridges to Enlightenment. The Spirit of the Renaissance, refreshed by classical culture and pointing the way to a social and political reality beyond feudalism, was exhausted by religious wars of nationalism. This was especially true in the case of Germany, where the Renaissance failed to bring about the long-awaited *neue Gemeinschaft*, generating, rather, a new epoch of despotic absolutism and rationalistic positivism. The Spirit of the Reformation, which Hegel identifies with the "great Protestant principle of the North," also lost its dynamic sense of freedom by drifting into a wooden orthodoxism no better than the threadbare scholasticism it discarded. Seventeenth-century religious orthodoxism and political absolutism produced, each in its own way, eighteenth-century reactions in Pietism and Romanticism respectively. The common element shared by both, as Hegel probably saw more clearly than anyone, was the subjectivism driving the excessive claims of the Enlightenment and the post-Enlightenment culture of individualism—especially the "virtuosity" (*Virtuosität*) of Schleiermacher, now become the substitute for *content* as the pious attacked those they perceived to be the "cultured despisers of religion" (*RP*, 160).

However lamentable the historic permutations of the Renaissance and the Reformation, both held, for Hegel, the keys to the ongoing task of Enlightenment. Renaissance and Reformation retain this power not as isolated historical events but as the performative symbols of reason and faith respectively: *sapere aude, fides intellegens*. Hegel dedicated his philosophical project to the realization of a more perfect union of these symbols in a revitalized concept of Spirit, and he made this intent clear from the outset in works propaedeutic to the *Phänomenologie* (1807)—especially the *Differenzschrift* (1801), *Glauben und Wissen* (1802), *System der Sittlichkeit*, and the so-called *First Philosophy of Spirit* (1802–03). The "mature" works—*Die Wissenschaft der Logik* (1812), the *Enzyklopädie* (1817), and the *Rechtsphilosophie* (1821), together with the various posthumously published *Vorlesungen*—therefore may be viewed as Hegel's concentrated and fully formalized attempt to realize his *intinerarium mentis ad deum* through a clarification of its particulars. Rarely has there been such consistency in the work of a philosopher.

Hegel's choice of Spirit as the metaphoric vehicle of this lifelong exercise in Transcendence, as we have seen, is by no means accidental or incidental. Spirit, in fact, is the principal mark of consistency in Hegel's philosophical project, Spirit alone having the capacity to encompass both faith and knowledge without being reducible to either. Spirit is identical with the power, the creative force, and the structural energy simultaneously at the bottom and at the top of things, and Spirit provides Hegel with the historic-conceptual means of attaining Absolute Consciousness. As such, Spirit Absolute and Free, for Hegel, is the cosmoteleological horizon or Absolute Encompassing within which transcending-thinking or critical Idealism is possible. Spirit provides the groundwork for the realization of this possibility because actualized Free Spirit is identical with the life of the concept (*Begriff*). The comprehensive self-articulation of critical Idealism through Spirit is Hegel's way of making idealism Absolute.

This Absolute Identity represents nothing less than the fusion of faith and reason in Spirit. For Spirit, as Hegel understands it, is the origin and the goal of consciousness as implied, for example, in the traditional doxological utterance "Preserve us O Lord in Thy Truth; all things begun and ended in Thee"—this truth being the truth of the Absolute Idea. It is precisely the consciousness of Spirit that gives rise to such notions, the consciousness of Spirit being, in Hegel's view, what differentiates humans from the beasts by providing humans with the ability to have eidetic notions of absolute objects such as God and Freedom.[3] Hence Spirit underlies the very order of things and provides philosophy with its fundamental task—"to arrive at the notion of its notion" (*E*, §12). Spirit has this power because "it is of the essence of the concept of Spirit," as Hegel asserts in one of his earliest definitions, "to *realize* itself." In fact, the "concept of Spirit" is just this "absolute union of absolute *singularity* (where multiplicity is negated) with the absolute *multiplicity* which is itself positive or implicitly universal, simple multiplicity" (*FPS*, 208–9).

Absolute consciousness, far from being the result of an immediate inspiration, can be achieved only through a reasoned, critical, continuous process of *mediation*. Its absoluteness therefore consists only in being critically aware of this process as distinct from being in some final blissful state of repose.[4] This processual element of continuous critical mediation is precisely what sets Hegel's philosophy of Spirit apart from philosophies of alleged "spiritual" immediacy. In its fully speculative transcendental mode, Hegel's philosophy of Spirit has the task of becoming fully conscious of "the circle of circles" (*E*, §15), which encompasses the circles of all lesser sciences of determinate particulars providing them with their own possibility. What makes this knowledge Absolute, however, is *not* an absolute knowledge of empirical particulars including the completion of history, as is sometimes thought. What makes it Absolute is the knowledge of what makes Knowledge-itself possible, including the knowledge of particulars, the knowledge of Spirit. Changes in status regarding the knowledge of particulars in no way falsifies the absolute knowledge of Spirit-itself. Indeed, Spirit-itself not only makes possible but also compels a growth of knowledge regarding the nature and meaning of sense particulars. Thus processual absoluteness is the only absoluteness possible since it is impossible ever to have an absolute knowledge of contingency—absoluteness being formally excluded from contingency.[5] The reality of Spirit or Transcendence-itself, therefore, is what makes immanent transcending possible in the first instance.[6]

Because of these features, Hegel's supremely mediational philosophy of Spirit can be productively considered, as I have argued throughout this study, as a speculative pneumatology in both the philosophical and the religious senses of the term. Hegel in fact identifies the first part of his system as a *phenomenology* of Spirit and the final part as a *philosophy* of Spirit, the middle portions being his articulation of *Geist in der Welt*. Less clear to many, however, are the theological elements underlying the dialectical unfolding between the *terminus a quo* and *terminus ad quem* of his system. In this study, we have attempted to provide a sense of how it is the case that Spirit, considered theologically, is precisely what provides the historic basis for the continuous mediation of one's consciousness of the Absolute. For a salutary mediation of self-consciousness is impossible, Luther believed, apart from the ongoing work of the Holy Spirit—this notion finding its biblical warrant in the Johannine saying that "the Spirit [*paraclete* or "comforter"] will guide you into all truth."[7] Hegel's agreement with this promise undergirds what I have called his *pneumatological transformation of dialectic*, and it is precisely in this sense that Holy Spirit and Absolute Spirit, for Hegel, are ultimately one and the same.

That Hegel's concept of Spirit has this theological-pneumatological sense can be discerned not only in his comments in the introduction to the *Enzyklopädie* regarding "the indwelling of the Holy Spirit" (*E*, §3), but also in his early remarks regarding "Spirit as Consciousness" in his *First Philosophy of Spirit* (1803), where he refers to the "call of Spirit" being manifest first at the primary level of "language" (*FPS*, 218). Luther, as we have seen, also limits the "call" of Spirit to a Word-event. By this limitation one notes that the nature of Spirit is phenomenologically akin to the power of breath giving rise to speech. Hegel in fact uses the metaphorical ethereal mediation of "the living word" to indicate that what takes place *intra nos* with respect to consciousness is possible only because of the reality of Spirit *extra nos*. As such, Spirit retains an Otherness distinct from what would be the case were he to rely upon objective theories of transubstantiation regarding the Sacrament, as in Catholicism, or subjective theories of immediacy and intuitionism, as in Pietism and Romanticism, with respect to the actual or substantial presence of Spirit. In just this sense, Hegel's absolute idealism outstrips both realism and idealism, his system being devoted to showing how both are the posited instantiations of Absolute Spirit.

The speculative character of Hegel's pneumatology may further be amplified by looking at the two symmetrically located comments in the *Enzyklopädie*, where he specifically addresses the topic of pneumatology, the first in the introduction, and the second at the beginning of his final section on philosophy of Spirit. In the former passage, Hegel laments the displacement of the medieval conception of pneumatology understood as "rational psychology" by the more recent "empirical psychology"—something to which all philosophy will soon be reduced, in his view, if the British have their way. Hegel's chagrin is reinforced in the latter reference, where he asserts that the "ancient science" of pneumatology (as "an abstract and generalizing metaphysics of the subject") erred only in its treatment of the soul as a "static substance" (*E*, §377). But the alleged staticism of substance ontology pales to insignificance when compared with the entirely static, sensate, atomistic particularism of [British] empirical psychology, which precludes altogether, he asserts, "any speculative treatment" of the soul (*E*, §378, Z). While there is some warrant for rejecting the classical doctrine of soul substance as the basis for metaphysics, the new empirical psychology, Hegel indicates, is itself grounded in an uncritical empirical atomism and cannot be viewed, therefore, as being "science" in the sense of *Wissenschaft*. The new psychology is science only in the restrictive instrumentalist sense, since it is only in this restricted sense that ontological and metaphysical questions can be so trivialized as to be excluded from philosophy altogether.

Hegel therefore perceives his own philosophy of Spirit as, among other things, a critical modification of the older doctrine of pneumatology understood as rational psychology. Furthermore, this pneumatological modification provides the means of rehabilitating the most important dimension of philosophy—speculative metaphysics—by way of a dialectical mapping of the soul now understood as *Selbstbewußtsein*. Furthermore, it is quite evident that Hegel views the reality of *Geist* or *pneuma* as the middle-term providing or generating, as in

Aristotle, the sense of wonder underlying the dialectics of scientific inquiry. Spirit has this power because it is identical with the paradoxical mystery, as Kierkegaard later put it, lying at the very center of self-consciousness. For Hegel, however, the meaning of this mystery cannot be explained through strictly developmental or atomistic analyses of nature and substance; neither can it be explained by the simple appeal to religion—even though the religious appeal, in his view, is distinctively superior to an appeal to empirical science. The meaning of Spirit can be broached critically only by attending to the nature of the concept qua concept (*E*, §377). Indeed, an analysis of religion "true to its concept" is the special place where Hegel finds major evidence regarding the speculative possibility of his *Begriffsphilosophie*; hence the religio-pneumatological context of the logic of the concept is the focal point of the numinous in the philosophy of Hegel (*SL*, 577).[8]

The fundamentality of the concept is mythically illustrated in the trinitarian procession of the Spirit "from the Father and the Son" whereby Spirit, moving out of itself into its Other, is reconciled to itself through individuals in community (*E*, §381, Z); and it is concretely documented at the level of universal history, especially in the history of religions, as one considers the shifts in consciousness implicit in the development from the religions of nature or sense-certainty to religions of art or subjectivity and finally to revealed religions.[9] Christianity is not viewed by Hegel, then, as the *consummate* revealed religion because of the *positive* (that is, extrinsic) quality of its various revelations. Its consummate character lies rather in the fact that the *structure* of Christianity's revelation permits religious consciousness, for the first time, to comprehend itself fully, and, in so doing, to comprehend the basis of its finitude and negation. Hegel asserts that Christianity is "true to its concept" in a consummate way, therefore, in having generated the means whereby it is able to comprehend itself precisely as *concept* within the structural dynamics of its own revelation and not from some position external to itself.

Hegel's philosophy of Spirit, responsive to this insight (which is nothing less than a hermeneutical elucidation of the "Speculative Good Friday" he notes in *Glauben und Wissen*), provides him with the basis for a theologically reconstructed and philosophically transformed pneumatology. Spirit, both Absolute and Free, is the horizon of all possible Transcendence since it provides the logical means, as illustrated in the case of its *Trinitätslehre*, whereby one can meaningfully describe the syntheses of Objective and Subjective Spirit in their fully actualized state. Hegel's mature philosophy of Spirit therefore represents the definitive *Übergang* of the phenomenology of Spirit by way of a speculative pneumatology or metaphysics, and in so doing he

also completes, as we noted in our beginning chapter, that most enigmatic and neglected orphan doctrine in Christian theology—the doctrine of the Holy Spirit.

If it can be said that Hegel symbolizes the so-called *end of philosophy*
(as in the views of Nietzsche and Heidegger), this end understood simultaneously as a completion should also have marked the beginning,
as Karl Barth once noted, of a uniquely speculative Protestant Christian theology.[10] This did not happen, of course, the reason being the
triumph of subjectivism, which dominates theology after the Enlightenment. Indeed, the abandonment of the trinitarian conception especially placed Christianity into the precarious position of having subverted its deepest metaphysical insights by institutional, political, and
individualistic concerns. Thus it was Schleiermacher and not Hegel, as
Tillich rightly notes, who captured liberal theology after the mid-nine-
teenth century, the chief concern of modernist theology no longer
being *truth* in the "quarrel between the ancients and the moderns," but
relevance.[11] Schleiermacher's emphasis upon experience, upon "feeling" and the subjectivity of the subject, was simply more in tune with
the egophantic outburst, as Voegelin calls it, which has dominated
post-Enlightenment individualism up to and including the present.

No one was more aware of the danger of losing theological *content*,
as we saw in the chapter on Enlightenment, than Hegel. Indeed,
Hegel's *in pejorem partem* attack on Schleiermacher was not really di-
rected at the particulars of his Berlin colleague's system. It was rather
an attack motivated by the apprehension that theology would soon be
swallowed up by a conception of Spirit reduced to mere subjectivity.[12]
This subjectivist reduction was particularly pronounced in christology
as articulated in popular piety (which continues unabated to this day),
whereby Christianity is reduced to an emotivistic mystery cult focused
on the personality of Jesus. Schleiermacher's *Glaubenslehre*, in Hegel's
view, further encouraged this subjectivism by failing to address ade-
quately the content implicit in the trinitarian conception. Hegel therefore opted, as I have maintained throughout this study, for speculative
pneumatology as the center of his system, since it was his conviction
that only Spirit, considered in its fullness, could reconcile without
compromise faith and knowledge.

Free Spirit, for Hegel, is nothing less than the actualization of this
reconciliation through the authentic individual in community. Therefore Hegel's invocation (or *benedictus*, as the case may be) of Aristotle
at the end of the *Enzyklopädie* (§577) is critical to understanding the
meaning of his system as a whole.[13] Indeed, the *noesis-noeton* corollary
of "thought thinking itself" and the "life of God," which he quotes
from Aristotle's *Metaphysics* (1072b.15–25 [xii.7]) provides the pneu-

matological corollary between Absolute Spirit and Holy Spirit, the sublation of subjective and objective, transcendence and immanence, in the fully actualized soul or Free Spirit (*E*, §§481, 482).

Hegel's discussion of subjective Spirit in fact begins with a discussion of the *soul*—the soul being understood through the older pneumatology (rational psychology) as a *pros hen* equivocal as in Aristotle. Deeply interfused with "nature in its idea," one should not, Hegel argues, think of the soul as a thing or a substance. The soul is rather a process—"the awakening of consciousness" (*E*, §387) in which the dialectic of Spirit is immediate and nondifferentiate.[14] Deeply embedded in nature, the soul's task is to move from immediacy to mediacy, this movement made possible by "desire" (*Lust*). Thus while Hegel is critical of Spirit embedded in nature (natural soul) or, more accurately, while he is critical of those who childishly avow a philosophy based upon vague, sensate intuitivism, he also recognizes feeling as the higher ground of experience in matters religious since it provides the initial groundwork for the development of soul qua Spirit. It all depends on the context of affirmation combined with the realization that in matters of truth (which is the goal of pneumatology) the "truth of nature is that nature has no truth" (*E*, §400). Indeed, the realm of nature or sensation (*Empfindung*), while it contains much that is good, also contains what is evil since nature or sensation in its immediacy is undifferentiate and value-free, good and evil being second order reflections. Hence Hegel believes that *feeling* and *nature*, as we have observed, are odd places for neo-Pietists and Romantics to locate the truth, since to posit something in feeling is simply to posit it in subjectivity, and to posit something in subjectivity is only the first step in demonstrating its truth.

This transitional stage of the natural soul's development is therefore one of "dreaming innocence" where one has the feeling of an "immediate, undifferentiated unity" (*unmittelbarer, unterschiedsloser Einheit*) in "the concrete life of nature." At this intermediate stage the soul is not yet in control of itself and, like Plato's charioteer in the *Phaedrus*, the undifferentiated soul can fluctuate chaotically between what we consider good and evil. Such a soul can even become what we would today call *obsessive*, and drift, as we have shown in the case of Hölderlin, into madness (*Verrücktheit*) as the soul "holds itself fast in the isolated particularity [wherein it *feels* it has] . . . actuality," even though this imagined actuality is a delusion (*E*, §402, Z: *sondern in einer einzelnen Besonderheit festgehalten, darin ihre Wirklichkeit habenden*). It is only when the soul becomes conscious of itself as the master of its corporeality (*Leiblichkeit*), that is, only when the soul is able to "control itself" through constructive habituation, that one is able to abstract what in the life-world actually does and does not properly belong to it.

The dream-world of the feelings (*Traumwelt*), as we recalled earlier, was particularly pronounced in the work of Hölderlin just prior to his breakdown—life becoming, for him, a dream about the absent gods: "Silent now," as he puts it in "Patmos," "is his sign on thundering heaven" (*Still ist sein Zeichen / Am donnernden Himmel*). But Hegel came increasingly to look upon such utterances as a *regressus ad uteram* the more he saw his poet friend sink into the infantile disposition of total dependency. Both Hölderlin and Hegel's sister, Christiane, were for Hegel painful testimonies to the fragility of Spirit's development—case studies as to how easily the middle-point of consciousness, as it were, can be truncated and overturned, the subject slipping back into a consciousness no different from infancy or senility.

Hegel's entire discourse on madness, as we have seen, anticipates a great deal of what later comes to be the general view of depth psychology—the obvious difference being that Hegel strenuously avoids positing the unconscious or the libido as being somehow foundational for the development of mature consciousness. The ultimate mystery of consciousness for Hegel is not insanity but sanity, this being his Cartesian generosity, as it were, since Hegel believed that while the grip of nature is intense, and the lure of evil seemingly insatiable, the power of Spirit is greater still. Hegel's preoccupation with this mystery can be seen in the frequency of his allusions to the biblical injunction from Genesis regarding "the heart of man [being] evil from its youth"—the heart qua *kardia* being synonymous with nature or the *thumos* of *psyche*. But inclination toward what is base does not negate the teleology of Spirit; it rather places the teleoeschatology of soul into bold relief. Nor does Hegel suggest that insanity is a necessary stage of mental development—even though this sometimes seems to be the case, given the wild abandon and intensity of youth combined with the surfeit of misjudgment by adults. He suggests rather that the phenomenologically rich *Zwischenwelt* of dreams, like "madness," is a both-and rather than an either-or reality with respect to whether it is a physical/natural or a mental/psychological phenomenon. These contradictions, isomorphic to the dialectic of Spirit and especially evident during the middle stages of its development, are at the heart of Hegel's distinctions between religion and philosophy since they are the raw material of transcendence and possible self-being.

"The aim of conscious mind," according to Hegel, "is to make its appearance identical with its essence, to raise its self-certainty to truth" (*E*, §416). This "raising up" or "elevation" (*Erhebung*), as he calls it with respect to the "concept of God" consists in the joining together of "consciousness in general" (*Bewußtsein überhaupt*) and its objects in "self-consciousness" in the sense of self-autonomy (*Selbstbewußtsein*) or what we call the Ego. This unity or binding together of object-consciousness and subject-consciousness as consciousness in-and-for-itself is the function of reason—that is, "*Vernunft, der Begriff des Geistes.*" With this affirmation, Hegel makes the transition from the sensate soul and reflective consciousness to the active essence of his doctrine of Spirit.

That this transition is theologically pneumatological, while being developed philosophically, becomes evident from the outset of his section on theoretical Spirit, where Hegel discusses *die Intelligenz*. The German equivalent of scholastic *intelligentia*, "intelligence" immediately calls to mind the distinction between *ratio* and *intellectus* as the equivalents of *soul* and *consciousness* developed in Parts 1 and 2. Hegel in fact states his intention as being one of clearly establishing the difference between "simple knowing" (*Wissen*) and "critical knowing" (*Erkennen*)—the difference between a consciousness of the "thatness" of things and their "whatness" (*E*, §445). There are "theologians," he says in a telling remark (repeated throughout the *Lectures on the Philosophy of Religion*), who continuously assert that we can know God exists "by reason alone" but refuse to say anything regarding "what" God is. Not content to remain with this perplexing distinction, such theologians nevertheless go on to develop elaborate theoretical proofs in order to show why it is impossible to do so while failing to recognize that the distinction itself rests upon quite arbitrary rational grounds (*E*, §445, Z).

Hegel demonstrates the speciousness of this notion by his doctrine of Spirit—a doctrine developed, as we have shown throughout this study, by way of the same dialetic informing Luther's understanding of the Holy Spirit. Luther strongly asserted, we recall, the "impossibility" of "believing . . . by [one's] reason or strength" (*Ich glaube, daß ich kann nicht, aus meiner Kraft oder Vernunft, glauben*) in the unity of the Father and Son, Creation and Redemption, abstract and particular. Obviously critical to this formulation is the meaning of "reason" (*Vernunft*) to know and the "power" (*Kraft*) of will to believe what is known. Ordinary knowing and willing presented Luther with little difficulty. However, in matters religious and metaphysical, Luther was utterly overwhelmed by the "bondage of the will" (*de servo arbitrio*) and by reason's inability either to know or to will the conditions necessary to actualize one's self-being or salvation. Furthermore, Luther's nominalistic conception of the power of reason is blended with an even stronger Augustinian sense of the vain striving for moral purity and the human inability to merit, by strength of moral will or intellectual acumen, the righteousness of God as the external condition for salvation. As a consequence, Luther did not formally explore the nature of reason by way of a theory of knowledge since he was convinced that such theories, as in the case of late medieval Scholasticism, had as their primary function the rational legitimation of the ecclesiastical mediational structure he considered wholly corrupt. Luther's rejection of the powers of reason as intrinsic to the *ordo salutis*, therefore, is not so much the result of epistemological reflection and insight as it was the product of his personal *Anfechtung* regarding the sorry state of the religious establishment.

But there is another dimension to Luther's formulation that caught the eye of Hegel in a way that led him to the conviction, late in life, that he was more Lutheran than the Lutherans. Protestant theology, in Hegel's view, had in fact become a pale reflection of its former self, especially with respect to the power of the Spirit undergirding Luther's passionate and imaginative theological assertions.[15] The key to this Spirit, as I have argued, lies in Hegel's instinctive appreciation of Luther's dialectical conception of Holy Spirit—the implicitly transcendental assertion that Spirit-itself overcomes the hiatus between the act of faith and what, in fact, is believed. As in other medieval postulations of *docta ignorantia*, Luther's assertion is transparent to the power of the *via negativa* in which the knowledge of nonknowledge is present as a datum of consciousness. Moreover, this transcendental understanding is fundamentally grounded in the biblical understanding of Spirit, whether in the Hebrew Bible, where the lighting of Being is the result of Spirit's (*ru'ah*) "hovering over the face of the deep," or the Johannine promise of the *Paraclete* as the "comforting spirit of understanding" that will "lead you into all truth."[16] Hegel is as firmly convinced as Luther, I think, of the general validity of these assertions—the fundamental difference being that Hegel goes on to demonstrate *how* and *why* it is the case that a complete cognitional theory can and should be developed through the category of Spirit, a category so central to the otherwise sparse philosophical reflections found in scripture.

The pneumatological correlation becomes fully explicit as Hegel develops his *Intelligenz* theory of *Geist* by way of three functions or operations: first, as *Anschauung* or "intuition" as distinct from mere "sensation" (*Empfindung*), and "attention" (*Aufmerksamkeit*) as distinct from "intention" (*Absicht*), for we are here dealing with "intuition proper," Hegel insists, as distinct from mere sensation, which is characteristic of the natural soul. Second, this "attentional" emphasis makes it possible to consider "representation" (*Vorstellung*) and the unity of the object by way of three suboperations—"recollection"

(*Erinnerung*), "imagination" (*Einbildungskraft*), and "memory" in the proper sense (*Gedächtnis*). Third, Hegel moves to a consideration of "concrete objectivity" by way of the "comprehensive intelligence" (*begreifenden Intelligenz*) and the triple functions of "understanding" (*Verstand*), "judgment" (*Urteil*), and "reason" (*Vernunft*)—considerations that pave the way to the full development of Spirit Objective.

Hegel therefore makes it clear in his discussion of *Anschauung* that feeling, far from being the external foundation of intelligence, is "included" within intelligence as one of its basic but not final moments; in other words, feeling is not a moment *sui generis*, but a moment needing differentiation through the life of the concept. Thus Hegel rejects all who claim for "feeling" special cognitive status as if, by being antecedent to or separate from rationality, it is pure and uncontaminated by reason. This, of course, was the basic contention of the Pietists and certain Romantics about whom Hegel makes clear, as does Luther in his pejorative comments regarding the *Schwärmerei*, that he has had quite enough. Indeed, if one has the misfortune of prolonged encounters with such *enthusiasts*, it is best simply to leave them alone since the terms of rational debate cannot be established (*E*, §447).[17]

But Hegel's emphasis upon the call of feeling in this passage is not without a special existential significance insofar as the call of the Holy Spirit is precisely what was at issue in the debate between Pietists and Orthodoxists generally. Luther's answer to the enigma of belief regarding the unity of the Father and the Son is precisely "the Holy Spirit which calls me through the Gospel" (*Sondern der heilige Geist hat durchs Evangelium berufen mich*). Conspicuously excluded, as we saw earlier, is any mention of the Sacraments as the sure and certain external agencies of this mediation. Conspicuously *included*, on the other hand, is Hegel's attention to the hermeneutical event of comprehending, through Spirit, the meaning of the Word through which Spirit calls. This Word qua *logos*, for Hegel, is nothing less than the concept of Spirit,[18] and it is Hegel's contention, as I have maintained throughout this study, that any pneumatology worthy of the name must be able to unpack the meaning of this comprehension. Hegel's logic is nothing less than the systematic working out of his pneumatological hermeneutic.

In sum, the proper work of the Holy Spirit is not emotive intensification as the Pietists would have it, nor does the Holy Spirit provide grounds for the legitimation of any specific kind of institutional authority. Feeling plays a role in this comprehension, but feeling is merely the first and not the final step. The fundamental task of pneumatology is demonstrating, through the logic of the concept, how it is the case that Spirit has the power to "bind together feeling's emotion" and "memory's reflective recollection" in "thought," to "be one with one's actions," as he puts it throughout his *Rechtsphilosophie*. Only by comprehending the genuine religious action (which is but an extension of Luther's attempt to comprehend justification will the truths of "revealed religion" be known and translated into Spirit Objective. For this to happen, sensation (*Empfindung*) must become "intuition proper" (*Anschauung*), the immediate, unmediated object must become external, must become object for consciousness. This is accomplished through "attention" (*Aufmerksamkeit*) since it is "attention" that makes things self-external (*sich-selber-Äusserlichen*) as "real" external realities with their own time and space. By this critical realism (through which Hegel believed he had refuted Kant's notion that space and time are merely the subjective forms of intuition), Hegel also thinks that he has overcome one of the major problems in critical idealism (*E*, §448, Z). Attention, as distinct from intention, provides the critical mediational step in the movement from mere sensation to intuition—especially as regards the possibility of education (*E*, §448, Z: *Die Aufmerksamkeit macht daher den Anfang der Bildung aus*), for apart from this distinction there would be no basis for the possibility of accuracy in "representation" (*Vorstellung*). Such a step therefore presupposes the mediational power of language as symbolized by the power of Spirit *to call* through the conceptual agency of the Word or language within the social context of the spiritual community.

Ricoeur has it right, therefore, when he suggests that a theory of representation is the critical center of Hegel's philosophy of religion, since Hegel himself asserts, "Representation is this inward intuition of the center [where] unmediated intelligence finds itself [initially] determined and then in its freedom as thought" (*E*, §451: *Die Vorstellung ist als die erinnerte Anschauung die Mitte zwischen dem unmittelbaren Bestimmt-sich-Finden der Intelligenz und derselben in ihrer Freiheit, dem Denken*). This means that the productions of *Vorstellungsdenken* are the property of *Intelligenz* in the final stages of its development, intelligence being the link between intuition and thought. Like Hegel, Ricoeur develops a theory of metaphoricity onto this doctrine of intelligent representation, for in Ricoeur's view, metaphor, as distinct from mere symbol (which remains buried in the unconscious), receives its meaning and identity from *logos*, that is, through the life of the concept even though it, like symbol, has its origin in feeling, and remains, in some sense, dependent upon it.[19]

Hegel enhances the dynamic process of Spirit through his tripartite doctrine of representation. First, there is simple recollection (*Erinnerung*), according to Hegel, where "images" (*Bilder*) are the product of the largely automatic or unconscious process of "imaging." But for recollection to become imagination in the proper sense, that is, *Einbildungskraft*, what is outer and external as the merely recollected image must become inner and subjective. Left to themselves, recollected or spontaneously produced images are simply an "unconscious mine" (*ein bewußtloser Schacht*) and not yet properly one's own. To become "consciously subjective" it is necessary for images to be "raised by thought" into the universal space-time configuration of consciousness from which they can be "recalled" (*E*, §§452, 453). Failure to do so consigns one to a life lived in the immediacy of sensation. Thus Hegel insists that we are not here dealing with immediate but with reconstructed images that have their unity by way of the educative *sign*. I. J. Gelb has, in fact, very effectively utilized Hegel's theory of representation in the formulation of a grammatology, maintaining that the key to phonetically encoded ancient scripts has precisely to do with comprehending the operations between "picture" or ideographic writing (*Vorstellungsschrift*) and the systematic introduction of the mnemonic sign as societies become more complex. With this comprehension, phonetic encodement is possible—and written languages become, for the first time, as Saussure puts it, "a substitute for discourse."[21] Language becomes in this instance the substitute not only for discourse, that is, for auditory or spoken language, but also for *seeing* or imaging itself. In other words, with the advent of *Vorstellungsschrift* mediated by the logic of the concept it is possible to see in written signs what is now twice removed from what is otherwise directly signified—removed, in the first instance, from living speech, and, in the second, from what speech is *about*.

Owing to the dialectics of negation, Hegel seems to be implicitly aware of this double effacement in his discussion of the active "reproductive," "associative," and "creative imagination." Imagination, he says, has to do with the active "voluntary" control of intelligence over its experience and, as such, is the "contact point" between what becomes known, in consciousness, as both "object" and "subject" (*E*, §455). As "reproductive," the imagination does its work "voluntarily" and without the immediate assistance of sense intuition, and as "associative," the imagination textures its productions with the moods of subjectivity. This process is fundamentally different from the "associationism" of empirical psychology (which, as we have seen, Hegel identifies with "the decline of philosophy"). What Hegel has in mind is closer to what might be called the "free associationism" that takes place in the stream of ordinary consciousness as distinct from the association of so-called clear and distinct ideas one finds in Locke (*E*, §455, Z). For "ideas," in the proper or critical sense, are the work of "memory" and presuppose, *a priori*, the "embodiment of intelligence" in the "creative imagination" (*zeichenmachende Phantasie*). This embodiment consists of the synthesis of what is given in "reproduction" and "association" in specific forms such as works of art (*E*, §456).

The products of the creative imagination, however, are still rooted in subjectivity; that is, such productions have not as yet been subjected to the analysis of formally constituted "truth" considerations. To do so requires a complete transition from imagination's productions as "symbol" to their consideration as "sign," and such a transition requires the activity of "memory proper" (*E*, §457, Z). In other words, while *Phantasie* remains the *Mittelpunkt* in which the inner and the outer, the universal and the particular, subject and object, are welded or "bound" together, this unification is accomplished by reason still "nominal" because its productions are partially subjective. Reason in the proper sense must intervene "to determine the truth of its content" (*E*, §457) by entering fully into the logic of the concept. In such a way, Spirit becomes Free Spirit.

Understood in terms of our prior grammatological illustration, this means that it is necessary to move to a theory of signs no longer tied to the visual or sensate signifier as in ideographic writing—a theory of signs that renders possible the production of alphabetized, phoneticized, written scripts or, as Hegel calls it, a "sign of signs" (*E*, §459), in order for reason to apprehend the truth of its content. "This sign-creating activity," he says, "may be distinctively termed 'productive' memory (abstract *Mnemosyne*) since memory, which in ordinary life is often used interchangeably and synonymously with recollection and even with conception and imagination, has always only to do with signs" (*E*, §458).

This reduction of "outwardness" to "inwardness" in alphabetic naming, then, depends upon abstract memory for the generation of what one might further designate (as does Wallace in his translation) *verbal* memory. This should not be taken to mean that verbal meanings are superior to visual, as is so frequently the case.[22] For Hegel makes it clear (in a rather extended discourse on hieroglyphic writing) that there is a surplus of meaning in the notations of so-called primitive or preliterate societies (*E*, §459). It is further the case, as Gelb also argues, that the movement from *Vorstellungsschrift* to a "sign of signs" becomes necessary in those civilizations wherein strictly ideographic (pictorial) writing is no longer functional. In other words, if one remains with imaginative, symbolical, pictographic representationalism, there is no limit to the number of characters one can invent to communicate experience and meaning. Partial phonetic encodement, therefore, necessitates some abstraction from the immediacy of the referential symbol, and full phonetic encodement, as Derrida and Ricoeur have also observed, demands a "complete effacement" between sign and signifier (as is the case in the "Speculative Good Friday," for example). Such a movement or effacement can be accomplished, in Hegel's terms, only by differentiating "recollection" (*Erinnerung*) from "memory proper" (*Gedächtnis*). Memory, then, is the third stage of *Vorstellung*, in which the unity of intuition and image is raised to intelligence through thought. For it is "memory" that, through its triple functions of "retention," "reproduction," and "mechanism," provides the basis for thought to rise to "understanding," "judgment," and "comprehension." Only then does Spirit rise to the "practical" level of being "free" (*E*, §481)—that is, free to actualize itself objectively.

The parallels of "free Spirit" to the fundamental work of Holy Spirit are obvious enough, for it is the "Spirit which makes free," to cite the biblical verse with which Hegel commences his investigations. The quality of one's freedom becomes manifest theologically only as Spirit becomes "objective" or actual in the process of sanctification, that is, in the concrete improvement of moral life as an individual in community. It is precisely here that Hegel's allusions to ecclesiology are instructive, for this is the "other half," so to speak, of traditional pneumatology in a theological context—precisely what Hegel goes on to develop in his *Philosophy of Right* in order to show, in the words of MacIntyre, how the "tradition constituted, tradition constituting" community of "rational discourse" is the only possible locus for translating moral inclinations into ethical life.

It is important to note that Hegel, in the final section of the *Enzyklopädie*, only sketches the outlines for the basis of fusing Church and state; he does not develop this notion materially and empirically, but in terms of complementarity and unity of purpose. Hegel is in agreement with Kant that most people tend to be inclined toward religion because of ethical and moral need. It would be counterproductive, therefore, to insist that there be a "wall of separation," to use the American constitutional phrase, between religious morality and a national social ethic. Indeed, Luther and the reformers, he observes, paved the way for this kind of complementarity since religion, after the Reformation, became sufficiently "inwardized" to make this transition possible.[23] This is in sharp contrast, for Hegel, to the situation that obtained prior to the Reformation, in which religion remained "external" as symbolized, for example, in the adoration of the host during the festival of *Fronleichnam*. Thus while Catholicism has the reputation of providing the basis for political stability, such a view, according to Hegel, is shortsighted since the future of social order depends upon the making subjective of social consciousness and morality prior to an adequate institutional objectification or actualization.

Against the in-itself morality of Catholicism, Hegel therefore views the Protestant principle as a constructive and, indeed, essential development in the history of religious and philosophical consciousness since the *Freiheits-Prinzip* has, as its goal, the goal of *Selbstbewußtsein* in the ethical sense. In other words, freedom of Spirit grounded in a rational autonomy no longer undermines community but improves it by way of a moral philosophy that naturally passes over into social ethics (*E*, §552)—a passing-over that is identical with the passing-over of Absolute Spirit into Free Spirit.

This working-out of Spirit is entirely consistent with pneumatology understood as providing a basis for ecclesiology—in Hegel's case, a philosophy of right made possible by dissolving the artificial dialectical tensions between Church and state by way of placing into relief the authentic dialectical relationship between morality and ethics. Spirit alone has the power to accomplish this because "the *concept* of Spirit has its *reality* in Spirit" (*Der* Begriff *des Geistes hat seine* Realität *im Geiste*) (*E*, §553), and the unity of Spirit both subjective and objective is to be found in the state still religious because here alone "God as Spirit [is] apprehended in community" (*daß Gott als Geist in seiner Gemeinde aufgefaßt Werden muß*) (*E*, §554).

It is important to note, finally, that Hegel rarely refers to the Church in his later writings. His concern rather is with the spiritual community, this being the term he consistently uses throughout his *Lectures on the Philosophy of Religion*. The reason he does this, as we have suggested throughout this study, is that pneumatology must not be a substitute for ecclesiology nor, conversely, should ecclesiology be the substitute for pneumatology. In Hegel's view, it is of the essence of Spirit to develop beyond traditional boundaries and instantiations— especially as these boundaries and instantiations are under stood by conventional theology. With this notion, the mature Hegel severely qualifies, even repudiates, the earlier Romantic motto shared with Schelling and Hölderlin—*hen kai pan* with ultimate union in "the invisible and not the visible."[24] Hegel now identifies Spirit-filled faith with "process" whereby the "witness" of Spirit (*Zeugnis*), initially manifest subjectively in "devotion" (*Andacht*) and manifest objectively in the "cultus" of worship, is now bound together in rational belief and ethical life in the state. Through this concrete mediation, Spirit, and its apprehension by the subject, "passes over" (*Übergang*) into its status as "free, reconciled, actualized Spirit" (*E*, §555). It is precisely from this Hegelian view that Tillich extrapolates his notion that "culture is the form of religion, and religion the substance of culture" as the never-ending dialectic informing the Protestant formula, *ecclesia semper reformanda est*.

Not just any religion, of course, will accomplish this self-transcending transformation for Hegel; only "revealed" religion—and by "revealed" he does not simply mean the so-called Judeo-Christian tradition as is commonly thought. He means rather religion within which the meaning of Spirit has become coherent. As Hegel puts it in one of his most important assertions regarding pneumatology, "If the word *Geist* is to mean anything at all, it must refer to God's self-revelation" (*E*, §564). This divine self-revelation is the "truth" underlying the meaning of *Wissenschaft* for Hegel—or, more precisely, the revelation in which the truth of science becomes clear, nothing more, nothing less. But the meaning of this truth would not be evident were it not for the centrality of the *Dreiheit* conception of dialectic implicit in the trinitarian conception of Christianity—precisely what is asserted in orthodox theology and what must be maintained at whatever cost against the ravages of subjectivism in theology, whatever form it might take. Indeed, this is why he can say of the older orthodoxy, its positivity notwithstanding, that a militantly "atheistical" philosophy is infinitely superior to the modern alliance between Rationalism and neo-Pietism in liberal theology where "everything seems to be God" (*E*, §573).

In sum, if the new altar of worship is to be feeling and subjectivism, Hegel will worship at the old one since the older, Orthodox Pietism is infinitely superior to *die neue Frömmigkeit* to the extent that it is simply secularism cloaked in a few insubstantial (*äusserlich*) religious rags. The religion that is truly "revealed" not only is self-critical but must have the power of becoming actual and concrete. The reality of Spirit in-and-for-itself cannot be locked up either in someone's idea of Orthodox objectivism or in the privatized world of Pietistic subjectivism: "Piety, in particular, which with its pious airs of superiority fancies itself free to dispense with proof, goes hand in hand with empty rationalism (which seems to be so much opposed to it, though both repose really on the same habit of mind)" (*E*, §573).

True Piety, for Hegel, is identifiable by its willingness to abandon "this emotional region as soon as it leaves the inner life, enters upon the daylight of the Idea's development and revealed riches, and brings with it, out of its inner worship of God, reverence for law and for an absolute truth exalted above the subjective form of feeling." Luther, according to Hegel, clearly understood the movement from "faith in feeling" to the "witness of Spirit," the dialectical movement through which, "as Spirit becomes mature" in the logic of the concept, faith recognizes that "reason is the rose of the cross in the present" (*RP*, preface).[25] Thinking-faith, for Hegel, is the comprehensive actualization of this chiasm in "the genuine religious action."

NOTES

Chapter One
INTRODUCTION

1. The index to the Suhrkamp Verlag edition of Hegel's *Werke in zwanzig Bänden* lists some fifteen pages (pp. 215–29) of indexed notations to *Geist*—more than any other single indexed term or category.

2. See Nicholas Berdyaev, *The Beginning and the End*, trans. R. M. French (New York: Harper and Row, 1957), p. 20. Berdyaev's assessment of Hegel is measured and, as such, stands in rather bold contrast to most philosophical assessments of Hegel during the 1940s and 1950s, especially in Britain and America. Henry Aiken's judgment, as found in the highly influential *Mentor Philosophers* series on the history of philosophy (six volumes, each selling for fifty cents!), may be taken as typical of the manner in which countless students were introduced to Hegel during the height of the Cold War: "Without Hegel, Marxism would be unthinkable; without him, therefore, the ideological conflicts of our own age would be hard to imagine. . . . As a human being, Hegel is uninteresting; he lived, apparently, for no other purpose than that of playing secretary to the Absolute." While Aiken's sketch improves a bit as one reads on, the message is clear: if one is hostile to totalitarianism, one better watch out for Hegel—and Fichte as well, since they are the alleged progenitors of all manner of absolutism. See *The Age of Ideology*, ed. Henry D. Aiken (New York: New American Library, 1956), p. 71.

3. See Jaspers's *Diagram of Being* in *Von der Wahrheit* reprinted in the appendix of my *Transcendence and Hermeneutics* (The Hague: Martinus Nijhoff, 1979). Jaspers was highly influenced by Hegel, and *Von der Wahrheit* is the unfinished attempt of Jaspers to write a *Logik* in the manner of Hegel. But as in the case of so many of his contemporaries in the early twentieth century, whether those of the existentialists (whom he emulated) or the neo-Marxists (for whom he had little admiration), he rarely acknowledges the extent of his debt to Hegel. See *Von der Wahrheit. Philosophische Logik. Erster Band* (Munich: Piper Verlag, 1947; 2d ed., 1958).

4. Hegel was always, for Heidegger, as Gadamer argues convincingly in *Hegel's Dialectic* (New Haven: Yale University Press, 1976), the ultimate object of "overcoming." Derrida obviously agrees with this assessment even though I will argue that Heidegger's return to "Spirit" and the "spiritual" can in no way be viewed as surpassing the mature Hegel's conception of *Geist*. It represents rather a return to the early Romantic Hegel, the Hegel of *Entschlossenheit* as represented, for example, in his 1796 poem "Eleusis: An Hölderlin," and to a primordialistic-Pagan account of Spirit by way of Schelling and Trakl. Derrida is entirely correct, however, in suggesting (both in *Of Spirit* and in earlier works—especially *Glas*) that the religious differences between Hegel and Heidegger (Lutheran Protestantism and Roman Catholicism respectively) are a point of irreconcilable tension between them. One of my primary tasks

throughout this study is to show how this is the case—especially with reference to the category of *Geist*. In making this point, however, it is absolutely essential to separate the "spirit" of these religious backgrounds from the "spirit" that drove National Socialism and with which Nazism tends to be identified. Victor Farías, and others bent on showing Heidegger's political culpability out of Roman Catholicism, fails to do this—*Geist* here being identified with neo-Pagan or neo-Romantic philosophy. Hegel's *Geist* can be contaminated by these later associations only by failing to read him in context. See Jacques Derrida, *Of Spirit: Heidegger and the Question*, trans. Geoffrey Bennington and Rachel Bowlby (Chicago: University of Chicago Press, 1989); also Victor Farías, *Heidegger and Nazism*, ed., Tom Rockmore and Joseph Margolis (Philadelphia: Temple University Press, 1989). The recent appearance in English of the Neske-Kettering collection, *Martin Heidegger and National Socialism* (New York: Paragon, 1990) is very helpful in providing some balance to Farías.

5. See Ricoeur's *The Rule of Metaphor* (Toronto: University of Toronto Press, 1975).

6. One of the common features of recent translations is the acknowledgment that *Geist* and its derivatives cannot simply be rendered as *mind*. Obviously this is no insignificant hermeneutical point when it comes to understanding Hegel. John E. Smith is particularly aware of consequences of failing to read Hegel "theologically," and that a *pneumatological* approach is precisely what is needed to clarify the "social" dimensions of Spirit. Smith is also correct, in my view, by way of focusing on Hegel's reflections on the so-called "sin against the Holy Spirit" in his *Lectures on the Philosophy of Religion*, viz., "that all sins can be forgiven if the natural world is relinquished except in the case where there has been a sin against the Holy Spirit (*nur nicht die Sünde gegen den Heiligen Geist, das Leugnen des Geistes; denn er nur ist die Macht, die alles aufheben kann*), for this transgression alone contains the power whereby everything can be negated and canceled." See Smith's article "Hegel's Reinterpretation of the Doctrine of Spirit and the Religious Community," in *Hegel and the Philosophy of Religion* (Wofford Symposium), ed. D. E. Christensen (The Hague: Martinus Nijhoff, 1970), pp. 157–85.

7. Obviously, it is highly unlikely that Jesus here speaks of the mediational power of a vast institutional apparatus, and far more likely that he alludes to the power of "understanding" and "blessedness" (even in the late testimony of Saint John's Gospel) with respect to what will and will not be accomplished by the arrival of the *paraclete* or "comforter."

8. In this regard, I think that my approach is similar to that of several other recent studies, including those of Tom Rockmore, *Hegel's Circular Epistemology* (Bloomington: Indiana University Press, 1986), and Robert Pippin, *Hegel's Idealism: The Satisfactions of Self-Consciousness* (Cambridge: Cambridge University Press, 1989). Both of these works attempt to elucidate Hegel by viewing his work in the "context" of his German philosophical contemporaries and in the wake of Kant's critical idealism. Terry Pinkard, in *Hegel's Dialectic: The Explanation of Possibility* (Philadelphia: Temple University Press, 1988), and William Desmond, in *Desire, Dialectic, and Otherness* (New Haven: Yale University Press, 1987), are also sensitive to context while also focusing on Hegel's relevance to

basic philosophical tasks. No one has been more influential in restraining recent speculative interpretations of Hegel than Klaus Hartmann—to whom all the previously mentioned studies are deeply indebted. Hartmann in fact proposes a Hegelian solution, so to speak, to the extremes of the metaphysical and value interpretations of the right and left, by way of a "hermeneutic of categories" that is, at the same time, an "ontology." In so doing, that is, by separating the man from his myth(s), Hartmann in fact elevates Hegel in a way that is entirely in keeping with Hegel's *Aufhebung* qua *Erhebung*. See Hartmann's essay "Hegel: A Non-Metaphysical View," in *Hegel: A Collection of Critical Essays*, ed. Alasdair MacIntyre (Notre Dame: Notre Dame University Press, 1976), pp. 101–24. See also the recent *Festschrift für Klaus Hartmann, Kategorie und Kategorialität*, ed. Dietmar Koch and Klaus Bort (Verlag Könighausen and Neumann, 1990), especially the article by Klaus Brinkmann, "Intersubjektivität und konkretes Allgemeines," pp. 131–69.

9. See Lawrence Dickey, *Hegel: Religion, Economics, and the Politics of Spirit, 1770–1807* (Cambridge: Cambridge University Press, 1987).

10. See H. S. Harris, *Hegel's Development*, 2 vols. (Oxford: Clarendon, 1972; reprint, 1983).

11. Jacques Derrida has recently commented on this in *De l'esprit* (Paris: Editions Galilée, 1987), trans. Geoffrey Bennington and Rachel Bowlby as *Of Spirit: Heidegger and the Question* (Chicago: University of Chicago Press, 1989).

12. See *Hegel Spiele*, ed. Heiner Höfener (Donauwörth: Rogner and Bernard Verlag, 1977).

13. As Shlomo Avineri points out, Gruppe's play was motivated in large part by anti-Semitism, as evidenced by the Jewish characters being duped by Hegel (who supported emancipation) into thinking they might pursue professional careers that afforded status beyond being mere peddlers and shopkeepers. See Avineri's article "Hegel Revisited," in the Alasdair MacIntyre collection, *Hegel* (Notre Dame: Notre Dame University Press, 1976); and also "A Note of Hegel's View on Jewish Emancipation," in *Journal of Jewish Studies* (April 1963).

Chapter Two
PNEUMATOLOGY

1. See Reinhold Seeberg, *History of Doctrines*, trans. Charles Hay (Grand Rapids: Baker, 1961; 1st German eds., 1895 and 1898), vol. 2, §69. As Seeberg points out, Luther's emphasis upon the "outer word" was made in the face of the many radical "spiritist" reforming groups of the early sixteenth century and does not necessarily represent his true position. Luther was far more inclined, I contend, to a position of *paradox*, in which the outer-inner, involuntary-voluntary dialectic is the mystery at the heart of the *Glauben als Bewußtsein* (faith as consciousness) conception of faith that runs throughout German Idealism.

2. In this brief discussion, I pick up on the suggestion of John E. Smith that Hegel's reinterpretation of the doctrine of Spirit and the religious community is a critical, if not the most critical, aspect of his work. I am also agreed with

Smith regarding the necessity of understanding Hegel's *Geist* against the ethos of this doctrine, namely, Pietism. See Smith's essay "Hegel's Reinterpretation of the Doctrine of Spirit," pp. 157–85. Robert Williams takes a position similar to that of Smith in his article "Hegel's Concept of *Geist*," in *Hegel's Philosophy of Spirit*, ed. Peter G. Stillman (Albany: SUNY Press, 1986), pp. 1–21.

3. See Paul Tillich, *A History of Christian Thought*, trans. Carl Braaten (New York: Simon and Schuster, 1967), pp. 64ff. Tillich therefore agrees with Harnack's view of pneumatology as the "orphan" doctrine of Christian systematic theology. See Adolf von Harnack, *History of Dogma*, vol. 4, pp. 108–34.

4. The strategies of what logicians call *evidentialism* and *presuppositionalism* are applicable here, subjective Pietists being allied with the former and objective Orthodoxists being allied with the latter with respect to the need for propositional grounding.

5. This underlies Berdyaev's intention to rescue the authentically speculative element in Eastern pneumatology—especially in thinkers such as Gregory of Nyssa, who believed that "Spirit is the conceptual part of man as distinct from his sensible soul and nutritive body. Thus *pneuma* becomes *nous*." Berdyaev therefore strenuously objects both to the excessively Platonic conception of Spirit as *theosis* and, especially, to the Western objectification of Spirit in the authority of the Church. His aim—*sobornost* or "the quality of community in men," which arises out of the *axiological* dimension of Spirit—is very close to the *praxis* element in German Pietism and, as I intend to show, to Hegel's conception of Free Spirit. See Berdyaev, *Spirit and Reality* (London: Centenary, 1939), pp. 23 and 38.

6. The original formulation of the Nicene Creed, it will be recalled, simply asserts in its third article (and following the complex *homoousian* christological formulation of the second), "I believe in the Holy Spirit"—and ends with a series of anathemas regarding the fate of those who do not accept the validity of the second article. See J.N.D. Kelly, *Early Christian Creeds* (New York: Harper and Row, 1960), pp. 223–251.

7. The great exception here, of course, is Origen, whose conception of Spirit is determined by *logos*—whom Hegel, in fact, cites in the context of true or authentic *Aufklärung* in the *Phänomenologie* (p. 422). Harnack's point is that the fundamental concern of the ancient Church was *fides implicita*, i.e., the development of the structural, observational, institutional norms for a system of belief; and with the Athanasian Creed "the doctrine of the Trinity as an article of faith to be inwardly appropriated, [is transformed] into an ecclesiastical legal statute the observance of which salvation depends" (*History of Dogma*, vol. 4, p. 136).

8. All references to this work are from Conn O'Donovan's translation of Part 1 under the title *The Way to Nicea: The Dialectical Development of Trinitarian Theology* (London: Darton, Longman, and Todd, 1976). I would argue that Lonergan is the most consistently Hegelian of all major recent Roman Catholic theologians, a point that has not gone unnoticed in the excellent study of Jon Nilson, *Hegel's Phenomenology and Lonergan's Insight: A Comparison of Two Ways to Christianity* (Meisenheim am Glan: Hain, 1979).

9. Herein lies the origin of what Heidegger calls *onto-theology* while remaining oblivious to the fact that it is precisely this paradox that keeps such questions alive.

10. This is the reason for the rejection of the trinitarian conception by many Christian groups down through the centuries, be they conservative biblicists on the one hand, or free-thinking liberals on the other.

11. Martin Chemnitz, the so-called Aquinas of sixteenth-century Lutheran Orthodoxy, is typical in his observation that "the Church departed from the simple usage of Scriptural words, not from any wanton affectation of novelty, but as Augustine elegantly and truly says, 'by the necessity of speech, these terms were acquired from the Greeks and Latins, because of the errors and snares of heretics'... The Church would have preferred to use such simplicity of speech, so that, as it believes, it might also speak, viz., that there is one God, the Father, Son, and Holy Ghost.'" *Loci Theologici (1591)*, vol. 1, p. 36, as quoted by Heinrich Schmid, *The Doctrinal Theology of the Evangelical Lutheran Church*, trans. Charles Hay and Henry Jacobs (Minneapolis: Augsburg, 1899), pp. 138–39.

12. As Hegel makes abundantly clear throughout in his *Lectures on the Philosophy of Religion*, the truth of religion depends entirely upon "how true" a given religion is to its concept. For Hegel the superiority of revealed traditions consists precisely in the ability of a given tradition to recognize and acknowledge the validity of the dialectical process whereby it comes to its own self-consciousness. Nowhere is this better evidenced than in Luther's comment "Faith is the dialectic which conceives the idea of whatsoever is to be believed." See Martin Luther's *Commentary on Saint Paul's Letter to the Galatians* (Middleton ed., 1575), trans. Philip Watson (London: James Clark, 1953), p. 460.

13. Lonergan, *The Way to Nicea*, pp. 5–6.

14. As we will show in the chapter on Absolute Spirit, Hegel is deeply aware of this phenomenological category by way of his exposition of the pre-Socratics.

15. Lonergan, *The Way to Nicea*, pp. 7 and 12. Lonergan is agreed with Ricoeur's notion that "pluri-vocity" is an essential feature of mythic-symbolic language—the function of which is, as Lonergan puts it, "to expand one's horizon." See Ricoeur's *Interpretation Theory* (1975) and *Rule of Metaphor* (1976).

16. The mythical precedent for this hidden essence, of course, goes back to Sinai, where the first version of the Law (hence the direct instantiation of Yahweh) was destroyed by Moses in his act or rage against the idolatry of Aaron and the children of Israel. The second version seems to have been the result of Moses functioning as a copyist—hence, the questions as to whether there is more unwritten, whether it can be captured in the oral tradition, and whether, in fact, the unwritten might be more important than what is written. See Exodus 31.18, 32.15–20, and 34.277–28. This element of Otherness in the Word, so important in the Talmudic tradition, is highly evident in the work of Derrida—especially Derrida's work on Hegel.

17. Lonergan, *The Way to Nicea*, pp. 43–44.

18. *Against Heresies* 8.3, as quoted by Lonergan, *The Way to Nicea*, pp. 46–47, observing that "such is the case with Marcion who introduces another God."

19. Lonergan, *The Way to Nicea*, pp. 48–49.

20. Ibid., pp. 54 and 89.

21. It was precisely such an intuition that led Irenaeus to differentiate, as Lonergan indicates, among three different modes of divine manifestation in the scriptures: God as revealed in the biblical literature as the covenant God of Law (objectivity); God as revealed in the prophets as the God of internal consciousness (subjectivity) in wisdom; and God as revealed as the incarnate God-man, Jesus of Nazareth. Ibid., pp. 113 and 120. This triple structure is mirrored in the medieval understanding of exigesis (*tropological, allegorical, anagogical*) and the medieval understanding of faith (*notitia, assensus, fiducia*).

22. Ibid., pp. 141 and 135.

23. See Heidegger's 1930–31 lectures on *Hegel's Phenomenology of Spirit* (Bloomington: Indiana University Press, 1988), where he argues that the preposition "of" is in no way to be construed as an "objective genitive" but as an "explicative genitive"; that is, neither experience nor spirit is the *object* of phenomenology or consciousness (in the Husserlian sense). The experience of Absolute Spirit is rather a phenomenology of consciousness "having an experience of itself" (25)—consciousness being "absolutely related to the Absolute" as in Kierkegaard, the "movement" or motion of this relation being the descriptive task of phenomenology.

24. This is particularly evident in Luther's *Freiheits-Prinzip* as articulated in the classic text "On the Freedom of the Christian," where he articulates what Ricoeur later refers to as the mystery of "being free yet bound," to wit, that "the Christian person is the free lord of all subject to none and also the perfectly dutiful servant subject to all." See also Gerhard Ebeling's excellent exposition of Luther's dialectical understanding of the Law in "Usus Triplex Legis," where he argues that Luther maintained the accusatorial function of the Law (*lex semper accusit*) in order to avoid an extrinsic notion of faith with respect to its proper object—the consciousness of Christ—as distinct from its improper object—works or the fruits of sanctification. See *Word and Faith* (Philadelphia: Fortress, 1963), pp. 62–78.

25. See Adolf Koberle, *The Quest for Holiness*, trans. John Mattes (Minneapolis: Augsburg, 1938). In Calvinism, it will be recalled, this verification came by way of the *testimonium spiritus sancti internum*, which, for Hegel and for Lutheranism, was an excessively subjective category.

26. Jaspers's rigorous critique of *Katholizität* is informed by precisely the same distinctions we find in Ritschl. See esp. *Der philosophische Glaube angesichts der Offenbarung* (Munich: Piper Verlag, 1962). During Hegel's "flirtation with Catholicism" during his Nuremberg period there is, for a moment (albeit purely on speculative, metaphysical grounds) an appreciation for what is possible, philosophically, when a society creates "space," as it were, for contemplatives to do their work unimpeded by the workaday world. See, for example, his critique of the exoteric philosophy of Kant in the preface to the *Science of Logic*, pp. 25–29.

27. Albrecht Ritschl, *Three Essays*, trans. Philip Hefner (Philadelphia: Fortress, 1972), p. 26.

28. Ibid., p. 86.

29. See Martin Luther, *Der kleine Catechismus*, "Der dritte Hauptartikel von der Heiligung" (various editions).

30. See the final section to Ricoeur's *Symbolism of Evil*. Twenty years later, in connection with his work on Hegel, Ricoeur said, "Now I know why and how the symbol gives rise to thought." See Ricoeur's "On the Status of *Vorstellung* in Hegel's Philosophy of Religion," in *Meaning, Truth, and God*, ed. Leroy S. Rouner (Notre Dame: Notre Dame University Press, 1983).

31. See Luther's edition of the *Frankfurter Tractate, Theologia Germanica*, trans. Bengt Hoffman (New York: Paulist Press, 1982). Luther's struggles with medieval realism and nominalism were squarely within the speculative neo-Platonic tradition of Rhineland mysticism, and the German translation of this treatise was his first publication effort in 1516. It was only when the Protestant Left reduced religiousness to pure subjectivity that he abandoned or, more accurately, sublimated his mystical interests in order to deal with practical, institutional matters.

32. Ibid.

33. Tom Rockmore develops his arguments in *Hegel's Circular Epistemology* (Bloomington: Indiana University Press, 1986) by way of the *Differenzschrift* (1801)—historically contextualized arguments with which I am entirely agreed. My point here is to show, by way of Lutheran Pietism, that the origins are deeper even than the debate between Fichte, Schelling, Jacobi, Bardili, and Maimon, going back to Luther and the Rhineland tradition of speculative mysticism.

34. See Heidegger, *Hegel's Phenomenology of Spirit*, p. 28.

Chapter Three
PIETISM

1. Hegel in fact says that this "contempt for man" happens only when the Church "abhors reason" (*ETW*, 143; *FS*, 187–88); in other words, the Church is contemptible if and only if it "teaches men to despise civil and political freedom as dung (*als Kot*) in comparison with heavenly blessings and the enjoyment of eternal life" (*ETW*, 138; *FS*, 182), or when, as in the case of Pietism, it attempts to "command feelings" as the substitute for understanding. The majority of Lutherans, however (and Hegel obviously identifies himself with them), have the "good sense" (*der gesunde Menschenverstand*) to reject such notions (*ETW*, 142; *FS*, 186), and in spite of these deformations, "the beautiful spark of reason" is precisely what shows itself most luminously in the history of religion (*ETW*, 145; *FS*, 190).

2. This famous—or *infamous*, depending on one's point of view—"canine" characterization of Schleiermacher's philosophy of religion (or "theology" as the case may be) is to be found in Hegel's *Vorwort* to H. F. W. Henrichs's *Die Religion im inneren Verhältnisse zur Wissenschaft* (Heidelberg: Groos, 1822). Most

of the texts surrounding this debate are to be found in a recent translation and commentary by Eric von der Luft entitled *Hegel, Henrichs, and Schleiermacher on Feeling and Reason in Religion: The Texts of Their 1821–1822 Debate* (Lewiston and Queenston: Mellen Press, 1987). An earlier translation of Hegel's foreword can be found in *Beyond Epistemology*, ed. Frederick Weiss (The Hague: Martinus Nijhoff, 1974), pp. 221–24.

3. The index to the Suhrkamp Verlag edition of Hegel's *Werke* lists only about a half-dozen entries for *Pietismus* and *Frömmigkeit* respectively, the former in volume 1 of his *Lectures on the Philosophy of Religion* and the latter in his *Lectures on the Philosophy of History* and in the famous preface and conclusion to his *Philosophy of Right*. But there are also numerous indirect references and these are what chiefly concern us here.

4. By this approach Emil Fackenheim, in his *The Religious Dimension in Hegel's Thought* (1967), follows the lead of Franz Rosenzweig in the latter's much neglected and still untranslated but highly significant early biographical study of Hegel in *Hegel und der Staat* (1920). Oddly enough, Fackenheim makes no mention of Rosenzweig. Nevertheless, it seems to be the case that Jewish commentators on Hegel have generally been much more careful to situate him against his religious environment than those who are nominally Christian. Alexander Altmann, deeply interested in Rosenzweig throughout his life, was engaged in a major reconstructive study of Hegel prior to his death in 1987. To be sure, formalist interpretations of Hegel have frequently been fueled by reactions to existential-biographical approaches designed to distort Hegel's views to the service of particular ends hence being driven by what Paul Ricoeur calls the "hermeneutics of suspicion" as in the works of George Lukacs and Walter Kaufmann. But this does not obviate the need for an integrative, constructive approach informed by what Ricoeur terms a "hermeneutics of sympathetic reenactment" such as Fackenheim's. Indeed, Jacques Derrida's unconventional *deconstructionist* reading of Hegel's *Phenomenology of Spirit* in *Glas* (1974) should be viewed, in this regard, as hermeneutically reconstructive.

5. See Johannes Hoffmeister, *Dokumente* (1936). Christiane, three years younger than her famous brother, is a primary source for much of the admittedly sparse firsthand biographical information on the early Hegel. The bond between them, however, was close and made closer, as I contend in the next chapter, by her frail emotional condition. Christiane never married and lived vicariously through her brother as women were particularly wont to do in those days. In fact, she suffered an emotional breakdown in 1814 and, like little Ludwig, Hegel's illegitimate son, found happy refuge through the Hegel household, Hegel's wife Maria apparently being congenial to both orphans. It is also unfortunately the case that the detailed notation Christiane provides on the life of her brother extends only through the Bern period (1796) since, being overwhelmed by her personal loss, she committed suicide on 2 February 1832, just two and a half months after Hegel's sudden death on 14 November 1831.

6. Philip Spener, the lifelong friend of G. W. Leibniz, published his now-classic work in 1675, a work that consists, in brief, of a careful delineation of

what is wrong with religion in Germany and how to fix it. See *Pia Desideria*, trans. Theodore Tappert (Philadelphia: Fortress, 1964).

7. F. Ernest Stoeffler, *German Pietism During the Eighteenth Century* (Leiden: Brill, 1973), p. 91. See also Stoeffler's *The Rise of Evangelical Pietism* (Leiden: Brill, 1965). For a definitive bibliography of primary sources see *Bibliographie zur Geschichte des Pietismus. Die Werke der Württembergischen Pietisten des 17. und 18. Jahrhunderts*, part 1, ed. Gottfried Mälzer (Berlin: Walter de Gruyter, 1972).

8. See Lawrence Dickey, *Hegel: Religion, Economics, and the Politics of Spirit, 1770–1807* (Cambridge: Cambridge University Press, 1987). Dickey is entirely correct in pointing out that Württemberg Pietism was of a unique type, being forged, as it were, between Orthodoxy and the separatist tendencies of many Swabian sects. As such, it was a Pietism with an extraordinary vocational-educational emphasis that, while much influenced by the chiliastic eschatological teachings so prominent following the Thirty Years War, had a more far-reaching effect by way of its presence in universities such as Halle and Tübingen.

9. Stoeffler, *German Pietism During the Eighteenth Century* (Leiden: Brill, 1973), pp. 92 and 96.

10. James Martin Estes, *Christian Magistrate and State Church: The Reforming Career of Johannes Brenz* (Toronto: University of Toronto Press, 1982), p. 16. See also *Johannes Brenz. Reformator und Organisator der evangelische Landeskirche in Württemberg*, ed. Hans-Martin Maurer und Kuno Ulshofer (Stuttgart, n.p., 1970).

11. See Christopher Friedrikus Sartorius, *Compendium Theologiae Dogmaticae* (Stuttgart: Mezieri, 1777 and 1782). The Sartorius compendium was the standard *Lehrbuch* in dogmatics at Tübingen during the beginning of Hegel's tenure there as a student. This classic exposition of the catholic symbols of confessional Lutheranism has a typically Protestant-Scholastic form and can in no way be viewed as "antispeculative" in the manner of the biblicist versions by which it was succeeded beginning with those of Storr and Flatt. Hegel, in fact, quotes Sartorius favorably in his "Treatise on the Augsburg Confession" (1830) penned and delivered at the tricentenary in Berlin just one year prior to his death. See *Blätter für württembergische Kirchengeschichte* (1980–81), pp. 204–78.

12. The *Brenzische Katechismum* (Reutlingen: Verlag von Fleischbauer and Spohn, 1860) in fact begins with a prayer for those in the "fellowship of the Holy Spirit" (*die Gemeinschaft des heiligen Geistes*) by making note of the fact that "the great prophet and teacher, Jesus" was "twelve years of age" when he went to the "Temple" to hear and establish "the basis of belief and the teaching of godliness" (*den Grund des Glaubens und die Lehre von der Gottseligkeit*), a feat accomplished by way of *der heilige Geist*, to whom students are exposed in the first section.

13. As Adolf von Harnack puts it with respect to the devotional literature of the period, "Even at the present day we cannot escape the charm that clings to such questions and answers; for they let us see into the living movement of the heart. But he for whom religion has become so serious a matter that he seeks, not for charms, but for nourishment, will not be inclined to exchange

Luther's *Small Catechism* and his hymns for all the wealth, beauty and freshness of the German devotional literature of the 14th and 15th centuries." See *History of Dogma*, vol. 6 (New York: Dover 1961; based on the 3d German ed., 1900), p. 117.

14. See Friedhelm Nicholin, ed., *Der junge Hegel in Stuttgart. Aufsätze und Tagebuchlaufzeichnungen, 1785–1788* (Marbacher Schriften, no. 3, 1970). See also the bilingual (Latin-German) text of Hegel's laudatory contribution to the tricentennary of the Augsburg Confession at the University of Berlin (1830), viz., *Traditae Confessionis Augustanae*, included in Stephan Strohm, "Freiheit des Christenmenschen im Heiligtum des Gewissens," in *Blätter für württembergische Kirchengeschichte* (1980–81), pp. 204–78.

15. See Hans-Georg Gadamer, *Truth and Method* (New York: Seabury, 1975), Part 3. Gadamer's stress on the importance of Pietism in the development of a hermeneutics inclusive of Aristotelian *phronesis*, this being what undergirds his notion of an "integrative" Hegelian hermeneutic. Gadamer makes a great deal of the importance of Luther's *Catechism* and Lutheran Swabian Pietism generally on the development of Hegel's dialectic, and the influence of this religious background in Hegel's rediscovery of the speculative element in Plato's *Sophist, Parmenides*, and *Philebus*. See also *Hegel's Dialectic*, pp. 7–33. Alasdair MacIntyre's recent work in moral philosophy is much influenced by Gadamer's views on Pietist hermeneutics as evidenced, for example, by MacIntyre's insistance that constructive moral theory can best be accomplished when the theorist is part of a "tradition constituted, tradition constituting community." We will say more on this in the chapter on Enlightenment.

16. See Friedrich Christoph Oetinger, *Die Lehrtafel der Prinzessin Antonia*, ed. Reinhard Breymayer and Friedrich Häußermann. *Texte zur Geschichte des Pietismus*, vol. 1, §7 (Berlin: Walter de Gruyter, 1977. In addition to presenting his own theosophy, Oetinger's views on Boehme, Newton, Malebranche, Leibniz, Wolff, Swedenborg, Zinzindorf, Spener and Friedrick the Great are included in this fine volume—together with the "pietistic art" of the princess. It is also interesting to note that one of Oetinger's nieces was Hölderlin's godchild.

17. Ernst Benz, *The Mystical Sources of German Romantic Philosophy*, trans. Blair R. Reynolds and Eunice M. Paul (Allison Park, Pa.: Pickwick Publications, 1983), pp. 50–55. Benz traces the chiliastic element in Bengel directly to Marx where it obviously becomes entirely secularized. See also the comments of Hajo Holborn on Reuchlin's place in the rise of German humanism, in *A History of Modern Germany*, vol. 1, *The Reformation* (Princeton: Princeton University Press, 1982), pp. 110ff.

18. See H. S. Harris, *Hegel's Development: Toward the Sunlight, 1770–1801* (Oxford: Oxford University Press, 1972), pp. 57–96.

19. Stoeffler, *German Pietism During the Eighteenth Century*, p. 108.

20. The principal protagonists of this kind of Pietism in Tübingen during Hegel's time were Johann August Urlsperger (1728–1806) and especially Johann Heinrich Jung-Stilling (1740–1817), who, while trained as a physician, was known as a "man of parts" and won the admiration of Goethe with respect to his "genius" on everything from medicine to economics, philosophy, and

literature. See Stoeffler, *German Pietism During the Eighteenth Century*, pp. 217–65.

21. Education by way of the *Sartorious Compendium*, as it was commonly called in the late eighteenth century, consisted, as in the case of compendia theology generally, of rote memorization of the propositional elaborations of the primary confessional symbols of Lutheran Orthodoxy in a manner not unlike the *Sentinarium* of Peter Lombard. But it was also assumed that the catholic symbols, once mastered, could stand on their own hermeneutically, so to speak, and did not have to be buttressed by additional proofs. C. F. Sartorious's *Compendium* is a masterfully symmetrical work developed in 35 sections, the first being propaedeutic to a general theology and cosmology, a christology, and a pneumatology/ecclesiology with precisely 11.5 sections being devoted to each person of the Holy Trinity. Hegel's *Enzyklopädie*, it will be noted, has the same general organizational shape.

With respect to the pseudo-Kantians, Dieter Henrich notes that the Stift Tutor, Immanuel Diez, probably had more negative influence on Hegel, Schelling, and Hölderlin than either Storr or Flatt, and that Schelling's early monograph, "Vom Ich als Prinzip der Philosophie," was written to protect Kant from harmonization with Lutheran Orthodoxy at the hands of the pseudo-Kantians. See "Some Historical Presuppositions of Hegel's System," in *Hegel and the Philosophy of Religion* (Wofford Symposium), ed. D. E. Christensen (The Hague: Martinus Nijhoff, 1970), pp. 25–60. Hegel's early essay, "On the Positivity of the Christian Religion" (1795–96), is certainly a reaction to these developments, especially to the movement toward biblicism in theology.

22. Hegel is not antihermeneutical in this view. He rather points to the speciousness of what Gadamer later called "the Enlightenment prejudice against prejudice," namely, that the philosophy and theology of the Enlightenment and post-Enlightenment "follows upon a period in which antipathy becomes once more a presupposition" (*LPR* 1, §66). His criticism is not lodged, therefore, against the necessary work of interpretation but against the conceptual deficiency of interpreters, i.e., that their "spirit" is deficient in not realizing that Spirit in its essence is *concept*.

23. F. S. Harris notes this possibility in his impressive biographical-textual study of Hegel. But Harris's contention that Hegel's "relative indifference" to orthodox theology "hardened into firm opposition while he was in Tübingen" holds true only if it is assumed that students were receiving an orthodox theological education at the time, "orthodox" in this case meaning a truly Lutheran education. But as we have already shown, this was not the case, the Catholic character of traditional theology already having been softened by Pietism. See *Hegel's Development*, vol. 1: *Toward the Sunlight, 1770–1801* (Oxford: Oxford University Press, 1972), pp. 57ff. In this connection, see also Eberhard Jüngel's brilliant treatment of "The Death of God" by Hegel and his contemporaries in *God as the Mystery of the World*, trans. Darrell Guder (Grand Rapids: Eerdmans, 1983), pp. 43–104.

24. Karl Barth may be viewed as the Christian thinker of the twentieth century most responsive to Hegel's critique—not least in giving his *Trinitätslehre* first position in the *Church Dogmatics*—a revisioning that repre-

sents a kind of ironic Swiss reversal for the motive that initially motivated the Brenz revision of Luther's *Catechism*. See Eberhard Jüngel, *The Doctrine of the Trinity*, trans. Horton Harris (Edinburgh: Scottish Academic Press, 1976), for a position that explores this view very effectively.

25. Hegel holds to this view throughout his life, especially in the later work, as evidenced by his assertion that the philosophy of Spirit "constitutes the essence of the entire doctrine of religion," that is, *concrete* Spirit, this concreteness being the *spiritual community* (*LPR* 3, §74).

26. See *Blätter für württembergische Kirchengeschichte* (1978), pp. 73–145. The archival documentation, by way of church records, is one of the primary features of this journal, viz., determining the extent to which Württemberg's leading eighteenth- and nineteenth-century literary and philosophical *lights* may or may not be aligned with Pietism. In Hegel's case, as Gerhard Schaffer puts it, the situation is "ambiguous."

27. Harris, *Hegel's Development*, pp. 1–2. Hegel's ancestors had originally immigrated to Württemberg from Austria, being of the Protestant minority there.

28. Such matters, together with a fine summation of Marxist and Freudian interpretations of Hölderlin, can be found in Helen Fehervary, *Hölderlin and the Left: The Search for a Dialectic of Art and Life* (Heidelberg: Carl Winter, 1977). Additional evidence can be found in the "Poems from His Madness," where the questions of *Schuld* and *Gottesmutter* are frequently the same.

29. *Briefe*, vol. 1, ed. Johannes Hoffmeister (Hamburg: Meiner, 1861).

30. Ibid.

31. See T. M. Greene's excellent biographical introduction in Kant's *Religion Within the Limits of Reason Alone* (New York: Harper, 1960), pp. xxvii–xxviii.

32. See Dieter Henrich, "Hegel und Hölderlin," in *Hegel Studien* (Bonn: Bouvier Verlag, 1974), pp. 29ff. I develop Henrich's fascinating observation regarding the silence of Hegel on Hölderlin at length in the next chapters, contending, to the contrary, that Hegel speaks *indirectly* on this matter—especially in his early "Spirit" essay and his extensive disquisition on "madness" (*Verrücktheit*) in the *Enzyklopädie*. Indeed, it is my thesis that between the former and the latter Hegel came to conclude that Romantic preoccupation with "feeling" and "subjectivity" can turn into insanity and that, in fact, he himself was preoccupied with a fear of madness throughout his life—this fear casting yet another angle upon the famous phrase of Hegel regarding the equivalence of the "rational" and the "real." Hence the necessity, in Hegel's view, of sublating sensation and the life of reflection to the logic of the concept and the tendency of Hegel throughout his mature works to identify evil with nature on the notion that "the truth of nature is that nature has no truth."

33. Although little is known about the personal relationship of Hegel and his pastor, it is important to note that the Rev. Griensinger went on to become a bishop. As the rector of the *Landeskirche* in Stuttgart, one might conjecture that he was a man of more than average ability and that his influence upon the young Hegel was considerable. See Franz Wiedmann, *Hegel: An Illustrated Biography*, trans. Joachim Neugroschel (New York: Pegasus, 1968), pp. 12ff.

34. See Harris, *Hegel's Development*, pp. 7–14. Gustav Müller notes, in his *Hegel. Denkgeschichte eines Lebendigen* (Bern: Franke Verlag, 1959), that

throughout his life Hegel never failed to commemorate his mother's birthday. Furthermore, since Hegel deferred the celebration of his own birthday on 27 August to after midnight in order to celebrate it on Goethe's, 28 August, it is clearly the case that Hegel was preoccupied with numerological and other symmetries and synchronicities—even to the point of superstition.

35. Clark Butler and Christine Seiler have caught a bit of this repressive element in their translation and commentary of Hoffmeister's *Hegel Briefe*. See *Hegel: The Letters* (Bloomington: Indiana University Press, 1984). Jacques Derrida's deconstructive reading of Hegel in *Glas* (1974), of course, is almost entirely based upon "suppressed" elements in the Hegelian *Aufhebung*, which, in turn, provided Freud with the structural features of his psychoanalytic method.

36. See *Hegels Briefe*. These points are not missed by Derrida in his deconstructive reading of Hegel in *Glas*. Hegel's first extensive courtship, of course, was with Nanette Endel of Stuttgart, who was Catholic. During this courtship, Hegel viewed his move to Bavaria as an opportunity to become "more familiar" with Catholicism and, we might speculate, with the place of the feminine in Catholicism.

37. The famous *hen kai pan* motto of the three, viz., "Let freedom and reason our watchwords be and the invisible Church our point of union," clearly suggests, of course, that they conceived for themselves a destiny far beyond the mundane fate of the parish ministry. Near the end of his life, Hegel came to regard this motto as being entirely superficial.

38. Ulrich Asendorf misses this point in his otherwise comprehensive but excessively linear *Luther und Hegel. Untersuchungen zur Grundlegung einer neuen systematischen Theologie* (Wiesbaden: Steiner Verlag, 1982).

39. See "Hegels eigenhandiger Lebenslauf" (September, 1804) in *Werke*, vol. 2 (Jena Schriften), pp. 582–83.

40. The letters of Hölderlin and Schelling to Hegel during the Bern period, for example, reveal contempt for "backward" Tübingen and the "dead" who reside there, in contrast, for example, to Jena and Frankfurt. See Hoffmeister, vol. 1, p. 15; Butler and Seiler, pp. 23–54.

41. In the "Positivity" essay, Hegel (anticipating Nietzsche) rejects piety and impiety, *pietas* and *impietas*, on the grounds that they have nothing in common with the Greek expressions *hagion* and *anhagion*, from which they are derived. For the Greeks (highly idealized and romanticized by Hegel prior to 1880), such feelings came from the heart and were not merely commanded— as was the case, Hegel believed, in Christianity. Hence *Frömmigkeit* and *Sünde*, "devotion" and "sin," as these terms are understood in popular religion, are inimical to what Hegel considers desirous in an authentic *Volksreligion* (see *FS*, 212–13; *ETW*, 163–64). But Hegel also recoils from his romanticized conception of the Greeks after his father's death in 1799 and the events of Frankurt (which we address in the next chapters), while clinging to the notion that emotivism in matters religious can lead to madness, viz., that "pious feelings commanded" can lead to an *Angst* culminating in madness (*FS*, 185: *ein Seelenzustand, der oft bis zum Wahnsinn getrieben wird*). These notions regarding "true religion" (and especially Hegel's understanding of the "genuine religious action") serve to establish the path to the *Phänomenologie*, the *Logik* and the *En-*

zyclopädie, as the continuation of this *Aufhebung*. If this is the case, then it is even less likely that he is the author of the much-debated *Systemfragment* (1800), and Dieter Henrich is correct in attributing this text to Hölderlin or, as others have held, to Schelling, since the mediative role of subjective feeling is central in this document. It might be added, finally, that Hegel was also keenly aware of the destructive potentiality of "feeling" in the case of his sister, Christiane—who, as we mentioned above, was frequently overwhelmed by persistent melancholy, and ultimately committed suicide just two and a half months after her brother's death. Even more astonishing is the fact that Hegel himself died on his mother's birthday, and that soon after, as mentioned earlier, his widow "took refuge with the [Berlin] Pietists." See Hegel's *Stammbaum* in Hoffmeister, *Briefe*, vol. 4. Maria Magdelena Louisa (*née* Fromm) Hegel was born on 14 November 1741 and died on 20 September 1783.

42. See especially Hegel's comments in "The Passing Away of the Community," in the *Lecture Manuscript* of his *Lectures on the Philosophy of Religion*, vol. 3, pp. 158–62.

Chapter Four
TRANSCENDENCE

1. The phrase "blazing presence of the Divine" belongs to Donald S. Carne-Ross. See his *Instaurations: Essays In and Out of Literature from Pindar to Pound* (Berkeley and Los Angeles: University of California Press, 1979).

2. Nathan Scott, Jr., *The Wild Prayer of Longing: Poetry and the Sacred* (New Haven: Yale University Press, 1971), p. 7.

3. *Bonaventure*, trans. Ewart Cousins (New York: Paulist Press, 1978), pp. 101–2.

4. Plotinus, *Enneads*, 1.3.1–6.

5. See "The Mystical Theology," in *Pseudo-Dionysius the Areopagite* (New York: Paulist Press, 1987).

6. See Gadamer's discussion of *überwinden* and *verwinden* with respect to the proper understanding of the Hegelian *Aufhebung* in his *Hegel's Dialectic: Five Hermeneutical Studies*, trans. P. Christopher Smith (New Haven: Yale University Press, 1976), pp. 100–102. Gadamer is entirely Hegelian in his understanding of dialectic as distinct from Jaspers, for example, in the latter's treatment of *Three Ciphers of the One* in *Chiffren der Transzendenz* (Munich: Piper Verlag, 1970). In this treatment, otherwise entirely dependent upon Hegel's tripartite mode of organization in his *Lectures on the Philosophy of Religion*, Jaspers argues that there are three paradigm ciphers (symbols) of the One, viz., the purely formal "Impersonal One," as in Plato and Plotinus; the "Personal One," as in the biblical tradition; and the "Incarnate One" of the mystery cults—including Catholic Christianity. But Jaspers rejects the "Incarnate One" as a fraudulent "corporealization of Transcendence," thus choosing to remain, as with Mendelssohn and Buber, with the Kantian dichotomy. Hegel's concern, of course, is with the overcoming of the dichotomy between Athens and Jerusalem through the development of a christological theory of dialectical diremption (*die Trennung*), a theory that shows its first mode of organization in the "Spirit" essay in the dialectics of renunciation.

7. See Flavius Josephus, *The Jewish War*, ed. Gaalza Cornford (Grand Rapids: Zondervan, 1982), book 6, p. 402. Hegel cites this image in the "Spirit" essay (1798–99) and attributes it to Pompey (*ETW*, 192; *FS*, 284), probably by way of Eusebius.

8. See Theodor Adorno, *Negative Dialectics* (New York: Seabury, 1973), esp. Part 1, *The Ontological Need*, and his polemic against Heidegger. Negativity in Adorno's dialectic (and also in the dialectic of Habermas, although to lesser degree) consists precisely in *renunciation of the ontological need*. This is in sharp contrast to what I am here suggesting, viz., that the dialectic of renunciation and the renunciation of renunciation in Hölderlin and Hegel respectively are alternative possibilities with regard to speculative metaphysics and ontology. For a similar inclination, see the arguments of the following: Karl Raschke, "The End of Theology," in *Journal of the American Academy of Religion* 42, no. 2, pp. 173ff.; David Ling, "Mysticism, Poverty, and Reason in the Thought of Meister Eckhart," in ibid., 46, no. 4, pp. 465ff.; the major study of *Abgeschiedenheit* by John Caputo in *The Mystical Dimension in Heidegger* (Athens: Ohio University Press, 1978); and finally Reiner Schurmann, *Heidegger on Being and Acting: From Principles to Anarchy* (Bloomington: Indiana University Press, 1988)—certainly the most intense linguistic study of Heidegger, at least in recent memory.

9. See Nikos Kazantzakis, *The Saviors of God: Spiritual Exercises*, trans. Kimon Friar (New York: Simon and Schuster, 1960); and Samuel Beckett's *Endgame* (New York: Grove Press, 1958). The stage works of Beckett's play, it will be recalled, are constructed to suggest that the players (and viewers) are within an empty skull looking out, from time to time, to see if anything of consequence is happening or, for that matter, if anything at all is happening. Beckett's "an/archaic" view here, to take Schurmann's phrase, is to convey the sense that *nothing* happens in a world bereft of foundations and that only "you . . . remain" as the nonevent in an eventless world.

10. Wallace Stevens, "Esthetique du Mal," in *Palm at the End of the Mind*, ed. Holly Stevens (New York: Random House, 1972), p. 257. Stevens plays brilliantly with the Hegelian and Marxian aspects of "negation" in this poem.

11. See Nathan Scott's negative version of Gerard Manley Hopkins's famous phrase in *The Wild Prayer of Longing*, p. 7.

12. Dante, *Paradiso*, canto 30, trans. Dorothy Sayers and Barbara Reynolds (London: Penguin, 1973), p. 321.

13. See Theodore Roszak, *Where the Wasteland Ends: Politics and Transcendence in Postindustrial Society* (New York: Doubleday, 1972), p. 449.

14. The allusion, of course, is to Richard Rorty's now-famous phrase and the notion that history, having come to an impasse, begs us to "start over." See *The Consequences of Pragmatism* (Minneapolis: University of Minnesota Press, 1983).

15. "This demand [of unsurpassability] obtains because values are essentially absoluteness-claiming: to experience their appeal is to experience the appeal of something that would attract us whoever we were and whoever we conceived ourselves as being, and which would attract us no matter what we happened to be personally interested in." See "The Notion of an Absolute," in J. N. Findlay, *Ascent to the Absolute*, pp. 27–28.

16. The great exception, of course, is Heidegger, whose essays on the poet have galvanized interest in Hölderlin more than any other single factor. See *Existence and Being*, trans. Werner Brock (Chicago: Regnery, 1949). Among the rich, recent German explorations, see Christoph Jamme, *"Ein Ungelehrtes Buch.* Die philosophische Gemeinschaft zwischen Hölderlin und Hegel in Frankfurt, 1797–1800," in *Hegel-Studien*, supplement 23, 1983. See also the recent translation of many of the prose works of Hölderlin during this period, *Friedrich Hölderlin: Essays and Letters on Theory*, trans. and ed. Thomas Pfau (Albany: SUNY Press, 1988).

17. There can be little doubt that both Hegel and Hölderlin greatly envied the glamorous academic life of Schelling in Jena—up to and including the celebrated divorce of Carolina from Augustus. The marriage of Augustus and Carolina, as Ernst Benz points out, had been one of convenience owing to political difficulties caused by her prior participation in events leading up to the French Revolution. Theirs was also the first civil divorce in Germany— being administered, on their behalf, by Goethe, the personal minister of the duke of Weimar. This celebrated divorce, Benz comments, was also "the first and at the time the only consequence of the French Revolution on German soil." *Mystical Sources of German Philosophy*, p. 15.

18. There is every reason to conclude, from the Bern correspondence, that Hölderlin feels he *needs* the rational sobriety of Hegel since, as Clark Butler indicates, it seems to be Hölderlin who initiates this correspondence (see *Letters*, pp. 44ff.). It might also be speculated that Hegel and Hölderlin represent for Heidegger (at least after the *Kehre*), the respective "mountains" of philosophy and poetry, which, he argues, must remain "separate."

19. I say "onerously" because the seemingly anti-Semitic character of assertions in Hegel's early essays has led many commentators to conclude that he was anti-Jewish. Such comments, I think, must be framed against the revolutionary spirit of the times and the general notion that the legacy of everything Byzantine and *Orientalisch* in Christianity was the chief impediment to the progress of the Enlightenment. In any event, Hegel leaves this kind of polemic behind him rather quickly and is himself accused of being a "lover of Jews" during the Berlin period as he champions the principles of emancipation and civil rights. See the insightful articles by Shlomo Avineri, "Hegel Revisited," in *Hegel: A Collection of Critical Essays*, ed. Alasdair MacIntyre (Notre Dame: Notre Dame University Press, 1976), pp. 329–48; and "A Note on Hegel's View of Jewish Emancipation," in *Journal of Jewish Studies* (April 1963). Avineri's reference to the O. H. Gruppe *Hegel-Spiel* (1832) is particularly important, I think, and has a measure of importance that goes far beyond the clarification of Hegel's political views.

20. Hölderlin, in fact, refers to Kant as "the Moses of our nation who leads it out of the Egyptian apathy into the free, solitary desert of his speculation and who brings the rigorous law from the sacred mountain." And he goes on to say, "Of course, they [the Germans] still dance around their golden calves and hunger for their meats, and he [*Kant als Volkeserzieher*] would have to emigrate with them . . . if they were to abstain from the dead customs and opinions which have become heartless and spiritless and under which their better,

more living nature moans as if in a deep dungeon." See *Friedrich Hölderlin: Essays and Letters on Theory*, p. 137.

21. See the conclusions of Albert Schweitzer, *The Quest of the Historical Jesus*, trans. W. Montgomery (New York: Macmillan, 1961), pp. 398–403; first published as *Von Reimarus zu Werde* (1906).

22. Bernard Reardon, *Hegel's Philosophy of Religion* (New York: Harper and Row, 1977), pp. 20ff. This is precisely the motif previously alluded to in Bonaventure.

23. See the fine development of the "educator of the people" motif in James Yerkes, *The Christology of Hegel* (Albany: SUNY Press, 1983), pp. 7–50. In contrast to Yerkes, my argument is that Spirit or pneumatology is the ultimate key to Hegel's *Trinitätslehre*, not christology.

24. See Butler, *Letters*, pp. 46–47. A photographic reproduction of the original draft of Hegel's poem can be seen in Theodor Lorenz Haering, *Hegel, sein Wollen und sein Werk. Eine chronologische Entwicklungsgeschichte der Gedanken und der Sprache Hegels* (Leipzig and Berlin: Verlag and Druck von B. G. Teubner, 1929), as a frontispiece to vol. 1. See Heidegger's commentary on the parallel line in Stephan George, *On the Way to Language*, trans. Peter Hertz (New York: Harper and Row, 1971), p. 67. Many of the principal lines and ideas from "Eleusis" reappear in the "Spirit" essay.

25. See Alessandro Pellegrini, *Friedrich Hölderlin. Sein Bild in der Forschung* (Berlin: Walter de Gruyter, 1965), pp. 75–116.

26. See Pfau, *Hölderlin: Essays and Letters*, pp. 33–116.

27. This is what ultimately underlies the "satisfactions of self-consciousness" for Hegel—not merely success as a category theorist as Robert Pippen implies. The latter, I would argue, is derivative of the former. See Pippin's *Hegel's Idealism: The Satisfactions of Self-Consciousness* (Cambridge: Cambridge University Press, 1989).

Chapter Five
DIALECTIC

1. Donald S. Carne-Ross, *Instaurations: Essays In and Out of Literature from Pindar to Pound* (Berkeley and Los Angeles: University of California Press, 1979), p. 13.

2. See *Friedrich Hölderlin: Poems and Fragments*, trans. and ed. by Michael Hamburger (Ann Arbor: University of Michigan Press, 1967), a bilingual edition based on *Hölderlin. Sämtliche Werke*, ed. Friedrich Beissner (Stuttgart: Kohlhammer, 1961). All subsequent citations of Hölderlin's poetry are from this work.

3. See Alessandro Pellegrini, *Friedrich Hölderlin. Sein Bild in der Forschung* (Berlin: Walter de Gruyter, 1965). The metaphysically speculative character of this poem is brought out in the following passage from his letter to Casimir Ulrich Bohlendorff (1802), where he says: "The contemplation of ancient statuary made an impression on me that brought me closer to an understanding not only of the Greeks, but of what is greatest in all art, which, even where movement is most intense, the conception most phenomenalized and the in-

tention most serious, still preserves every detail in tact and true to itself, so that assuredness, in this sense, is the supreme kind of representation" (quoted by Hamburger, ibid., p. 13). The hymns of Hölderlin were all written in the period immediately following his departure from the Gontard family in 1798 after his difficulties arose.

4. See "On the Difference Between Poetic Modes," in Thomas Pfau, ed., *Hölderlin: Essays and Letters* (Albany: SUNY Press, 1987), p. 83.

5. This is nothing less than the "Greek/Jew is Jew/Greek" dialectic pondered by Derrida. See Jacques Derrida's essay "Violence and Metaphysics" in *Writing and Difference*, trans. Alan Bass (Chicago: University of Chicago Press, 1978), pp. 79–153. Derrida's deconstructive reading of Hegel, especially in *Glas* (1974), is very close to what I attempt to do with Hölderlin here.

6. See Heidegger's famous essay on this passage, "What are Poets for?" in *On the Way to Language*. The beginning of an age guided by Lessing's axiom (1776), viz., "the accidental truths of history cannot be substituted for the necessary proofs of reason," Hegel, and after him, Kierkegaard, are the two post-Enlightenment thinkers most responsive to the dilemmas posed by historicism.

7. Perhaps an ironic allusion to the exchange of Fichte for the incipient *Naturphilosophie* of Schelling?

8. See Walter Biemel, "Poetry and Language in Heidegger," in *On Heidegger and Language*, ed. Joseph Kockelmans (Evanston: Northwestern University Press, 1972), pp. 65–105. In Biemel's words, "The soundless language of the silence is [for Heidegger] the language of abiding Being" (p. 91).

9. Gadamer relates the personal insight that just prior to the publication of "Remembrance of the Poet" (1942) Heidegger attended a lecture in which he [Gadamer] presented an interpretation of *Heimkunft* quite contrary to Heidegger's with respect to the meaning of *nicht*. Heidegger, he said, nodded his head ponderously saying, "Then I am wrong!" Nevertheless he also went on, Gadamer observed, to publish the essay "without changing a word."

10. See Michael Hamburger, *Hölderlin: Poems and Fragments* (Cambridge: Cambridge University Press, 1966), p. 15.

11. This rendering would come closer to the *ousa eiden* of John the Divine's utterance in Revelation 1, 2, viz., "as much as I saw" as distinct from the "all that I saw," which is common in many English translations. See also Hölderlin's "Patmos" in Hamburger.

12. Heidegger, of course, does not think so; it is rather for him the location of place prior to the commencement of ontotheology.

13. "Final," in this case, means the works prior to Hölderlin's committal to the psychiatric clinic in Tübingen in 1807. However, the "poems from his madness," as Hamburger calls them, are also be included here.

14. See Heidegger's "Remembrance of the Poet," in *Existence and Being*, ed. Werner Brock (Chicago: Regnery, 1949), p. 261.

15. This reappropriation, I suggest, concerns Lutheran Pietism—a point overlooked by Heidegger probably because (owing to his problematical Catholic identity) he does not want to recognize this dimension in Hölderlin. For the "overcoming" of metaphysics, for Heidegger, is also the "overcoming" of Protestant Christianity in Germany (as Gadamer also implies), since the grand

tradition of German Idealism is basically the working-out of *Freiheits-Philoso-phie* or what Hegel so frequently refers to as the "Great Protestant Principle of the North." Hence Hegel, as Heidegger makes clear in *Hegel's Phenomenology of Spirit* (Bloomington: Indiana University Press, 1987), and as Gadamer also comments in the last chapter of *Hegel's Dialectic*, is the ultimate object of "overcoming" in a philosophical, religious and, indeed, even a geographical sense for Heidegger. Heidegger's infamous comment regarding the "wonderful hands" of the corporal from Linz, Austria, has something to do with Heidegger's southern German origin—the region from which he scarcely ever strayed his entire life. One can adduce additional support for this surmise from Jaspers's comments on Heidegger in the new edition of the Schilpp festschrift, *The Philosophy of Karl Jaspers*, augmented edition (Peru, Ill.: Open Court, 1981), pp. 75–84, not least Heidegger's refusal to meet with Jaspers in Paris after the war in order to work out their differences. The most recent development of this theme, of course, is in Victor Farías, *Heidegger and Fascism* (Philadelphia: Temple University Press, 1989), where the author attributes Heidegger's anti-Semitism to his "Old Catholic" roots in Swabia. As a kind of deterministic thesis, Farìas's argument is clearly overstated; that provincialism is a problem for Heidegger, as it is for most of us, is certainly true enough.

16. Heidegger, in *Existence and Being*, "Remembrance of the Poet," pp. 251 and 258.

17. See Hans-Georg Gadamer, *Dialectic and Dialogue*, trans. P. Christopher Smith (New Haven: Yale University Press).

18. I do not here discount or minimize the significance of the expressly Catholic character of *gratia praeveniens* as it appears in this poem, for that dimension is clearly present here—especially in the sacramentalistic images of Nature that abound throughout the poem. Nor should it be forgotten that Hegel also expresses interest in finding out more about Roman Catholicism seeking to live, as he puts it during the late Jena period, in a "Catholic city" (Bamburg-Nurenberg) in order to obtain a better understanding of this side of German Christianity. This desire is initially attributed, by Butler and others, to his interest in Nanette Endel, who was Catholic and whom he is courting during the time Hölderlin writes *Heimkunft*; but it may also be attributed to the interest of both Hegel and Hölderlin in the incipient *Naturphilosophie* of Schelling and in that sector of Christianity where images of nature abound, viz., Roman Catholicism. See *Letters*, pp. 57–62.

19. Karl Rahner is very directly influenced by Heidegger's notions regarding the "linguisticality of Being" and language as the "house of Being"—especially in *Hörer des Wortes* and *Geist in der Welt*, the first editions of which appear during the war years. "Spirit" and "Word" respectively are explored phenomenologically as a means of reconciling some of the differences between Catholic and Protestant.

20. Karl Löwith, *From Hegel to Nietzsche: The Revolution in Nineteenth-Century Thought*, trans. David E. Green (New York: Holt, Rinehart and Winston, 1964), p. 19.

21. *Geistlicher Kirchengesang* (Cologne, 1599), trans. Theodore Baker in *Service Book and Hymnal of the Lutheran Church in America* (Minneapolis: Augsburg, 1958). See also the fine article by John Caputo, "The Rose is With-

out Why: An Interpretation of the Later Heidegger," in *Philosophy Today* 15 (1971): 3–15. Caputo views the rose as a "pivotal metaphor" in Heidegger and the line out of Angelus Silesius, which defines Heidegger's *Der Satz vom Grund* (1957). My exposition of the "rose" in Hölderlin vis-à-vis Luther may be viewed as additional evidence to support Caputo's thesis.

22. This joy may be profitably contrasted with the "joy" of Hegel at self-consciousness become "Absolute Consciousness," viz., the "joy of consciousness seeing itself in Absolute Being" in the *Phenomenology*, p. 761.

23. "Jesus, my joy, pasture of my heart, my jewel; how long, how long has my heart longed for you!" BWV 227 (18 July 1723).

24. One of the distinctive features of Hegel's speculative metaphysics, of course, is his insistence that "conceptual comprehension" is not the same as "grasping comprehension"; in other words, that a philosophy of mind or spirit (*Vernunft*) is different from the philosophy of reflection (*Verstand*). Rodolphe Gasché has brought out this point as well as anyone in his *The Tain in the Mirror* (Cambridge: Harvard University Press, 1986) where he correctly, in my view, aligns Derrida with Hegel with respect to a notion of "altarity" that preserves and does not negate the otherness of the Other.

25. See Paul Ricoeur, *Interpretation Theory: Discourse and the Surplus of Meaning* (Fort Worth: TCU Press, 1975), and *The Rule of Metaphor* (Toronto: University of Toronto Press, 1976). Ricoeur follows Hegel here; that is, *symbol* is the product of a dynamic interaction between *Empfindung* and *Vorstellung*, and *metaphor* is the product of the dynamic interaction of *Vorstellung* and *Begriff*. See Ricoeur's important essay, "The Status of *Vorstellung* in Hegel's Philosophy of Religion," in *Meaning, Truth, and God*, Boston University Studies in Philosophy and Religion (Notre Dame: Notre Dame University Press, 1982).

26. See Paul Ricoeur, "The Hermeneutics of Testimony," in *Anglican Theological Review* 61, no. 4 (1979): 431–61. This essay, first published in French in 1972, is now included in *Essays in Biblical Interpretation*, ed. Louis Mudge (Philadelphia: Fortress, 1980). This would seem to be the force of Ricoeur's modification of Hegel's dialectic, namely, "that there is no unitary intuition, no absolute knowledge, in which consciousness would grasp both the consciousness of the absolute and consciousness itself" (p. 456). On the other hand, more recently, Ricoeur acknowledges that it was Hegel, more than any other thinker, who recognized the "inner dynamism" in representational thinking; a dynamism that has led him to recognize not only "that" the "symbol gives rise to thought" but "how" this happens. Thus Ricoeur now concludes that it is "the description of the inner dynamism of the figurative mode that constitutes the Hegelian hermeneutics of religion" (see "On the Status of *Vorstellung* in Hegel's Philosophy of Religion," in *Meaning, Truth, and God*, vol. 3, Boston Studies in Philosophy and Religion [Notre Dame: Notre Dame University Press, 1982])—a point reaffirmed at the end of *Time and Narrative*, vol. 3. (Chicago: University of Chicago Press, 1987). As such, the hermeneutical project may be likened to what we have termed the "genuine religious action" in Hegel; viz., the continuous project of "binding together" experience and representation in "thought." But herein also lies the limit of dialectic, for while the inner dynamism of mythopoetic discourse gives rise to thought (and while

meta-phor presupposes the work of the concept qua *logos*), "the concept is the endless death of representation" for "the concept is nothing apart from the dying process of the representation." And because of the parasitic dependence of the concept on the representation, and the representation on experience, we have, at an epistemic level, an insight into the structural necessity of "circularity" in the hermeneutic process, namely, as Ricoeur asserts in the *Vorstellung* essay, "the necessity of starting from, and returning to, the moment of immediacy in religion, be it called religious experience, Word-Event, or Kerygmatic Moment."

27. See the Gifford Lectures of J. N. Findlay, *The Discipline of the Cave* and *The Transcendence of the Cave* (London: Allen and Unwin, 1967), esp. the latter, pp. 200–220.

28. See Paul Ricoeur, *The Symbolism of Evil*, pp. 306ff.; and *The Conflict of Interpretations* (Evanston: Northwestern University Press, 1974), pp. 227–334.

Chapter Six
MADNESS

1. See Hoffmeister, *Briefe*, vol. 1, esp. nos. 38 and 97. This does not mean, of course, that Hölderlin was not otherwise discussed. It simply means that there is no longer an extant record of such references. But since Hegel died in 1831 and Hölderlin in 1843, it was possible for Hegel to see him during twenty-three of the thirty-five years of Hölderlin's confinement. The other glaring omission in Hegel's works is reference to Ludwig van Beethoven, born in Bonn in the same year as Hegel, 1770. This omission is much less troubling for two reasons: first, the fact that Beethoven's father lied about his age, stating that he was born in 1775 (the same year as Schelling) in order to give the impression that he was at least as much of genius as Mozart; and second, Hegel's seemingly limited or underdeveloped musical taste, as William Desmond has pointed out, ran toward Rossini! It is the visual sense that captures Hegel's concept of beauty and Rossini probably provided this for him in a rather uncomplicated way. See *Aesthetics*, vol. 2, pp. 888–958, and William Desmond, *Art and the Absolute: A Study of Hegel's Aesthetics* (Albany: SUNY Press, 1986).

2. See Dieter Henrich, "Hegel and Hölderlin," in *Hegel im Kontext* (Frankfurt: Suhrkamp Verlag, 1971), pp. 9–40. The dominant aesthetical and mythological themes in this "fragment" regarding a "System-Program for German Idealism" (*FS*, 234–36) evidence the Romanticism driving the views of Hölderlin, Schelling, and Hegel during the early part of the Frankfurt period. But because both Hölderlin and Schelling were more "fixed" in these views than Hegel, and because Hegel quickly departed Romanticism after 1800, it might be speculated that if Hegel is the author, especially of the *Systemfragment* dated in the same year, he is merely playing with the views of Hölderlin or Schelling in a tentative manner. See Otto Pöggeler's argument for Hegel's authorship, "Hegel, der Verfasser des altestern Systemprogramms des deutchen Idealismus," in *Hegel-Studien*, supplement 4. But even if this fragment is the copy of

a portion of Hölderlin's 1797 treatise "On Religion," as the editors of the Frankfurt edition of Hölderlin's works contend, what is significant for our purpose is determining the extent of thematic parallel in these works and the "Spirit" essay of Hegel dated between 1797 and 1800. The sudden break at the end of this essay, in addition to Hegel's attempt to rewrite the final section of his "Positivity" essay, might also suggest a break with the aesthetical-mythological theme of the work; hence its fragmentary condition.

3. It should be pointed out that Hegel's style, on such matters, does not vary in his personal correspondence—even with "matters of the heart," as can be easily noted in his letters to Nanette Endel during the Frankfurt period, and in the letters to his betrothed, Maria von Tucher, during the Nuremberg period. See the letters in Butler and Seiler under the heading "Hegel's Idea of Marriage: Science or Ideology?" pp. 234–53.

4. See Michael Shodell's article, "The Clouded Mind," in SCIENCE 84. The Tübingen neurologist, Alois Alzheimer, first described the disease in an article entitled "Concerning a Unique Illness of the Brain Cortex" in 1906. "Alzheimer was the first to show," Shodell writes, "that senile dementia was not just a natural wearing out of the mind," and that the "inability to remember recent events" is the first sign of onset. One of the most remarkable features of Hölderlin's dementia was the fact that when Sinclair told him (in 1802) that Susette had died, he seemed unable to connect with its implication. See Adolf Beck, ed., *Hölderlins Diotima, Susette Gontard* (Frankfurt: Insel Verlag, 1980), pp. 156–62.

5. Hegel's comments on "siderism" to Schelling in the letter of 1 May 1807 and the "magnetic fusion" of "higher and lower natures" may have something to do with the "treatment" Hölderlin is receiving in Tübingen. See Hoffmeister, *Briefe*, vol. 1, no. 95; Butler, *Letters*, p. 79.

6. Hegel spells this out in detail in his *Rechtsphilosophie* (1821), in which the subjective conditions of morality (and conscience) are formally transitional to "ethical life" (§§105–41).

7. As we have previously noted, Hegel was preoccupied with the name Maria, the given names of his maternal grandmothers for several generations being Maria Magdalena. See Hoffmeister, *Briefe*, vol. 1, no. 186, pp. 367–69.

8. See Soren Kierkegaard's *Philosophical Fragments*, trans. David Swenson (Princeton: Princeton University Press, 1936) and, of course, its predecessor, *Concluding Unscientific Postscript*. Kierkegaard's subscript about whether "a historical point of departure can lead to an eternal consciousness or whether it is of merely historical interest" is inspired by Lessing's "broad ugly ditch," to wit, that "accidental truths of history cannot be substitute for the necessary truths of reason." A similar enigma exists for Hegel but Hegel's point of reference is to the Parmenidean-Plotinian tradition of speculative mysticism in which the *mathematici* have supremacy over the *acousmatici*.

9. For example, in the lengthy *Zusatz* to the *Enzyklopädie*, §408, Hegel says that the most important question regarding the philosophical meaning of madness is not "how does the mind become insane. . . . Rather the converse, namely, how does the soul, shut up in its *inwardness* and is immediately identical with its individual world, emerge from the merely *formal*, empty difference

of the subjective and the objective and attain to the *actual* difference of these two sides, and thus to the *truly objective* rational and intellectual consciousness?" The answer, he says, comes in the "last four paragraphs of the first part of the doctrine of subjective spirit," namely, *Der freie Geist* (*E*, §§481, 482). We will comment more on this in the final chapter, *Free Spirit*.

10. J. N. Findlay was convinced that Hegel was wrong on this point, namely, that the typical distinction between humans and other sentient creatures (especially the higher domestic mammals) with respect to feeling and mental reflection was and is another form of self-serving anthropocentrism. Findlay's favorite illustration came from the observation of cats not only "enjoying themselves" but "knowing that they are enjoying themselves." Even if Findlay is correct on this point (and I am inclined to believe that he is), this does not invalidate the observation of Hegel that what we call "evil" is deeply rooted in the dialectic of feeling and self-feeling, in other words, that feeling's first mediation is in the lower mental state of first reflection and "too sunk" into nature to know the difference between the "in-itself" and the "for-itself" with respect to determining whether an action is properly constructive or destructive as, for example, in the case of a dog that "goes bad." See Findlay's essay "Confessions of Faith and Life," in *Meaning, Truth, and God*, ed. Leroy Rouner (Notre Dame: Notre Dame University Press, 1984).

11. See *Lectures on the Philosophy of History*, where this criticism is particularly explicit.

12. Jaspers's famous statement from *Die Atombombe und die Zukunft des Menschen* "Philosophy alone yields clarity against the perversion of reason," is informed by the Hegelian distinction regarding the superiority of *Vernunft* to *Verstand*, the former being inclusive of moral consciousness whereas the latter is not. See my article "Glasnost and Enlightenment," in *Philosophy Today* 34, no. 2 (Summer 1990): 99–110.

13. See Terry Pinkard, *Hegel's Dialectic: The Explanation of Possibility* (Philadelphia: Temple University Press, 1988). I am entirely in agreement with Pinkard's thesis that, for Hegel, "philosophy is primarily a particular form of explanatory enterprise"—and what makes it different from other forms of explanatory enterprise is showing how it is the case that "beliefs" are possible (p. 4).

14. It is the *concept* that is important here, not merely the *idea* or *logos* in the general sense. For mentally deranged individuals also have access to some form of *logos*; what they lack is the ability to differentiate true ideas from false ideas conceptually.

15. His generally pejorative usage of *Leiblichkeit* obviously also indicates how far Hegel has traveled from his earlier infatuation with the speculative neo-Pietism of Oetinger and Schelling.

16. Hegel's predilection for the kenotic christology of Saint Paul is entirely consistent with this view. See *Phänomenologie* and the famous treatment of *Kenosis* there; see also James Yerkes, *The Christology of Hegel* (Albany: SUNY Press, 1983).

17. As such, the cosmological element in Plato and the teleological element in Aristotle are reconciled in the eschatology of Spirit, as it were.

18. The implication, for Hegel, is that empiricism necessarily follows from the British soul being "stuck" in nature or sense-certainty.

19. It is interesting to note that Findlay regards this section as somewhat "confused" (possibly owing to Hegel's pejorative references to the British), especially as regards the "barely noticeable transition" from the "feeling soul" to "self-feeling" manifest as "insanity" or madness. However, if Hölderlin is viewed as a critical point of historical reference, a key element in this transition may be located in Hegel's comment that when the soul is especially "sunk" into itself, trapped within emotion, it seems to want "to have itself . . . in another person" (*E*, 297). The absent Other is particularly manifest in Hölderlin's eloquent poem "Menon's Lament for Diotima," where, as we have seen, he hovers at the edge of this dialectic without being finally able to overcome it—the reason being, as Hegel would have it, that the dialectic is ultimately controlled by the image of what is lost and not by the concept.

20. Dietrich von Englehart, for example, argues that Hegel's notion of illness and medicine hovers "somewhere between empiricism and metaphysics"—an observation that has merit only if it is assumed that illness can only be properly understood as an empirical reality. Here we are concerned with psychological states that have yet to be domesticated by the so-called exact sciences, and Hegel's position still has much to commend it when viewed within an overall theory of consciousness that, obviously, was his primary intention. See "Hegel's Philosophical Understanding of Illness" (*Krankheitsbegriff*), in *Hegel and the Sciences*, ed. Robert S. Cohen and Marx Wartofsky, Boston Studies in the Philosophy of Science, vol. 64 (Dordtrecht: Reidel, 1984), pp. 123–41. See also Hegel's "Confessions Regarding Hypochondria," in Hoffmeister, *Briefe*, vol. 1, pp. 314–15.

21. This parallels the "return to the womb" sensibility identified by psychologists after Freud (who, no doubt, was greatly influenced by this section). The womb experience, for Hegel, is his primary example of "self-feeling in its immediacy" (*E*, §405, Z) and the biogenetic reference point for "dream states" in which not only temporal order is dissolved but also the "otherness of the Other," since the soul of the child and the mother are one. The spiritual goal of philosophy, then, is the recovery of this unity once sundered in birth *not* through immediacy (as Jesus also suggests in his famous discourse with Nicodemus in Saint John's Gospel 3.1–15) but through the mediation of Spirit.

22. The biblical parallel to Hegel's analysis, of course, is the cogent reflection of Jesus that "the Spirit is willing but the flesh is weak," for, as we will see, madness is ultimately a deficiency in Spirit—Hegel's understanding of Spirit obviously being far more interfused with *logos* than was the case with Jesus, St. John the Evangelist's prologue notwithstanding.

23. Hegel's fascination with the "unforgivable sin" and the blasphemous "sin against the Holy Spirit" parallels his discussion of madness and his rational understanding of *Geist* is brought to bear upon it in a similar way. According to Lutheran theology, "one is utterly lost," so to speak, when one has willfully placed oneself in the unhappy position of no longer being able to respond to the "call" of Spirit, the dialectic of Spirit having collapsed, as it were, just as consciousness collapses in madness. Although such a position raises questions in the area of theodicy, it also affirms the reality of freedom.

Hegel thought that rationalists had "trivialized" this doctrine to the point of making it theologically inconsequential, the reason being that theologians no longer understood Spirit: "for Spirit alone is the power that can itself sublate everything. Spirit has only to deal with itself in the element of the soul, of freedom, of spirituality; it does not continue to stand over against natural being or action and deed. Only Spirit is free; its energy is not restricted. There is no power that is equal to it or that can come against it; no mechanistic or spiritless relationship is possible." See *Lectures on the Philosophy of Religion*, vol. 3, §165; see also §§77–79.

24. It was precisely this discontinuity that so astonished Schlegel and Teick, who noted, by way of Sinclair in 1807, that Hölderlin's poetry still remains "incomparable." See Hoffmeister, *Briefe*, vol. 1, no. 97.

25. See *Hölderlin*, ed. Bernard Zeller, Marbacher Kataloge, no. 33, (Munich: Kösel Verlag, 1980), pp. 82–83. Hölderlin's *Reisepaß* (passport) for his trip between Nürtingen and Regensburg during the fall of 1802 provides the following information about his person: *6 Fuß hoch, braunen Haaren, hoher Stirne . . . braunen Augen, gerader Nase, röthlichen Wangen . . . schmalen Lippen, angelaufenen Zähnen . . . runden Kinn, länglichtem Angesicht, breiten Schultern, und ohne Gebrechen.*

26. One can also abstract from this "individualized" understanding of the soul's development to the development of society generally. Indeed, it would certainly be Hegel's view that the society that venerates "individualism" more than any other value, that places "free expression" first on the scale of rights irrespective of moral consequences, is a society gone mad. One may have *Gesellschaft* in the formal sense, but no *Gemeinschaft*, since a "community" of fellowship presupposes the kind of constructive moral habituation that makes a "civil society" possible. See Hegel's *Rechtsphilosophie*, §182–256.

27. This condition is particularly evident in the confused agitation of Alzheimer's victims, viz., how in the midst of their confusion they somehow know that they are confused but are now unable to do anything about it—the loss of "constructive habituation" being progressive and ultimately complete. The plea of "temporary insanity" (admittedly controversial) is also based on the notion that people can and do sometimes lose control of their faculties—in this case, *moral* faculties—becoming strangers to all that is human with respect to judgment and value.

28. These issues, of course, are explored at length in the *Rechtsphilosophie*, which, in the context of Hegel's philosophy as pneumatology, may be viewed as his substitute for the ecclesial articulation of the meaning of Spirit in the *Dritte Hauptartikel* of the *Credo*.

29. Jaspers's notion of *periechontology* is directly dependent upon Hegel's notion of the *encyclos* or "circling round" of thinking. Hegel obviously would have difficulty with the *ontology* part of this construction, *pneumatology*, in my estimate, being closer to what is the case. See Tom Rockmore, *Hegel's Circular Epistemology* (Bloomington: Indiana University Press, 1986), on the matter of "circularity" in Hegel's epistemology.

30. See E. M. Butler, *The Tyranny of Greece over Germany: A Study of the Influence Exercised by Greek Art over the Great German Writers of the Eighteenth, Nineteenth, and Twentieth Centuries* (Cambridge: Cambridge University Press, 1935;

reprint, Boston: Beacon Press, 1958). "There was something unearthly" about Hölderlin, she writes; "other [great] poets have greater range . . . but no one has ever reached the same dizzy heights . . . he was almost that spiritual freak, a pure poet." Perhaps that is why no one could understand him, why Schiller and Goethe were "threatened" by his vision and why, when he fell, like Icarus, "he fell so far" (p. 206).

Chapter Seven
ENLIGHTENMENT

1. Alasdair MacIntyre, *After Virtue* (Notre Dame: Notre Dame University Press, 1981), p. 87. MacIntyre's arguments on this and related topics in ethics and moral philosophy continue in *Whose Justice? Which Rationality?* (Notre Dame: Notre Dame University Press, 1988), and most recently in his 1988 Gifford Lectures, *Three Rival Versions of Moral Enquiry: Encyclopedia, Genealogy, and Tradition* (Notre Dame: Notre Dame University Press, 1990).

2. See Alasdair MacIntyre, *Three Rival Versions of Moral Enquiry*, p. 225.

3. Ibid., p. 230. The preliberal university was, therefore, a combination of "enforced and constrained agreements"—"enforced" with respect to discriminatory practices that were and are clearly "wrong," but "constrained" with respect to whether a given rationally justified conclusion was "good" for the community.

4. Ibid., p. 88.

5. The most startling recent example of this, of course, is the near-total rejection of Marxian functionalist conceptions of the state in Eastern Europe on the grounds of being nonfunctional. Another example is evidenced by the neoconservative shift in major segments of the black community in America upon discovering that the overall quality of communal life in the black neighborhoods of urban America was in many ways better "prior" to the time social programs were designed to improve it. For obvious reasons, social scientists dominated by instrumentalist rationality are unable to see the larger implications of this pragmatic judgment since it places instrumentalist rationality into question.

6. In the late 1980s, this once-theoretical objection has become "material," so to speak, as those societies, themselves the products of positivistic planning and applied Marxist "totalism," desperately strive to throw off the yolk of self-imposed oppression. The great irony to appear out of Marx's material "inversion" of Hegel's dialectic of Spirit, then, is that it swallows up dialectic. Hence Marx's critique of Hegel, as applied, becomes the basis of its own falsification through the loss of Spirit. See my article "Glasnost and Enlightenment," in *Philosophy Today* 34, no. 2 (Summer 1990): 99–110.

7. Not all social scientific projects, to be sure, claim emancipatory power; many are simply diagnostic. Nevertheless, the assumption underlying the justification for such exercises is linked to tacit acceptance of the truth of Marxist and neo-Marxist rhetoric regarding "false consciousness"—it being assumed that what is the case should not be and that social science can both identify the causes and supply the remedies. Obviously this assumption today is being dra-

matically turned against itself by those who are themselves the products of so-called emancipatory praxis (especially in what was formerly identified as the Soviet Bloc) as the reformers of Marxian economics are confronting the momentous task of weaning individuals away from the paternalistic, bureaucratic mind-set generated by "collective consciousness."

8. See *Whose Justice? Which Rationality?*, p. 339. This argument is continued very effectively in MacIntyre's Gifford Lectures by way of pointing out that the shortcoming of the encyclopaedist and the genealogical approaches to moral theory lies in being unable to move beyond what is "good" for research and "good" for the individual to questions of the "common good." To do so requires one to be connected or hermeneutically reconnected with the "tradition constituted, tradition constituting" community—which is precisely what the marginalized critic refuses to do.

9. I say "cautiously" in order to avoid a direct identification of MacIntyre with Jean-Francois Lyotard—to whose analyses of the dilemmas of postmodernity MacIntyre's views are at some levels strikingly similar, but from whose answers (or the lack thereof) they are completely different. MacIntyre obviously is quite unsympathetic with most of what transpires in the discourse of postmodernity—especially deconstruction, since it pursues genealogy with a vengeance. He cites, for example, the "bad faith" of Giles Deleuze's "nomadic strangers," who, like Jacques Derrida, "choose" to remain "within" while remaining "strangers" to the "already constructed social and intellectual edifice . . . but only in order to deconstruct it from within." See *Whose Justice? Which Rationality*, p. 369.

10. It is Cicero, of course, who, in the sufficiently pluralistic context of the Greco-Roman world, comes up with *relegare* ("to tie back or bind") as the expression best suited to what we would call religious behavior in the service of *numen* or the gods. Hegel himself would later conclude, on the basis of Cicero's observations, that far from being the "most religious," the Romans were probably the "least religious" of peoples, the Roman religion of "expedience" being synonymous with the instrumental devaluation of the sacred. See *Lectures on the Philosophy of Religion*, vol. 2. MacIntyre, in fact, makes this connection in *Three Rival Versions* with respect not only to religion but also to art (p. 191).

11. The absence of a convincing "metanarrative," of course, is precisely Jean-Francois Lyotard's argument in *The Postmodern Condition* (Minneapolis: University of Minnesota Press, 1979).

12. See Gadamer's analysis of Pietist hermeneutics in *Truth and Method*, and my chapter on Pietism.

13. See Hayden White, *Metahistory: The Historical Imagination in 19th Century Europe* (Baltimore: Johns Hopkins University Press, 1973).

14. The media—especially television, given its vast influence—is particularly vulnerable to the charge of deformation since the structures of format convention are designed exclusively for the marketing of commercial products. See *Video Icons and Values*, ed. Alan M. Olson, and Christopher and Debra Parr (Albany: SUNY Press, 1990).

15. As MacIntyre observes, post-Enlightenment diagnosticians of alienation and "normlessness"—even up to and including Durkheim, could not per-

ceive the time in which anomie would itself become the normative intellectual condition and even be "assigned the status of an achievement" (*Whose Justice? Which Rationality?*, p. 368). Those involved with teaching in the humanities nowadays should be able to recognize the spuriousness of preoccupation with criticism when dealing with classic texts since students rarely have any first-hand familiarity with these texts. This is a marked departure from the time when this familiarity could be presupposed, a period that gave rise to the remarkable century of criticism that unfolded between 1850 and 1950, and within whose context such efforts made sense. What has now taken place, however, as Jaspers was one of the first to note, is degeneration into "the dead-end of interpreting interpretations" (see the *Entmythologisierung* debate between Jaspers and Bultmann in *Myth and Christianity* [New York: Noonday Press, 1958]).

16. See Peter Berger, *The Capitalist Revolution: Fifty Propositions about Prosperity, Equality, and Liberty* (New York: Basic Books, 1986).

17. See John R. Silber, "The Mythic Roots of Morality," in *Meaning, Truth, and God*, ed. Leroy S. Rouner (Notre Dame: Notre Dame University Press, 1982); and Peter Berger, *The Homeless Mind* (New York: Doubleday, 1979).

18. See Jean-Francois Lyotard, *The Postmodern Condition: A Report on Knowledge*, trans. Geoffrey Bennington and Brian Massumi (Minneapolis: University of Minnesota Press, 1984).

19. For example, Allan Bloom in *The Closing of the American Mind* (Chicago: University of Chicago Press, 1986).

20. *Whose Justice? Which Rationality?*, p. 398.

21. This is the aforementioned Achilles' heel, of course, to all arguments regarding the revitalization of "moral education" in strictly academic contexts either through a return to a "Great Books" curriculum or through "applications" of ethics. For as MacIntyre points out very effectively, it is not a question of *content* that is deficient, but *how to read, criticize*, and *interpret* classical or any other content. The deficiency, in short, is hermeneutical. With this judgment, MacIntyre seems to agree entirely with Hans-Georg Gadamer—his major difference being that it is Scottish Enlightenment, and not the German, that affords his historical point of reference. Nevertheless, Gadamer's distinction between the "reconstructive" option afforded by Schleiermacher and the "integrative" option afforded by Hegel parallels MacIntyre's distinction between genealology and encyclopaedia—encyclopaedia, in Gadamer's case and Hegel's, being understood not in the sense of the French and British encyclopaedists but in Hegel's sense, in which tradition is encompassed by Hegel's unique understanding of *Encyklopädie*. See Gadamer, *Truth and Method*, part 1.

22. See Stanley Rosen, *G.W.F. Hegel: An Introduction to the Science of Wisdom* (New Haven: Yale University Press, 1974). "One cannot understand Hegel's philosophy of history, nor his political and religious teaching," Rosen argues, "without understanding his logic" (p. 46). Rosen's way into Hegel as a philosopher of history, as in the case of Klaus Hartmann, is through his "science of logic" or what he terms, perhaps more accurately, "science of wisdom" (p. 16). Although it is not always clear what Rosen means by "wisdom," he is correct in asserting that Hegel's logic is different from ordinary logic, in the sense of

NOTES TO CHAPTER SEVEN **191**

being existentially and metaphysically "integrative," as Gadamer would put it. For it is Hegel's intent, according to Rosen, to develop a mode of logic that will "resolve" the "conflict between the ancients and the moderns" (p. 16). In so doing, Hegel does not reach for an occult, primordial kind of "wisdom," at least not as that term is understood by some. It arises rather out of Hegel's familiarity with the classics and, indeed, his return to the classics, as I also attempt to show in the final chapters on Absolute and Free Spirit. As such, Hegel is to Kant what Plato was to the Eleatics, with Heraclitus being the "key" mediating figure; indeed, Zeno prepares the way for Heraclitus as Kant prepares the way for Fichte and Schelling. For Hegel, according to Rosen, sees an inversion of the insight of the Skeptics in these two epochs; the former being skepticism regarding the nature of the external world but confidence in the principle of contradiction, whereas the latter skepticism has confidence regarding phenomena but skepticism regarding the nature of mind. To this end, then, Hegel develops an encompassing theory of consciousness that can "resolve" this conflict through the development of a theory of consciousness rooted, as Rosen argues, in his philosophy of Spirit (p. 21). Consciousness is the "bond of Being," so to speak, which encompasses "identity and non-identity" and without this, viz., consciousness qua *Geist* or *logos*, one necessarily sinks into nihilism (p. 25).

I take issue, however, with Rosen's contention that Hegel's primary motive, from the outset, is the development of a revolutionary kind of logic. Certainly it is primary in his works after 1800, but "how" this comes to be the case becomes evident only if one pays close attention to the early so-called theological writings. While Rosen is certainly wise in commending the reader to avoid some of the numerous studies of the "early" Hegel, especially what he terms "intellectual biographies" and the highly speculative notions informing these works, one cannot so easily discount the religio-biographical factor in Hegel's development. Thus against Rosen's contention that christology, for Hegel, is a sign of the "harmony" between the temporal and the eternal (p. 14), and against Rosen's suggestion that Hegel is an "anti-mystic" (p. 15), I would argue precisely the contrary. Obviously, the weight of such a counterposition presupposes agreement with respect to such terms as "christology" and "mysticism"—which is not easy to achieve, especially in the case of Hegel. In my view, christology has to be understood, in Hegel, very strictly through Luther, where, far from being a sign of "harmony," it is a sign of scandal, conflict, and paradox—not "paradox" in its extreme Kierkegaardian form, even though Kierkegaard depends on Hegel for this formulation. It is pneumatology that provides the basis for what Rosen calls "harmonization," that is, a philosophy of Spirit—not in the sense of harmonization, rather, as the basis for coherent comprehension. Similarly, one must differentiate between "mysticism" in the ordinary sense and "speculative" mysticism, a differentiation that may be best understood by way of the four primary models of yoga: Bhakti and Karma corresponding to what I call conventional, devotional mysticism; and Raja and Janna corresponding to what I term speculative, conceptual mysticism. That Hegel himself became aware of such subtleties is clearly evident in the difference between his 1827 and 1831 *Lectures on the Philosophy of Religion*.

Finally, given the fact that Rosen views Hegel's *Trinitätslehre* as the "paradigm" for the overcoming of the subject-object problem in Hegel's doctrine of Spirit, I find his antireligious interpretation somewhat odd (pp. 47ff.). What Rosen fails to appreciate, as in the case of so many commentators, is the extent to which the very early Hegel is influenced by Pietism and the symbolical residue of Luther's exposition of the *Credo*. To be sure, Hegel's treatment of the conventional symbols of dogmatical theology is "novel" and highly speculative. But the motive for this treatment is clearly religious—otherwise Hegel would have abandoned altogether his theological background. Hence Rosen's conclusion that "if Hegel was a Christian, he belonged to a sect of which he was the only member" (p. 10) betrays an undisclosed notion of what he thinks it means to "be a Christian" in the first instance. Hegel's Christianity, I would argue, is entirely consistent with Kant's views on the Enlightenment, viz., the "speculative" hermeneutical treatment of "Orthodoxy" as precisely the dialectic between *Glauben* and *Wissen*. One cannot have the one without the other.

23. See Bernard J. F. Lonergan, *Insight: An Inquiry into Human Understanding* (New York: Philosophical Library, 1956).

24. See editor's note no. 255 in Hegel's *Lectures on the Philosophy of Religion*, vol. 3, trans. Peter Hodgson, and the reference to Schelling's treatise *On University Studies*, trans. E. S. Morgan (Athens: Ohio University Press, 1966).

25. See especially Jürgen Habermas, *The Philosophical Discourse of Modernity* (Cambridge: MIT Press, 1987).

26. Quotations from Kant's essay on Enlightenment are from the Modern Library edition of *Kant's Moral and Political Writings*, ed. Carl Friedrich (New York: Random House, 1949).

27. Ibid., p. 133.

28. See Karl Jaspers, *Chiffren der Transzendenz* (Munich: Piper Verlag, 1970). See also my *Transcendence and Hermeneutics: An Interpretation of the Philosophy of Karl Jaspers* (The Hague: Martinus Nijhoff, 1979).

29. Karl Popper, Leo Strauss, Eric Voegelin, Karl Jaspers, and Hermann Cohen are much closer to Kant than to Hegel on the meaning of Enlightenment—even though this proximity is frequently based on "totalistic" misinterpretations of Hegel, or come indirectly by way of deferral to the authority of the Marxist or neo-Marxist interpretations of Hegel (so influential in the mid-twentieth century) as being the inevitable consequence of Hegel's positions. Moreover, Hegel, for all of the above (including Jaspers, although he never develops Hegel's philosophy in any systematic way even though Jaspers's own system can be viewed as but an existentialized version of Hegel), remains suspect if not the arch-villain of the post-Enlightenment since his displacement of the moral law in Kant by the dialectic of consciousness opens the way, in their view, for the "new tribalism," as Popper puts it, and the "black magic," in Voegelin's view, that culminates in national socialism. What is significant about their views regarding Hegel is the extent to which such distortions and misinterpretations were lionized by the "free West" during the post–World War II "Cold War" period. This was particularly the case with exiles (Paul Tillich being a notable exception), who tended to look upon the tradition of German Idealism as the primary source of the world's difficulties. Other dialectical thinkers, most notably the Frankfurt group—Adorno, Horkheimer, and Ben-

jamin—remained elitist within the very system that made "critical thinking" possible—while ever longing, so it seems, and however aesthetically, for the very totality that would falsify it.

30. See Luther's "Treatise on Christian Liberty," in *Three Treatises* (Philadelphia: Fortress, 1943).

31. Ibid., pp. 134–36.

32. This notion follows from the Pauline assertion in Galatians 5.1: "For freedom Christ has set us free; therefore stand fast and do not again submit to the yoke of bondage"—the notion that informs not only the classic Lutheran distinction between Law and Gospel but also Luther's *Freiheits-Prinzip* as this notion is carried over into both Kant and Hegel. In his *Commentary on Galatians* (1535) Luther in fact asserts that "faith is the dialectic which conceives the idea of whatever is to be believed," the rhetoric of faith (hope) being its practical, existential application (faith active in love). These elements are to be kept formally distinct, according to Luther, especially when it comes to understanding the nature of freedom, which, he asserts in the same commentary, has strictly to do with matters of conscience and consciousness (see *WA*, 40, 3, and 11; and *WA*, 40, 27, and 18, in *Middleton Text* [1575] prepared by Philip S. Watson [London: James Clarke and Co., 1953], pp. 441–64). See also Gerhard Forde, *The Law-Gospel Debate: An Interpretation of Its Development* (Minneapolis: Augsburg, 1969).

33. See *Religion Within the Limits of Reason Alone*, trans. T. M. Greene and H. H. Hudson (New York: Harper and Row, 1960).

34. Jaspers's position in *Vernunft und Widervernunft in unserer Zeit* (Munich: Piper Verlag, 1950) is thoroughly Kantian in this regard.

35. Ibid., pp. 138–39.

36. See T. M. Greene's introduction to *Religion Within the Limits of Reason Alone* (New York: Harper and Row, 1960), p. xxx. Nevertheless, in fairness to Kant, this comment need not be taken in the pejorative sense in which it was probably reported. It is rather the case that the *Small Catechism* was regarded by Kant and Hegel as being superior in content and implication to most of the theological writings of the day.

37. I share the view of Peter Fuss and John Dobbins (the translators of some of the first essays of Hegel, including a portion of the so-called "Tübingen" essay on *Volksreligion* and *Christentum* (1793–94), that the mature Hegel's thinking is entirely consistent, at least in religious and metaphysical intent, with his earliest works. In other words, Hegel may have changed his mind about the meaning of empirical particulars, but the overall intentional structure of his horizon does not change in any dramatic way. The most dramatic change, with respect to empirical particulars (if it may be so called), has to do with his attitude toward Romanticism. See *Hegel: Three Essays, 1793–1795* (Notre Dame: Notre Dame University Press, 1984).

38. See Findlay's Gifford Lectures, *The Discipline of the Cave* and *The Transcendence of the Cave* (London: Allen and Unwin, 1966 and 1967 respectively), and *Ascent to the Absolute* (London: Allen and Unwin, 1970).

39. See Ricoeur's *The Rule of Metaphor* (Toronto: University of Toronto Press, 1975), especially the final studies on Heidegger.

40. In raising this question, Hegel of course anticipates the dilemma of

Nietzsche's Madman in *Die fröhliche Wissenschaft* as he ponders "sacred games" adequate to memorialize the implications of the Enlightenment deicide.

41. See *Whose Justice? Which Rationality?*, p. 369.

42. It was Hegel's ability to elucidate what was most deficient in the Enlightenment—the inability of Enlightenment to have faith in anything other than itself and, a fortiori, the obvious inability of Enlightenment to provide a working basis for morality become "actual" (*wirklich*) or concrete in the life of community, which permanently endeared him to Karl Barth. See *Protestant Thought from Rousseau to Ritschl* (New York: Harper and Row, 1959).

43. John Silber gets at the same problem in his discussion of Kant's apophatic definition of freedom, namely, the failure "to comprehend the incomprehensibility" of freedom—the essence of freedom being, in this instance, identical to the essence of God, and our knowledge of God being, as Cusanus observed, the "knowledge of our ignorance of God." See "The Ethical Significance of Kant's *Religion*," in Kant's *Religion Within the Limits of Reason Alone* (New York: Harper and Row, 1960), p. cxi. However, for most people "freedom" is not particularly "mysterious" and, in the wake of Toland's and other deistic demystifications of religion, Hegel's choice of *Geist* is his means, I think, of augmenting the ontological fact of this mystery present to consciousness at its deepest level.

44. Hegel believed that comprehension of the Protestant Principle was impossible in Catholic countries—which was the reason, of course, that they remained Catholic! While one may argue with this, the extremities in modern French philosophy, as related by Vincent Descombes for example, are certainly due in part to the unresolved continuation of the sacred-secular dichotomy that begins in Descartes, reaches its high point of extremity in the French Enlightenment, and continues through poststructuralism to the present. See *Le Meme et L'Autre* (Paris, n.p., 1979); trans. under the title *Modern French Philosophy* (Cambridge: Cambridge University Press, 1980); see also my essay "The Shape of Modern French Philosophy," in *International Journal for the Philosophy of Religion* (Fall 1984), pp. 173–79.

45. This is precisely what is implied, it seems to me, in Gadamer's notion of the *wirkungsgeschichtliche Bewußtsein*, namely, that consciousness in which history is ever effective in the determination of what can be reasonably asserted to be moral. See *Truth and Method*, part 3.

Chapter Eight
ABSOLUTE SPIRIT

1. See Nicolas Berdyaev, *Spirit and Reality*, trans. George Reavey (London: Geoffrey Bles, 1939), p. 28.

2. While Tillich's reading of Hegel is excessively Schellingean, he is correct, I think, in calling Hegel's logic "a philosophy of the inner divine life," that is, an essentialist description of "the dynamic process of the inner divine life in which all realities in their essence are present before they are actual in time and space." *A History of Christian Thought* (New York: Simon and Schuster, 1967), p. 124.

3. Heidegger acknowledges the scope of Hegel's achievement by his well-known comments in the introduction to *Sein und Zeit* (pp. 19–27) while also maintaining, erroneously in my view, that this greatness largely consists of the manner in which Hegel merely "reworks" the understanding of Being in Western tradition. In fairness to Heidegger, however, it must be pointed out that he soon modifies this view in his 1930–31 lectures on *Hegel's Phenomenology of Spirit* (trans. Parris Emad and Kenneth Maly [Bloomington: Indiana University Press, 1988]) by more clearly identifying Hegel's "philosophy of the experience of consciousness" with his own project of fundamental ontology (pp. 17–23). This positive assessment quite possibly rises out of a kind of resignation as he began to realize the impossibility of completing the project of *Sein und Zeit* as originally conceived, viz., working out a notion of primordial "lived time" as distinct from the "timeless" Aristotelian but remarkably nonstatic doctrine of essence in Hegel's *Logik*. Nevertheless, one cannot fail to notice the uncharacteristically modernist assumption implicit in Heidegger's earlier comment that no good will come out of merely "reworking" of the tradition and that true creativity and originality must find someplace to stand outside of the ontotheological tradition. Were it not for Heidegger's primordialism, such a notion would appear to be nonsense by dint of his own conception of the so-called hermeneutic circle.

4. Vol. 1 of the *Enzyklopädie*, of course, has an extensive preface designed to explain *Die Wissenschaft der Logik* in its initial form, especially vis-à-vis conventional logic. One of the more notable features of the *Encyclopedia Logic* is Hegel's organization of its three parts (Being, Essence, and Concept) as "subdivisions" (*Abteilungen*) of a single unitary science; whereas in the *Science of Logic* the three parts are presented as distinct *doctrines*.

5. The distinguishing feature of the account of creation in the *Rig Veda*, of course, is the poet's playfully subjunctive mood. The philosopher's serious "mood" is characteristically indicative—even imperative. That Hegel became increasingly interested in the speculative philosophical texts of South Asia (Hinduism and Buddhism) is clearly evident from the critical edition of his *Lectures on the Philosophy of Religion*, 3 vols. (Berkeley and Los Angeles: University of California Press, 1984, 1985, and 1987).

6. See Sarvepalli Radhakrishnan and Charles Moore, "Hymn of Creation," in *A Source Book in Indian Philosophy* (Princeton: Princeton University Press, 1957), pp. 23–24. Hegel is clearly captivated, and also somewhat confused, by his consideration of Indian philosophy in his *Lectures on the Philosophy of Religion* (1821, 1824, 1827, and 1931). He is captivated by the fact that images of nothingness and negation seem to function in ways that are directly contrary to the Western use of Being, especially the assumption, as in Anselm, that "Being is in all ways superior to non-Being." But he is also confused by the inaccuracy of historical dating processes regarding ancient Eastern manuscripts that characterized Asian research at the time. This causes him to reverse sequences and interactions between Hindu and Buddhist philosophy even though what he adduces, from a strictly logical standpoint, is quite accurate.

7. Hegel devotes more time to the priestly account of the Creation Story

than to any other section of the Bible—especially when challenged, as he was during the Berlin period, by rival accounts in his study of comparative religions. See Hegel's section on "determinate religions" in the *Lectures on the Philosophy of Religion*, vol. 2.

8. The recent article by Victor Weisskopf, "How the Universe Began," where he assesses the present state of cosmology and astrophysics, is notable in this regard. See the *New York Review* 36, no. 2 (16 February 1989): 10ff.

9. See Rosenzweig's *Star of Redemption*, which, of course, represents the author's rejection of Hegel after his reconversion to Judaism.

10. See the schematic diagrams of changes regarding the organization of these lectures provided by Peter Hodgson in Hegel's *Lectures on the Philosophy of Religion*.

11. That Hegel detects something akin to what Jaspers later identifies as the "axial time" is also evident in Hegel's reorganization of the 1831 *Lectures on the Philosophy of Religion*, where the major Eastern religions of founders or neofounders are removed from the categories of "nature" and "magic" and placed into the category having to do with the "internal rupture of religious consciousness," that is, with intellectual conversion. See also Jaspers's *The Origin and Goal of History*, trans. M. Bullock (New Haven: Yale University Press, 1953).

12. Walter Wili, "The History of the Spirit in Antiquity," in *Spirit and Nature* (*Eranos-Jahrbücher*), (New York: Pantheon, 1954), p. 77. Hegel himself was not impervious to these etymological nuances, especially out of Indo-Iranian origins, as Peter Hodgson points out in his comment on Hegel's use of *paradeisos* with respect to the *Tiergarten* in the biblical account of creation, *paradeisos* in Xenophon's *Anabasis* 2.1.7, and in the *Septuagint* deriving from the Persian *pairi daeza* or "zoological garden enclosed by a wall." See *LPR*, vol. 2, §424, no. 30.

13. See Ernst Cassirer, *The Philosophy of Symbolic Form*, esp. vol. 1, *Language*, and vol. 2, *Mythical Thought*, trans. Ralph Manheim (New Haven: Yale University Press, 1955). The current debate on *nostratic theory* in protolinguistics is not unrelated to Cassirer. See Philip E. Ross, "Trends in Linguistics: Hard Words," in *Scientific American* (April 1991): 139–47.

14. See Jung's "Phenomenology of Spirit in Fairy Tales," in *Spirit and Nature* (New York: Pantheon, 1954), p. 5. Jung's negative assessment of Hegel, in the 1946 essay "The Spirit of Psychology," is striking. This negativity probably accounts, at least in part, for the total exclusion of Hegel studies in the two volumes of Eranos yearbooks devoted to a study of Spirit. For example, Jung states: "The victory of Hegel over Kant dealt the gravest blow to reason and to the further spiritual development of the German and then of the European mind, all the more dangerous as Hegel was a psychologist in disguise who projected great truths out of the sphere of the subject into a cosmos he himself had created." Then, alluding to the twin postwar powers of atheistic Existentialism and Marxism, which occupied the intellectual stage in postwar Europe after the disaster of national socialism, he goes on to say, "We know how far Hegel's influence extends today. The forces compensating this calamitous development personified themselves partly in the later Schelling, partly in

Schopenhauer and Carus, while on the other hand that unbridled *bacchantic God* whom Hegel had already scented in nature finally burst upon us in Nietzsche" (p. 381). Jung correctly sees that for Hegel, it is the work of the concept to sublate the unconscious, which, left to itself, is bereft of truth—a notion that Jung, obviously, could not abide.

15. Wilhelm Dilthey, for example, concludes that the alchemical "mysticism of Spirit" discernible in Hegel by Boehme and Schelling is what makes it "wrong." Dilthey is right but for the wrong reasons, Hegel's mysticism of Spirit being a nonsubstantialistic mysticism of the logic of the concept. See Wilhelm Dilthey, *Gesammelte Schriften*, vol. 4 (Leipzig, B. G. Teubner, 1921), pp. 248–50.

16. I say "quasi-Hegelian" because he is more Romantic and therefore more Schellingian in his observations regarding the principle of identity. See Walter Wili, "The History of the Spirit in Antiquity," p. 82.

17. At the mythical level, of course, these dynamical elements are profoundly expressed (and presupposed) in the conception and infancy narratives of Luke and John, where the *Jungfrau Maria* (qua *theotokos*) conceives the God–man, by way of the *Heiliger Geist wird über dich kommen* (Luke 1.35)—Spirit traversing the distance, as it were, between the uranic and the chthonic, Transcendence and Immanence.

18. As we consider in some detail Hegel's treatment of the pre-Socratics, this point will become more evident. Obviously, this is also what makes Hegel's position controversial from the standpoint of more orthodox Christian theology—evangelical orthodoxy having as its primary interest the demonstration that the Trinity is in all ways unique as a historically discrete revelation or dispensation of its persons takes place. This kind of *positivity* with respect to the meaning of *Offenbarung*, in Hegel's view, is what makes the Trinity an absurdity as distinct from being the source of deepest philosophical truth, which, in fact, is what a "standing-under" (*hypo-stasis*) signifies with respect to "under-standing."

19. Hegel identifies Taoism with the philosophy of "measure" in his *Lectures on the Philosophy of Religion*.

20. The conclusions of Marx, of course, are precisely the opposite of Hegel's. In fact Marx probably wrote his doctoral thesis as an explicit refutation of Hegel's readings of the pre-Socratics—especially the atomistic materialism of Democritus, arguing that it was precisely the grounding of dialectic in the material order that made it superior to what followed in Parmenides. See Marx's thesis "The Difference Between the Democritean and Epicurean Philosophy of Nature," in Karl Marx and Friedrich Engels, *Werke* (Berlin: Dietz, 1968), supplemental volume, part 1.

21. See Plotinus's Tractate on Beauty *Enneads*, vol. 1, 6.

22. The mystical or metaphysical properties of so-called perfect odd numbers, especially the three in one–one in three characteristic of the Trinity (and Augustine), are not what makes them decisive "in themselves" for Hegel. The triad, as a *fundamentum in re*, is a dialectical truth more in keeping with the syllogistic thinking of Aristotle; in other words, the *Dreiheit* functions as the principle of actualization. See Karl Rosenkranz's comments on *Das Fragment vom göttlichen Dreieck* (*JS*, 534–39).

23. Heidegger's *Daseinsanalyse* in *Sein und Zeit* seems clearly indebted to Hegel on this point.

24. See Hegel's *Gottesbeweise* lectures at the end of *VPR* 2, 347–535.

25. Hegel makes it clear from the outset of the *Logik* and at various points throughout the *Enzyklopädie*, as well as in his "Lectures on the Proofs for the Existence of God," that he is unimpressed with Kant's refutation of Anselm and the ontological argument. Kant's assertions regarding existence not being a predicate may work in the realm of real and imaginary thalers, but it does not work with God unless the being of God is conceived as having being akin to that of a thaler, in both the conceptual and the actual realms. But God's being is not the same as that of a thaler in either realm; as *actus purus* ((Hegel follows Aquinas here) God is the only being that exists in the unity of Being and Nothing. Thus Kant's argument fails because of a disproportionate analogy (*WL*, 84–92).

26. See Martin Heidegger, *Sein und Zeit* (Tübingen: Max Niemeyer Verlag, 1984), 34–39. See also Michael Theunissen, *Sein und Schein. Die kritische Funktion der Hegelschen Logik* (Frankfurt: Suhrkamp Verlag, 1980), esp. pp. 95ff.

27. One of the clearest indications of this can be found in Hegel's *Lectures on the Philosophy of Religion*, where Hegel's earlier sacramental meditations of the late 1790s, when both he and Hölderlin were heavily under the influence of Romanticism and agonizing over the moribund *Moralität* of Christianity and its extrinsic *Positivität*, are developed squarely within the context of faith. For example, Hegel's extensive discussion of "faith as mediation" in the 1824 lectures on "Cultus" (§242ff.) is not "out of place," as Hodgson tends to suggest, but simply different from what he chooses to discuss in 1827. Indeed, in the 1824 lectures Hegel picks up on fundamental issues in Lutheran theology that, in fact, ultimately separate him from Schleiermacher (who was much on his mind during the early 1820s) and also from Kant; this discussion also provides additional support for my argument regarding the catechetical-pneumatological foundations of Hegel's dialectic.

In the 1824 lectures, Hegel develops the "concept of faith" as the "inner kernel" of the cultus, viz., "Faith is the witness of Spirit concerning Absolute Spirit" (*LPR* 2, §242). It is, therefore, the "concept" that brings about "this unity," Hegel insists, "which is expressed in the witness of Spirit concerning its essence, the witness of Spirit concerning Absolute Spirit, is the unity of pure self-consciousness and consciousness. Or it is the infinite form of knowledge as such and of the absolute content [God]. The unity of the two is the absolute content, which is the form of self, i.e., it is knowledge of itself, and hence defines itself as universal as opposed to singular, so that the latter exists simply and solely as semblance. This unity, then, is what lies at the basis of faith. This is what is innermost, what is at the heart of speculation, the deepest point which in this regard must come to speech. It is a point that can only be apprehended speculatively. If it is not so apprehended, then misunderstandings can arise—and it may seem as if these lead to forms [of reflective thought] that we have already dealt with earlier" (*LPR* 1, §243)—"philosophies of reflection" or neo-Kantian theologies such as Schleiermacher's.

This mystical, speculative unity lies at the heart of the "concept" of faith—faith being the actual working-out of this concept, *Glauben als Bewußtsein*. Hegel believes, furthermore, that Protestant theologians have utterly forgotten this dimension even though it was known to medieval Catholic theologians and especially to Meister Eckhart, whom Hegel quotes as follows: "The eye with which God sees me is the eye with which I see him; my eye and his eye are one and the same. In righteousness I am weighed in God and he in me. If God did not exist nor would I; if I did not exist, nor would he. But there is no need to know this, for there are things that are easily misunderstood (and that can be grasped only in the *concept*)" (*LPR* 1, §248).

28. See my chapter on Pietism. See also the reconstruction of Hegel's academic program at Tübingen by Betzendörfer and Fuhrmans in H. S. Harris, *Hegel's Development*, vol. 1 (Oxford: Oxford University Press, 1983), p. 89.

29. Transcendental Thomism, especially Lonergan's version of it, as we saw in the first chapter, comes closest to the Hegelian understanding of the relation between reason and Spirit.

30. Two weeks prior to his death Hegel writes, in the preface to the second edition of his *Science of Logic*, "The most important point for the nature of Spirit is not only the relation of what it is *in itself* to what it is *actually*, but the relation of what it *knows itself* to be to what it actually is; because Spirit is essentially consciousness, this self-knowing is a fundamental determination of its *actuality*" (*SL*, 37). The task of the science of logic or, as I here call it, speculative pneumatology, is to move from the former state, in which categories of external relation seem to have priority, to the latter, namely, what *actually* provides the groundwork for this relation, Spirit qua consciousness or *Selbstbewußtsein*. Hegel's *Trinitätslehre* therefore follows the general rule set down by Aristotle—that while questions of Being are last in the order of time (Spirit being the final mode of self-determinacy in the Trinity), they are first (a priori) in the order of logic (Spirit being, in the case of the Trinity, the precondition for its initial modes of self-determinacy).

Chapter Nine
FREE SPIRIT

1. Just how prominent this quasi-Romantic sense is can be noted in Hegel's preface to the first edition of his *Science of Logic* (*WL*, 13–18), where one would normally think such allusions least likely to occur. But then this is no ordinary logic.

2. With respect to external events, it is interesting to note that the major event in 1821 (when Hegel published his *Rechtsphilosophie* and first delivered his *Lectures on the Philosophy of Religion*) was the death of Napoleon on Saint Helena. Napoleon was born just one year earlier than Hegel, in 1769, and it was Napoleon to whom Hegel referred as "the world-spirit on horseback" when he reportedly caught a glimpse of him at the Battle of Jena in 1807. Perhaps it was the diminution of this revolutionary epoch that stands behind "the shape of things grown old" and Hegel's perception of how the most elab-

orate hopes and dreams of men ultimately come to nothing—that the great promise of the French Revolution had deteriorated into "absolute freedom and terror," as he put it in the *Phänomenologie*. And Hegel mentions Napoleon directly at least four times in the *Rechtsphilosophie*, one of the more dramatic being his attention to Napoleon's response to the German envoys at Erfurt in 1808: *Je ne suis pas votre prince, je suis votre maître!* (§281, Z). The officers were blissfully unaware that everything had changed, and, as Germany stumbled toward its own political redefinition during the next century and a half, Hegel certainly would have shared with Yeats the view that "while the best lack all conviction, the worst are full of passionate intensity."

3. See J. N. Findlay, *Ascent to the Absolute* (London: Allen and Unwin, 1970), esp. "Three Lectures on Absolute Theory," pp. 13–77.

4. This processual element greatly troubled Kierkegaard as evidenced by *The Sickness unto Death* (1843) in which every possible configuration of the "self's relation to itself" is cause for and the manifestation of *Angst*. The Platonistic-Augustinian element is far more pronounced in Kierkegaard than in Hegel, needless to say, since for Hegel the *cor inequietum* endemic to Pietism is necessarily modified by Aristotle and Thomas, this modification consisting not of final resolution but of delight in the life of the concept and the continuous mediation of thinking. Hegel's essentialism therefore turns out to be a truer form of existentialism by providing existentialism with the terms of its own possibility.

5. It might be objected, along Sartrean lines, that the order of contingency is formally absolute since it is the only order that exists. To speak of absolute contingency and to say that the contingent is absolute, however, are not the same. Moreover, one cannot make either assertion, as Thomas shows in his third proof, apart from a position that posits itself as absolute, this positing presupposing antecedent grounding in the Absolute.

6. This is the view of both Nicholas Berdyaev and Karl Jaspers—Berdyaev on the "realist" side and Jaspers on the "idealist" side—both being critical of Hegel, upon whom both are dependent for their views. When I wrote *Transcendence and Hermeneutics* (The Hague: Martinus Nijhoff, 1979), I was not aware of the extent to which Jaspers was dependent on Hegel. Now it is clear to me, however, that Jaspers's disincarnate notion of *das Umgreifende* makes him more rather than less subject to charges of pantheism than Hegel since it is a notion that, by its very nature, introduces images of spatialization and containment—precisely what he attempts to avoid with respect to fraudulent "corporealizations of Transcendence." Berdyaev, on the other hand, is entirely candid with respect to his debt to Hegel, the latter's "formalized" philosophy of Spirit being the place where "biblical spiritualism and Greek intellectualism come together." Berdyaev's critique of Hegel, on the other hand, is aimed at his doctrine of "objective spirit," which introduces a "deterministic" factor that Berdyaev, qua neo-Platonist, would otherwise avoid. See Berdyaev's *Spirit and Reality* (London: Geoffrey Bles, 1939), pp. 26–30.

7. The Fourth Gospel, as John Findlay was fond of pointing out—especially with reference to Hegel—is the "philosopher's Gospel." This quasi-pentecostal theme has led one of my recent graduate students to typify Hegel's

concept of the Absolute as the *"parousia* of consciousness." See Kimiyo Murata-Soraci, *Re-Marking the Beyond: A Study of Difference, Translation, and Transference in Nietzsche, Heidegger, and Derrida* (Ann Arbor Microfilms, 1991).

8. In his critique of the so-called pronominal language of Hegel, Eric Voegelin overlooks the fact that the language of the *concept*, in Hegel, is analogous to and in fact embodies the same mystery that Voegelin attributes to the *metaxy*, the only difference being that in Hegel the "mythic" qualities of this mystery are bracketed. See Voegelin's *Order and History*, vol. 5, (Baton Rouge: Louisiana State University Press, 1987).

9. Hegel's tacit acceptance of the *filioque* clause in the trinitarian formulations of the Western Church would also serve as a point of distance between himself and Berdyaev, Spirit for Berdyaev remaining ontologically "Other" in a dualist sense. Hegel is therefore more Catholic (at least in the Rahnerian sense) in having a conception of *Geist in der Welt* through the series of diremptions that makes it absolute. *Hörer des Wortes* and *Geist in der Welt* (in many ways the masterworks of Karl Rahner) are a couplet inconceivable, in my view, apart from the influence of Hegel.

10. In his *Protestant Thought from Rousseau to Ritschl*, trans. H. H. Hartwell (New York: Harper and Row, 1959), pp. 268–305, Karl Barth ponders "why" it should be the case that Hegel never became for Protestantism what Aquinas became for Catholicism. The reason implicit in his rhetorical question, of course, has to do with the displacement of Hegel by Schleiermacher in nineteenth- and twentieth-century theology—the "displacement" of objective *content* by subjective *form*, i.e., the narcissistic character of modern thinking. Hegel may, in fact, have attained this status if one maintains that the "invisible" and not the "visible Church is our point of union," for Protestant ecclesiology has fundamentally to do with the dismantling of visible institutional forms regarded as being "identical" with Spirit. This argument is implicit in the work of Thomas J. J. Altizer. See his *Gospel of Christian Atheism* (Philadelphia: Westminster, 1966) and more recently *The Self-Embodiment of God* (New York: Harper and Row, 1977).

11. See Paul Tillich, *Perspectives on 19th and 20th Century Protestant Theology*, edited by Carl Braaten (New York: Harper and Row, 1967), pp. 90–114.

12. It was the fate of Hermann F. W. Hinrichs to have his book *Die Religion im inneren Verhältnisse zur Wissenschaft* (1822) largely eclipsed by its *Vorwort* for it is here that Hegel makes his acerbic "canine" allusion regarding those sentient beings naturally predisposed to appreciate Schleiermacher's *Abhängigkeitsgefühl*, viz., the "feeling of absolute dependence." While Hegel's celebrated *Hinrichs-Vorwort* has previously been translated (by A. V. Miller in the F. G. Weiss collection of essays on Hegel, *Beyond Epistemology* [The Hague: Martinus Nijhoff, 1974]), a new English translation, together with a critical edition of its five different German versions and, for the first time, the text it was promoting—Hinrichs's *Religion in Its Internal Relation to Systematic Knowledge*—is available in *Hegel, Hinrichs, and Schleiermacher on Feeling and Reason in Religion: The Texts of Their 1821–1822 Debate*, including a new critical edition of the German text of Hegel's *Vorwort*, edited, translated, and introduced by Eric von der

Luft. *Studies in German Thought and History, vol. 3* (Lewiston and Queenston: Edwin Mellen Press, 1987).

In the first half of this impressive work, von der Luft provides a detailed description of Hegel's relationship with Hinrichs, extensive expository commentaries on Hegel's *Vorwort* and Hinrichs's text, and some highly germane selections from Schleiermacher's *Glaubenslehre*—"germane" because they are drawn from the first edition (1821–22) out of and against which Hegel and Hinrichs direct their invective, as distinct from the better known but dramatically altered second edition upon which the English translation is based. This is an extremely important point since, as von der Luft indicates, Schleiermacher radically adumbrates the highly undifferentiated rhetoric of a primordial *Abhängigkeitsgefühl* in the first edition of his *Glaubenslehre* by carefully attending to the mediational problematic of *Selbstbewußtsein* in the second edition. Thus the second edition, according to von der Luft, is clearly a "premeditated" response to the criticism of Hegel and Hinrichs, noting that in it Schleiermacher "is very careful to defend this feeling [*Abhängigkeitsgefühl*] whenever he invokes it, and is less prone to use it as a panacea for difficulties of explanation" (pp. 284ff.). Therefore, far from being a misunderstanding of Schleiermacher, it seems more likely that the position with which he becomes identified historically is very directly the result of coming to terms with the criticism of Hegel and Hinrichs—something that, quite obviously, the numerous theological followers of Schleiermacher in the twentieth century have failed to do.

13. James Hutchinson Stirling, in his exhaustive albeit idiosyncratic study of Hegel, identifies this as the "secret" of Hegel: "As Aristotle, with considerable assistance from Plato, made *explicit* the *abstract* Universal what was *implicit* in Socrates, so Hegel, with less considerable assistance from Fichte and Schelling, made *explicit* the *concrete* Universal that was *implicit* in Kant." See *The Secret of Hegel: Being the Hegelian System in Origin, Principle, Form, and Matter*, 2 vols. (London: Longman, Green, and Roberts, 1865).

14. Spirit here posits soul as "the other of itself" in a way that calls to mind the so-called loneliness of the primordial deity, Atman, in the *Chandogya Upanishad* and also Prajapati's account of the same in the *Brhadaranyaka Upanishad*. In these accounts the primal deity is "lonely" in not seeing anything other than himself and therefore "longs" for something "other than himself" and posits itself as "Other." See Sarvepelli Radhakrishnan and Charles Moore, *A Source Book in Indian Philosophy* (Princeton: Princeton University Press, 1957), pp. 64–95. This longing is synonymous with the birth of the theogonic dialectic, the precondition for cosmogony and anthropogony, whether the originating ground of this dialectic be conceived as the *Eros* that arouses *Uranos* and *Gaea* in Hesiod's *Theogony*, the *Mumu* that blends the cosmic oceans of *Apsu* and *Tiamat* in the *Enuma Elish*, or the *thanna* that fuels *samsara* in Hinduism and Buddhism.

15. This distinction is thematic throughout Hegel's first major essay, "On the Positivity of the Christian Religion" (1795–96). See also Hegel's 1826 letter to the neo-Pietist theologian Tholuck in Butler, *Letters*, pp. 519–20.

16. Throughout his writings, Hegel is preoccupied with these cosmo-eschatological passages more than any others in the New Testament—as evi-

denced especially in the various versions of his *Lectures on the Philosophy of Religion*.

17. Hegel in fact sides with Luther against Kantian and Fichtean voluntarism regarding the primacy of the "good will." Hegel asserts that it seems to be much more the case that we have an "infinite capacity in speculation" and a very "finite capacity in willing" ("the Spirit is willing but the flesh is weak": Jesus to Peter, echoing Luther's position regarding *de servo arbitrio*: "The sphere of my moral activity is [actually] a limited one. [But] in religion the good is [found] in and for itself; God is The Good." See the 1924 *Lectures on the Philosophy of Religion*, vol. 1, §§249, 250).

18. Both Karl Rahner and Gerhard Ebeling rightly understand Luther's pneumatology and his concept of faith through a doctrine of linguisticality, that is, as a *word event*. Far more important than Heidegger, however, is the contribution of Hegel to this reading of Luther.

19. Ricoeur's tensive theory of metaphor is, in fact, unintelligible apart from Hegel's dynamic theory of consciousness. This is why, for Ricoeur, metaphors, or the semantically impertinent predications of metaphor, have more philosophical significance for Ricoeur than symbols. Indeed, the "symbol gives rise to thought" only because of this dynamic structure and not because of the archaic primordialism that informs Romantic and other forms of symbolical foundationalism. But Ricoeur also attempts to accommodate Schleiermacher through his hermeneutics of "sympathetic reenactment" and, as such, maintains that the "concept" is the "endless death of the representation" and is, in some sense, parasitic upon them. See Paul Ricoeur, "On the Status of *Vorstellung* in Hegel's Philosophy of Religion," in *Meaning, Truth, and God*, ed. Leroy S. Rouner (Notre Dame: Notre Dame University Press, 1983); Ricoeur's *The Rule of Metaphor* (Toronto: University of Toronto Press, 1976); and my article "Ricoeur's Tensive Theory of Metaphorical Truth," in *Myth, Symbol, and Reality*, ed. Alan M. Olson (Notre Dame: Notre Dame University Press, 1980).

20. See I. J. Gelb, *A Study of Writing*, 2d ed. (Chicago: University of Chicago Press, 1963), esp. pp. 24–59 and 150ff.

21. See Ferdinand Saussure, *Course in General Linguistics* (New York: Philosophical Library, 1959).

22. See Janet L. Olson, *Envisioning Writing* (Portsmouth, N.H.: Heinemann, 1992).

23. This is reflected in Hegel's distinction between morality and ethical life in the *Philosophy of Right*, the latter "externalization" being entirely dependent upon the "inwardization" of the former.

24. See Hegel's comments on what he now calls (in 1827) a "shoddy unphilosophical view" in his *Lectures on the Philosophy of Religion*, vol. 3, §469.

25. This allusion stands on its own and does not have to be attributed to the Rosicrucians (as Knox does out of Lasson in the *Philosophy of Right*, p. 303). On the contrary, it may be properly understood, as we have argued throughout, as Hegel's speculative pneumatological encounter with the tradition within which he lived and died.

SELECT BIBLIOGRAPHY

Asendorf, Ulrich. *Luther und Hegel. Untersuchungen zur Grundlegung einer neuen systematischen Theologie*. Wiesbaden: Steiner Verlag, 1982.

Avineri, Shlomo. *Hegel's Theory of the Modern State*. Cambridge: Cambridge University Press, 1972.

Barth, Karl. *Protestant Thought from Rousseau to Ritschl*. New York: Harper & Row, 1959.

Beck, Adolf, ed. *Hölderlins Diotima. Susette Gontard*. Frankfurt: Insel Verlag, 1980.

Benz, Ernst. *The Mystical Sources of German Romantic Philosophy*. Trans. Blair R. Reynolds and Eunice M. Paul. Allison Park, Pa.: Pickwick Publications, 1983.

Berdyaev, Nicolas. *Freedom and the Spirit*. Trans. Oliver Fielding Clark. New York: Charles Scribners, 1935.

———. *Spirit and Reality*. Trans. George Reavey. London: Geoffrey Bles, 1939.

Brecht, Martin, and Jörg Sandberger. "Hegels Begegnung mit der Theologie im Tübinger Stift." In *Hegel-Studien* 5 (1969).

Bubner, Rüdiger. *Dialektik und Wissenschaft*. Frankfurt: Suhrkamp Verlag, 1973.

———. *Modern German Philosophy*. Cambridge: Cambridge University Press, 1981.

Cohen, Robert S., and Marx Wartofsky, eds. *Hegel and the Sciences*. Dordrecht: Reidel, 1984.

Congar, Yeves M. J. *I Believe in the Holy Spirit*. 3 vols. Trans. David Smith (New York: Seabury, 1983; London: Chapman, 1983). Originally published as *Je crois en l'Esprit Saint* (vol. 1, *L'experience de l'Esprit*; vol. 2, *Il est Seigneur et Il donne la vie*; vol. 3, *Le Fleuve de Vie coule en Orient et en Occident*). Paris: Les Editions du Cerf, 1980.

Comoth, Karharina. "Hegels 'Logik' und die spekulative Mystik." In *Hegel-Studien* 19 (1984).

Derrida, Jacques. *Glas*. Trans. John Leavey and Richard Rand. Lincoln and London: University of Nebraska Press, 1986.

———. *Of Spirit*. Trans. Geoffrey Bennington and Rachael Bowlby. Chicago: University of Chicago Press, 1989.

Desmond, William. *Desire, Dialectic, and Otherness*. New Haven: Yale University Press, 1987.

Dewar, Lindsay. *The Holy Spirit and Modern Thought: An Inquiry into the Historical, Theological, and Psychological Aspects of the Christian Doctrine of the Holy Spirit*. London: Mowbray, 1959.

Dickey, Laurence. *Hegel: Religion, Economics, and the Politics of Spirit, 1770–1807* (Cambridge: Cambridge University Press, 1987).

Ebeling, Gerhard. *The Nature of Faith*. Philadelphia: Fortress, 1961.

Fackenheim, Emil. *The Religious Dimension in Hegel's Thought*. Bloomington: Indiana University Press, 1967.

Findlay, J. N. *Ascent to the Absolute*. London: Allen and Unwin, 1970.

———. *The Discipline of the Cave* and *The Transcendence of the Cave* (Gifford Lectures). London: Allen and Unwin, 1967.

———. *Hegel: A Re-examination*. London: Allen and Unwin, 1958.

———. "Thoughts Regarding the Holy Spirit." In *Essays in Phenomenological Theology*, ed. Steven W. Laycock and James G. Hart. Albany: SUNY Press, 1986.

Gadamer, Hans-Georg. *Hegel's Dialectic. Five Hermeneutical Studies*. Trans. P. Christopher Smith. New Haven: Yale University Press, 1976.

———. *Truth and Method*. New York: Seabury, 1975.

Harris, H. S. *Hegel's Development*. Vol. 1, *Toward the Sunlight, 1770–1800*, and vol. 2, *Night Thoughts, 1801–1806* (Oxford: Clarendon Press, 1972 and 1983).

Hartmann, Klaus. *Die ontologische Option. Studien zu Hegels Propädeutik, Schellings Hegel-Kritik, und Hegels Phänomenologie des Geistes*. Berlin: Walter de Gruyter, 1976.

Hartmann, Nicolai. *Die Philosophie des deutschen Idealismus*. 2d ed. Berlin, Walter de Gruyter, 1960.

Heidegger, Martin. *Hegel's Concept of Experience*. New York: Harper and Row, 1970.

———. *Hegels Phänomenologie des Geistes*. Bonn: Bouvier, 1974.

Henrich, Dieter. "Hegel und Hölderlin." In *Hegel-Studien* (1974): 29–45.

———. *Hegel im Kontext*. Frankfurt: Suhrkamp Verlag, 1971.

———. *Hegels Philosophische Psychologie*. Bonn: Bouvier, 1979.

———. *Die Wissenschaft der Logik und die Logik der Reflexion*. Bonn: Bouvier, 1978.

Heron, Alasdair I. C. *The Holy Spirit: The Holy Spirit in the Bible, the History of Christian Thought, and Recent Theology*. Philadelphia: Westminster, 1983.

Höfener, Heiner, ed. *Hegel Spiele*. Donauwörth: Rogner and Bernhard, 1977. Contains the plays of G.F.L. Lindner, *Der von Hegel'scher Philosophie durchdrungene Schuster-Geselle oder Der Absolute Stiefel* (1844); Karl Rosenkranz, *Das Centrum der Spekulation* (1840); and O. H. Gruppe, *Der Wind, oder ganz absolute Konstruction der neuern Weltgeschichte durch Oberons Horn* (1832).

Hoffman, Bengt, ed. and trans. *Theologia Germanica*. Martin Luther's edition of the *Frankfurter Tractate* (1516). New York: Paulist Press, 1982.

Hoffmeister, Johannes, ed. *Dokumente zu Hegels Entwicklung*. Stuttgart: Frommann, 1936.

Holborn, Hajo. *A History of Modern Germany*. 3 vols. Princeton: Princeton University Press, 1982.

Hyppolite, Jean. *Genesis and Structure of Hegel's Phenomenology of Spirit*. Trans. S. Cherniack and J. Hackman. Evanston: Northwestern University Press, 1974.

Inwood, M. J. *Hegel*. London: Routledge and Kegan Paul, Ltd., 1983.

Jaeschke, Walter. *Die Religionsphilosophie Hegels*. Darmstadt: Wissenschaftliche Buchgesellschaft, 1983.

Jamme, Christoph. "Ein ungelehrtes Buch: Die philosophische Gemeinschaft zwischen Hölderlin und Hegel in Frankfurt, 1797–1800." In *Hegel-Studien* 23 (1983).

Jennings, Theodore W. *Beyond Theism. A Grammar of God-Language*. New York: Oxford University Press, 1985.

Jüngel, Eberhard. *The Doctrine of the Trinity. God's Being Is in Becoming*. Trans. Horton Harris. Edinburgh: Scottish Academic Press, 1976. First published as *Gottes Sein ist im Werden*. Tübingen: J.C.B. Mohr (Paul Siebeck), 1966.

———. *God as the Mystery of the World. On the Foundation of the Theology of the Crucified One in the Dispute between Theism and Atheism*. Trans. Darrell Guder. Grand Rapids: Eerdmans, 1983. First published as *Gott als Geheimnis der Welt*. Tübingen: J.C.B. Mohr (Paul Siebeck), 1977.

Kantzenbach, Friedrich Wilhelm. *Orthodoxie und Pietismus*. Gutersloh: Gutersloher Verlaghaus Gerd Mohn, 1966.

Kaufmann, Walter. *Hegel: A Reinterpretation*. New York, Doubleday, 1965.

Kojeve, Alexandre. *Introduction to the Reading of Hegel*. Trans. J. H. Nichols, Jr. New York: Basic Books, 1960.

Kroner, Richard. *Von Kant bis Hegel*. 2 vols. Tübingen: J.C.B. Mohr (Paul Siebeck), 1961.

Küng, Hans. *Menschwerdung Gottes. Ein Einführung in Hegels Theologisches Denken als Prolegomena zu einer künftigen Christologie*. Freiburg im Breisgan: Verlag Herder, 1970.

Lauer, Quentin. *Essays in Hegelian Dialectic.*. New York: Fordham University Press, 1977.

———. *Hegel's Concept of God*. Albany: SUNY Press, 1982.

Lonergan, Bernard J. F. *The Way to Nicea: The Dialectical Development of Trinitarian Theology*. London: Darton, Longman, and Todd, 1976.

Löwith, Karl. *From Hegel to Nietzsche: The Revolution in Nineteenth-Century Thought*. Trans. David Green. New York: Holt, Reinhart, and Winston, 1964.

———. "Hegels Aufhebung der christlichen Religion." In *Hegel-Studien*, 1 (1962).

Lucas, George R., ed. *Hegel and Whitehead: Contemporary Perspectives on Systematic Philosophy*. Albany: SUNY Press, 1986.

Lukacs, Georg. *The Young Hegel*. Trans. R. Livingstone. London: Merlin Press, 1975.

MacIntyre, Alasdair, ed. *Hegel: A Collection of Critical Essays*. Notre Dame: Notre Dame University Press, 1976.

Mälzer, Gottfried, ed. *Die Werke der Württembergischen Pietisten des 17. und 18. Jahrhunderts*. Berlin: Walter de Gruyter, 1972.

Mann, Golo. *The History of Germany Since 1789*. Trans. Marian Jackson. New York: Praeger, 1968.

Massey, James. "The Hegelians, the Pietists, and the Nature of Religion." In *Journal of Religion* 59 (1978).

Moltmann, Jürgen. *The Trinity and the Kingdom: The Doctrine of God*. Trans. Margaret Kohl. New York: Harper and Row, 1980. Originally published as *Trinität und Reich Gottes*. München: Christian Kaiser Verlag, 1980.

Müller, Gustav. *Hegel. Denkgeschichte eines Lebendigen*. Bern: Franke Verlag, 1959.

Oeing-Hanhoff, Ludger. "Hegels Trinitätslehre. Zur Aufgabe ihrer Kritik und Rezeption." In *Theologie und Philosophie* 52 (1977).

Oeing-Hanhoff, Ludger. "Licht der Philosophie im Schatten Hegels." In *Theologische Quartalschrift* 2, "Hegel und die Theologie" (1982): 146–62.

Olson, Alan M. "Glasnost and Enlightenment." In *Philosophy Today* 32, no. 4 (Summer 1990): 99–110.

———. "Metaphysics and Renunciation: An Examination of the Role of Dialectic in Hegel and Hölderlin During the Frankfurt Period." In *Man and World* (Spring 1983): 123–46.

———. "Faith and Postmodernity." In *Journal of the American Academy of Religion* (Fall 1990): 37–53.

———. *Transcendence and Hermeneutics*. The Hague: Martinus Nijhoff, 1979.

Pannenberg, Wolfhart. "Die Subjektivität Gottes und die Trinitätslehre." In *Kerygma und Dogma* 23 (1977).

Pinson, Koppel S. *Modern Germany: Its History and Civilization*. 2d ed. Prospect Heights, Ill.: 1989.

Pippin, Robert B. *Hegel's Idealism: The Satisfactions of Self-Consciousness*. Cambridge: Cambridge University Press, 1988.

Pöggeler, Otto. *Hegels Idee einer Phänomenologie des Geistes*. Freiburg: Karl Alber, 1973.

———, ed. *Hegel in Berlin*. Exhibit. Berlin: Staatsbibliothek, Preussischer Kulturbesitz, 1981.

Rahner, Karl. *The Trinity*. Trans. Joseph Donceel. New York: Herder, 1970.

Rauch, Leo. *Hegel and the Human Spirit: A Translation of the Jena Lectures on the Philosophy of Spirit (1805–1896)*. Detroit: Wayne State University Press, 1983.

Reardon, Bernard M. G. *Hegel's Philosophy of Religion*. London: Macmillan, 1977.

Ricoeur, Paul. "The Status of *Vorstellung* in Hegel's Philosophy of Religion." In Leroy S. Rouner, ed., *Meaning, Truth, and God*. Notre Dame: Notre Dame University Press, 1982.

Ritschl, Albrecht. *Three Essays*. Trans. Philip Hefner. Philadelphia: Westminster, 1972.

Ritter, Gerhard. *The Sword and the Scepter*. 4 vols. Trans. Heinz Norden. Miami: Miami University Press, 1969.

Rockmore, Tom. *Hegel's Circular Epistemology*. Bloomington: Indiana University Press, 1986.

———. "Idealistic Hermeneutics and the Hermeneutics of Idealism." In *Idealistic Studies* 12, no. 2 (1982).

Rosen, Stanley. *G.W.F. Hegel: An Introduction to the Science of Wisdom*. New Haven: Yale University Press, 1974.

Rosenkranz, Karl. *G.W.F. Hegels Leben*. Berlin: Verlag Duncker und Humblot, 1844; reprint, Darmstadt: Wissenschaftliche Buchgesellschaft, 1977.

Rosenzweig, Franz. *Hegel und der Staat*. Vol. 1, *Lebensstationen, 1770–1806*; vol. 2, *Weltepochen, 1806–1831*. Munich: Oldenbourg Verlag, 1920.

———. *The Star of Redemption*. Notre Dame: Notre Dame University Press, 1985.

Rotenstreich, Nathan. "On Spirit—An Interpretation of Hegel." In *Hegel-Studien* 15 (1980).

Schlitt, Dale M. "Hegel on the Kingdom of God." In *Église et Théologie* 19 (1988).

Shestov, Leo. *Athens and Jerusalem*. Trans. Bernard Martin. Athens: Ohio University Press, 1966.

Simon, Josef. *Anerkennung als Prinzip der praktischen Philosophie: Untersuchungen zu Hegels Jenaer Philosophie des Geistes*. Stuttgart: Kohlhammer Verlag, 1966.

———. "Hegels Gottesbegriff." In *Theologische Quartalschrift* 2, "Hegel und die Theologie" (1982): 82–104.

Smith, John E. "Hegel's Reinterpretation of the Doctrine of Spirit and the Religious Community." In D. E. Christensen, ed., *Hegel and the Philosophy of Religion* (Wofford Symposium). The Hague: Martinus Nijhoff, 1970.

Solomon, Robert C. *From Hegel to Existentialism*. Oxford: Oxford University Press, 1987.

———. *In the Spirit of Hegel: A Study of GWF Hegel's Phenomenology of Spirit*. Oxford: Oxford University Press, 1983.

Steinkraus, Warren, and Kenneth Schmitz, eds. *Art and Logic in Hegel's Philosophy*. New York: Humanities Press, 1980.

Stirling, James Hutchinson. *The Secret of Hegel: Being the Hegelian System in Origin, Principle, Form, and Matter*. 2 vols. London: Longman, Green, and Roberts, 1865.

Stoeffler, F. Ernst. *German Pietism During the Eighteenth Century*. Leiden: Brill, 1973.

———. *The Rise of Evangelical Pietism*. Leiden: Brill, 1965.

Taylor, Charles. *Hegel*. Cambridge: Cambridge University Press, 1975.

———. *Hegel and Modern Society*. Cambridge: Cambridge University Press, 1979.

Theunissen, Michael. *Hegels Lehre vom absoluten Geist als theologisch-politischer Traktat*. Berlin: Walter de Gruyter, 1970.

———. *Sein und Schein: Die kritische Funktion der Hegelschen Logik*. Frankfurt: Suhrkamp Verlag, 1980.

Tillich, Paul. *A History of Christian Thought*. Trans. Carl Braaten. New York: Simon and Schuster, 1967.

Tugendhat, Ernst. *Selbstbewußtsein und Selbstbestimmung. Sprachanalytische Interpretation*. Frankfurt: Suhrkamp Verlag, 1979.

Voegelin, Eric. "On Hegel—A Study in Sorcery." In *The Study of Time*, ed. J. T. Fraser, F. C. Haber, and G. H. Müller. New York: Springer Verlag, 1972.

Von der Luft, Eric. *Hegel, Hinrichs, and Schleiermacher on Feeling and Reason in Religion. The Texts of Their 1821–1822 Debate*. Lewiston and Queenston: Mellen Press, 1987.

Von Harnack, Adolf. *History of Dogma*, vol. 6. 3d ed. New York: Dover, 1961.

Westphal, Merold. *History and Truth in Hegel's Phenomenology*. New York: Humanities Press, 1978.

Williams, Robert. "Hegel's Concept of *Geist*." In *Hegel's Philosophy of Spirit*, ed. Peter G. Stillman. Albany: SUNY Press, 1986.

Yerkes, James. *The Christology of Hegel*. SUNY Press, 1983.

———. "Glauben und Genuss: Hegel, Luther, and the Holy Spirit." In *Christian Scholar's Review* 12, no. 3 (1983).

INDEX

Abraham (biblical figure), 133
Absolute: and consciousness, 201n.7; and
  Enlightenment, 123, 124, 125; Findlay
  on, 56, 177n.15; Hegel on, 28, 34, 68,
  120, 121, 125, 140–41, 148; in Hölder-
  lin's poetry, 78; and the medievals, 53–
  54; other philosophers on, 163n.2,
  168n.23, 200n.5; and reason, 68, 120;
  -Unconditioned, 29
Absolute Encompassing, 147
Adorno, Theodor, 54, 177n.8, 192n.29
Aesthetic du Mal (Stevens), 81
Aesthetics: Lectures on Fine Art (Hegel), 95
Aiken, Henry, 163n.2
All-Comprehensive, 4
All-Encompassing, 4
Altizer, Thomas J. J., 201n.10
Altmann, Alexander, 170n.4
Alzheimer, Alois, 86, 184n.4
Alzheimer's disease, 86, 184n.4, 187n.27
Anabaptists, 6, 26, 38, 39
Anabasis (Xenophon), 196n.12
Anaximander, 132, 134
Anaximenes, 132, 134
Anselm of Canterbury, Saint, 56, 137,
  195n.6
Antigone (Sophocles), 48
anti-Semitism, 165n.13, 178n.19, 181n.15
Antonia, Princess of Württemburg, 42,
  172n.16
Apostles' Creed, 16
Aristotle: on Being, 3, 22; compared to
  Hegel, 93, 102, 150, 152, 185n.17,
  197n.22, 202n.13; on habit, 102; influ-
  ence of, on Hegel, 11, 13, 94, 151,
  195n.3, 199n.30, 200n.4; Luther on, 30;
  MacIntyre on, 110, 112; on Parmenides,
  22, 136; in Pietist hermeneutics,
  172n.15; and Scholasticism, 24, 25; on
  soul, 93, 94, 102, 185n.17; on virtue,
  111
Arius, 17
Arndt, Johann, 38
Asendorf, Ulrich, 175n.38
"As on a Holiday . . ." (Hölderlin), 71, 73,
  74, 78
Athanasian Creed, 16, 166n.7

Athanasius (Athanasians), 17, 18, 19, 22,
  23–24
Atman (diety), 202n.14
*Atombombe und die Zukunft des Menschen,
  Die* (Jaspers), 185n.12
Augsburg Confession, 41
Augustine, Saint, 103, 125, 154, 167n.11,
  197n.22, 200n.4
Autenreith, Professor, 84
Avineri, Shlomo, 165n.13, 178n.19

Baader, Franz Xaver von, 142
Bach, Johann Sebastian, 79, 80, 182n.23
Barth, Karl, 151, 173n.24, 194n.42,
  201n.10
Battle of Jena, 57, 145, 199n.2
Beantwortung der Frage: Was ist Aufklärung
  (Kant), 115
Beckett, Samuel, 53, 55, 177n.9
Beethoven, Ludwig van, 183n.1
Being: Aristotle on, 3, 22; and conscious-
  ness, 122; and dialectic, 54, 130,
  181n.19; Hegel on, 9, 67, 68, 92, 122,
  129–32, 135–37, 195nn. 3 and 6,
  199n.30; Heidegger on, 73, 131,
  180n.8, 181n.19; Hölderlin on, 74, 78,
  82; -in-and-for-itself, 67; and Meaning,
  19; Nietzsche on, 128; and nothing,
  130–31, 195n.6, 198n.25; and Other,
  67, 130; pre-Socratics on, 135–36;
  Rosen on, 191n.22; self-, 153; and
  Spirit, 3, 56, 129, 155; and Transcendence, 122; and the Trinity, 18
Benedict, Saint, 112
Bengel, Johann Albrecht, 39, 42, 43, 46,
  172n.17
Benz, Ernst, 42, 172n.17, 178n.17
Berdyaev, Nicolas: compared to Hegel, 6,
  201n.9; on Hegel, 5, 129, 163n.2,
  200n.6; on pneumatology, 166n.5; on
  Spirit, 3–4, 129, 201n.9
Berger, Peter, 107
Berlinische Monatsschrift, 115
Bible: Galations, 193n.32; Genesis, 131,
  153; Hegel on, 195n.7–196n.7; John,
  155, 202n.16; Luke, 19; Matthew, 63;
  Revelation, 180n.11; on Spirit, 155

Lectures on the Philosophy of History (Hegel), 170n.3

Lectures on the Philosophy of Religion (Hegel): on Asian religions, 132, 191n.22, 195nn. 5 and 6, 196n.11, 197n.19; Christianity in, 164n.6, 170n.3, 198n.27, 203n. 16; comparative religion in, 11; on God's existence, 154; Hegel's first delivery of, 199n.2; organization of, 176n.6, 196n.11; on spiritual community, 161; on truth of religion, 167n.12

"Lectures on the Proofs for the Existence of God" (Hegel), 198n. 25

Left, 5, 26, 37, 165n.8, 169n.31

Lehrbuch (Sartorius), 40, 44

Leibniz, Gottfried Wilhelm, 131, 170n.6, 172n.16

Lessing, Gotthold Ephraim, 123, 180n.6, 184n.8

Levinas, 20

"Life of Jesus" (Hegel), 58

Locke, John, 119, 158

Lonergan, Bernard Joseph Francis, 18, 19–23, 141, 166n.8, 167n.15, 168n.21, 199n.29

"Love as the Transcendence of Justice and the Reconciliation of Fate" (Hegel), 64

Löwith, Karl, 75–76

Lukacs, George, 170n.4

Luke, Saint, 197n.17

Luther, Martin: and Brenz, 39; on christology, 191n.22; compared to Hegel, 125, 126, 127, 141; compared to Hölderlin, 80; compared to Oetinger, 43; on the *Credo*, 192n.22; on Divine Spirit, 141; Ebeling on, 203n.18; in education, 41; on Enlightenment, 128; on faith, 14, 25, 28–32, 41, 165n.1, 167n.12, 193n.32, 203n.18; on feeling vs. content in religion, 45; on freedom, 27; on *Geist*, 118; Harnack on, 172n.13; Hegel on, 121, 193n.36, 203n.18; on Holy Spirit, 10, 15–16, 28, 32–33, 75, 79, 143, 154–56; influence of, on Hegel, 5, 12, 27, 28, 29–30, 155–57, 172n.15, 203nn. 17 and 18; influence of, on Hölderlin, 75, 76, 77, 78, 182n.21; influence on Kant, 117, 193n.32, 193n.36; on justification, 157; on Law, 63, 168n.24; and

mysticism, 169n.31, 169n.33; Paradox-itself in work of, 18; and Pietism, 156, 169n.33; pneumatology of, 203n.18; on power of the will, 30; Rahner on, 203n.18; on reason, 29, 30, 34–35, 154–55; Ritschl on, 26; on Romanticism, 156; on Saint Paul, 79; on Spirit, 9, 126, 127, 128; on the Trinity, 32, 41; on *Vernunft*, 29, 30–31, 34–35

Lutheran Confessions, 14

Luther und Hegel. Untersuchungen zur Grundlegung einer neuen systematischen Theologie (Asendorf), 175n.38

Lyotard, Jean-Francois, 111, 189nn. 9 and 11

MacIntyre, Alasdair: compared to Lyotard, 111, 189n.9; on Enlightenment, 107–13, 115, 117, 124, 126, 190n.21; Gadamer's influence on, 110, 172n.15; on Hegel, 160

madness, 84–106; in dialectic, 91, 102; and Enlightenment, 12, 35, 57, 85; and *Geist*, 88, 186n.23; Hegel on, 35, 48; Hegel on feeling and, 91, 185n.14, 186n.19; Hegel on habit and, 101–3, 187n.27; Hegel on religion and, 175n.41, , 23; in Hegel's *Enzyklopädie*, 85, 88–91, 97–100, 103, 104, 174n.32, 184n.9; Hegel's fear of, 12, 85, 174n.32; Hegel's types of, 98–100; Heidegger on, 57; and Holy Spirit, 87, 88; and Pietism, 103, 156; and pneumatology, 105. *See also* Hölderlin, madness of

Maimon, Salomon, 169n.33

Malebranch, Nicolas de, 172n.16

Maria Magdalena (biblical figure), 48, 63, 64, 65, 87

Maritain, Jacques, 141

Martin Heidegger and National Socialism (Neske-Kettering), 164n.4

Marx, 108, 122, 145, 177n.10, 188n.6, 192n.29, 197n.20

Marxism, 163n.2, 172n.17, 188nn. 5, 6, and 7, 196n.14

Matthew, Saint, 87

Melanchthon, Philipp, 14, 42

Melissus, 135

Mendelssohn, Moses, 176n.6

"Menon's Lament for Diotima" (Hölderlin), 69–70, 73, 77, 186n.19